the
complete
book of

colour

the

complete

book of

colour

Using colour for lifestyle, health, and well-being

S U Z Y   C H I A Z Z A R I

ELEMENT

Shaftesbury, Dorset • Boston, Massachusetts • Melbourne, Victoria

NOTE FROM THE PUBLISHER

Any information given in this book is not intended to be taken as
a replacement for medical advice. Any person with a condition
requiring medical attention should consult a qualified practitioner
or therapist.

Designed and created with
The Bridgewater Book Company Limited

ELEMENT BOOKS LIMITED
Creative Director *Ed Day*
Managing Editor *Miranda Spicer*
Senior Commissioning Editor *Caro Ness*
Project Editor *Finny Fox-Davies*
Production Manager *Susan Sutterby*

THE BRIDGEWATER BOOK COMPANY
Art Director *Peter Bridgewater*
Designer *Glyn Bridgewater*
Editorial Director *Sophie Collins*
Managing Editor *Anne Townley*
Project Editor *Caroline Earle*

Printed and bound in Great Britain by Butler and Tanner,
Frome, Somerset UK

Library of Congress Cataloging in Publication
data available

ISBN 1 86204 250 0

To my husband David,
who has given me unfailing support
and encouragement during
my many travels while pursuing
the study of colour.

ACKNOWLEDGMENTS
With thanks to
Maria Andersson, Michael Attree, Phillip Auchinvole, Patricia
Blunt, Gary Brown, Adam Carne, Rukshana Chenoy, Kathleen
Cooper, Roger Cooper, Gemma Davis, Kate Davis, Rachel Dyker,
Tracy Ejuetami, Angela Enahhoro, Hazel Fairchild, Alexandra
Grant, Trevor Gunn, C. Hawes, Pat Infanti, Amanda Jones, Iana
Kaskero, Mette Lauritzen, Sarah McGowan, A. Mackay, Oliver
Milne, Richard Moss, Elin Osmond, Anna Owen, Jackie Oxley,
Joshua Oxley, Bethany Pool, Lauren Pool, Barbara Price, Rebekkah
Ryan, Michelle Sawyer, Emma Scott, Francesca Selkirk, Bethany
Sword, Lauren Sword, Sheila Sword, Louise Williams
for help with photography

Make-up artist: Tracy Ejuetami

With thanks to:
Alexandra Workwear, Brighton; Aura-Soma Colour Therapeutics;
Horncastle, Lincolnshire; Bright Ideas, Lewes; C&H Fabrics,
Brighton; Evolution, Brighton; Farnworths, Brighton;
The Floor, Brighton; Floor and Wall Design, Hawkhurst, Sussex;
Just Pine, Hove; Lands' End Direct Merchants, Rutland;
The Pier, Abingdon, Oxon; Wendy Rose Ltd, Brighton
for the kind loan of props

PICTURE CREDITS

AKG: 43B

A–Z Botanical: 34 (backdrop), 35 (backdrop), 168T, 169L, 170T,
171BR, 173B, 174TL, 178T, 227 (circular backdrop)

Bridgeman Art Library: 246

Werner Forman Archive: 208T, 222B, 238TR

Garden Picture Library: 168–187 (small detail), 169R, 170B,
171(CTL, CBL, BL, TR, CTR&CBR), 172T, 174 (BL, TR,&BR),
175 (all four), 176L&R, 177L&R, 178B, 179R, 180, 181, 207BR

Houses & Interiors: 108T&B, 111T, 113T, 114T, 118, 121, 123T,
125T&B, 130 (TL, TC, BC&BR), 131 (TC, BL, BC
&BR), 135T, 136, 140TL&TR, 141, 142T, 146B, 147T&B,
148T&B, 159, 161TR, 246

The Hutchison Library: 164TR

The Image Bank: 12–25 (small detail), 12, 23T&B, 24, 25B, 26,
27 (backdrop), 37 (backdrop), 39BR, 70TL, 112T, 131TL,
139TL&TCL, 161BL, 186T, 195R, 196T&B, 235T

Images Colour Library: 2,3 (backdrop), 8&9 (small detail), 9, 16,
17TL, 22TL, 25T&C, 36 (backdrop), 54, 57T, 68TL, 82T, 115T,
122, 126T, 130TR, 139TCR&TR, 149T, 152TL, 164BL, 166,
167 (backdrop), 171TL, 173T, 179L, 190L&R, 191, 195L, 212T,
214T, 226 (circular backdrop), 234 (backdrop),
235 (bottom backdrop), 246–256 (small detail)

The Interior Archive: 105B, 106, 107 (backdrop), 109, 116T&B,
119L&R, 129, 130BL, 131TR, 132, 133T&B, 134, 135B, 143,
146T, 149B, 153

NHPA: 22TR&B

Science Photo Library: 14L&R, 193L, 240TC&CR

Aliki Sapountzi: 165

Winfalcon's Healing Centre: 212B

CONTENTS

ABOUT THIS BOOK

Nature has provided us with colour to feed both the body and the spirit. It nourishes our whole system, supplying a vital energy that is an essential and wonderful part of life. As highly colourful beings, our forms are made up of ever-changing vibrating colours and we respond to colour actively or passively in all that we do. Light waves affect us every minute of our lives and penetrate our energetic system whether we are awake or asleep, sighted or blind. Our growth, blood pressure, body temperature, muscular activity, sleep patterns, and immune system are all affected by light rays. The coloured rays affect not only our physical bodies but our emotions, moods, and mental faculties.

We all have a personal relationship with colour. We often give ourselves an instinctive colour treatment by choosing clothes of a certain colour, or by surrounding ourselves with certain colours in our homes and gardens. Most of our reactions are, however, unconscious and it is only when we start to use the qualities of colour in an informed way that we can harness this wonderful vital force to improve the quality of our life and our well-being.

There are many ways we can introduce colours into our system. By understanding the meanings and the physiological and psychological effects of colours, you will be able to select colours for your dress,

*RIGHT **It is vital to be aware of colour. The colours we choose will affect our whole being – our health, self-esteem, and energy.***

your home and work environments, and your garden that will promote prosperity, success, personal growth, self-esteem, and the release of your creative energy. You can also ingest colour energy in food and drink. Everyone can learn to use colour to get more enjoyment and fulfillment out of life.

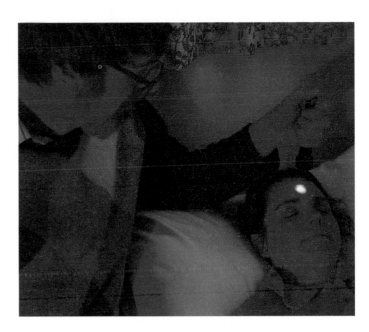

Finally, we can use the techniques of colour healing to maintain health and alleviate many disorders and imbalances. Using colour for healing is not a new idea; as there were many ancient systems of colour healing developed all over the world. We are rediscovering this knowledge, and colour researchers and therapists are using light for healing in a form that is relevant for today. You don't have to be a trained therapist to experience the benefits of colour therapy. The basis of good health revolves around balance and harmony in both the body and mind, and we can introduce colour energy into our system at times when we are "off colour" or when we feel washed out. Although light can be measured and manipulated in a physical way it also has a spiritual quality that has always been a source of wonder and inspiration. Through the pages of this book I wish to share with the reader my love and understanding of colour, and I hope it will bring wonderful changes to your life as it has done mine. If we learn the universal language of colour and understand the messages the colours convey, we can learn a great deal about ourselves and begin to use colour therapeutically.

ABOVE *A colour therapist uses light to stimulate the energy in a room suffused with healing colour.*

SUZY CHIAZZARI

PART ONE

INTRODUCING COLOUR

Across every continent and in every culture, the ancient language of colour dominates and permeates our lives. But few of us realize this. In our fast-moving world we are constantly bombarded by colour, yet many of us have lost touch with its meanings. Colour surrounds us, it feeds and nourishes our senses. We see it, feel it, and absorb it. Our minds, bodies, and spirits are profoundly affected by it. The impact of colour on us is multifarious.

Our bodies are stimulated and energized by some colours, or calmed and relaxed by others. Colours can be healing — and they can be harmful. The health of our internal organs, the circulation of the blood, the nervous, lymphatic, and endocrine systems — all the workings of the body are constantly altered by the colours to which we expose ourselves. Mentally and emotionally colour works on a deep level, changing our mood and our sense of well-being, as well as others' perception of us. Spiritually, too, colour is of immense significance. Employed in religious ritual throughout time, colour is the language of the soul. From the saffron robes of Tibetan Buddhist monks and the royal blue of the Virgin Mary's cloak in Christianity, to the black and white worn to represent death, birth, and renewal the world over, the beliefs that colours symbolize are communicated with an extraordinary immediacy which words can never match.

But humans are not the only creatures on our planet who are affected by colour. In the animal and plant worlds colour can mean survival or extinction. Colour is used to attract, camouflage, ward off danger, and send sexual signals. Colour is intrinsic to life, and it is as important to our species as it is to the plant and animal kingdoms. It is a lost language we must relearn for our own health, happiness, and perhaps even survival on this planet.

WHAT IS COLOUR?

*The Universe is a magnetic field of positive and negative
charges, constantly vibrating and producing electromagnetic waves.
Each of these has a different wavelength and speed of vibration;
together they form the electromagnetic spectrum.*

LONG WAVES		VISIBLE SPECTRUM	SHORT WAVES		
RADIO WAVES	INFRA-RED		ULTRA-VIOLET	X-RAYS	GAMMA WAVES
INVISIBLE		VISIBLE RAYS OF DAYLIGHT	INVISIBLE		

*RIGHT We can see
only 40 percent of
colours. These are
contained in sunlight
and range from red
through orange,
yellow, green, and
blue to violet.*

THE ELECTRO~ MAGNETIC SPECTRUM

We can see about 40 percent of the colours,
contained in sunlight. So although white light
appears colourless and intangible, it is made up
of distinct colour vibrations, which have not only
wavelengths but also a "corpuscular structure."
The radiant energy of pure white sunlight is a
vital factor in nourishing our bodies, our minds,
and our spirits, and each colour vibration has its
own healing qualities.

*BELOW The
rainbow colours form
just one octave of colours
in the electromagnetic
spectrum. There are 60
or 70 octaves in total.*

The colours in light

One way colours in sunlight are made visible to
us is to pass white light through a prism. Because
each of the colours has a different wavelength,
each is bent by a different amount. Rainbows are
formed when water droplets in the sky act as
natural prisms. As sunlight passes through the
droplets, each of the different rays is bent by a
different amount, creating a rainbow. The
rainbow colours form one "octave" of light and
are known as the "true hues."

Red is the longest wavelength we can see and
it has the slowest frequency of vibration. Its
magnetic energy is warming and stimulating.
Violet has the shortest wavelength and the
quickest vibration. It is cooling and cleansing.

Beyond the visible spectrum

At either end of the visible spectrum are many
wavelengths we cannot see. Ultraviolet light is
just beyond violet, and farther beyond this are
electromagnetic rays with increasing frequencies
as the wavelengths get progressively shorter;
these include X-rays and gamma rays.

At the opposite end, infrared light is found
just beyond red light. Like red it has warming
qualities although it gives off more concentrated
heat; these qualities are utilized in infrared lamps.
Beyond this are electromagnetic rays with
increasing wavelengths and decreasing frequencies; these include radio waves.

Mystics have long believed that we can see
colours well outside our normal range of vision
by opening our "third eye" during meditation.

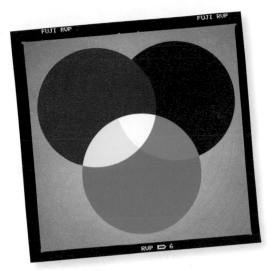

MAKING COLOURS

White light can be separated into three basic or primary colours: red-orange, green, and blue-violet. When these colours of light are projected together (e.g. if a lighting engineer in a theater were to merge spotlights of these colours together), they create white light. This is called additive mixing of colours; it is used, for instance, by colour therapists healing with coloured light.

The colours that make up the pigments we use in paints, fabrics, and other materials are different; they are obtained by subtraction of light. This effect produces a different trio of primary pigment colours: red, blue, and yellow; they are considered primary because they cannot be made from other colours. When these are combined as paints, they produce black. Subtractive mixing of colours is used, for instance, when working with paints or objects like clothes or furnishings.

COLOUR WHEELS

If we arrange all these colours around a circle we have a colour wheel. Looking at the colour wheel we can see that certain colours fall opposite to each other. Each colour has a complementary or opposite hue. So on the colour wheel we have three complementary pairs.

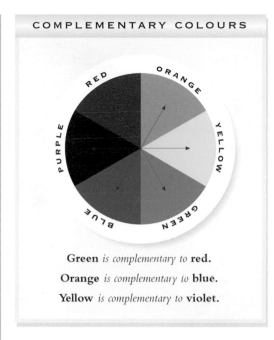

COMPLEMENTARY COLOURS

Green *is complementary to* **red.**

Orange *is complementary to* **blue.**

Yellow *is complementary to* **violet.**

Just as positive and negative magnets attract each other, so do complementary colours. You can prove this for yourself by staring at each colour in turn and then quickly moving your gaze to a white piece of paper. For a few moments you will be able to see an after-image of the complementary colour on the paper.

You could keep mixing adjacent colours to produce colour wheels with 12, 24, 48, or more variations; each time the difference between two adjacent colours becomes more subtle.

You can also make another colour wheel from the additive colours of light. The colours featured on this alternative wheel would be the three primaries of red, green, and blue-violet, and the secondary colours of turquoise, yellow, and magenta.

If you combine any two primary colour pigments, you end up with another trio of pigments: red and yellow make orange, yellow and blue make green, and red and blue make violet. These are the three secondary colours.

FAR LEFT When the three primaries are projected together on a screen, they create white light. This is called additive mixing.

LEFT When primary colours red, blue, and yellow are combined together as paints they make black. This is called subtractive mixing.

HOW DO WE SENSE COLOUR?

Our eyes are undeniably our primary sense organs, for without sight we find living harsh and difficult. It is primarily through our eyes that natural sunlight enters the body, although we also take in light through our skin and through the air we breathe.

RIGHT *Light travels through the pupil to reach the lens. The lens bends the rays of light, so they come to a focus on the retina covering the back of the eye.*

THE IRIS MUSCLES CONTROL THE AMOUNT OF LIGHT ENTERING THE EYE

THE LENS PROVIDES FOCUSING POWER AND BENDS LIGHT RAYS

THE LIGHT RAYS ARE FOCUSED WHEN THEY REACH THE RETINA

SENSING COLOUR THROUGH THE EYES

When light rays arrive at the eye they travel through the pupil and the fluid in front of the eye to reach the lens. Like the lens of a camera, the eye lens bends (refracts) the light rays, so they come to a focus on the retina, a layer of cells at the back of the eye.

When light reaches the retina it stimulates the cells there. These cells contain pigments that are sensitive to light. The cells are of two types: rods and cones. Rods are more highly light sensitive and allow us to see in dim light, but do not record colour, only shades of gray. Cones, which are less numerous, are comprised of three types, each of which is sensitive to one of the three primary colours of light – red-orange, green, and blue-violet. The cones that are sensitive to green light are situated directly in the middle of the retina, allowing light to fall into the center of the eye. This makes the colour green the most relaxing colour for the eyes and, in turn, the mind.

RIGHT *The cells of the retina are made up of rods and cones. Rod cells (orange) are highly light sensitive but only gather shades of gray. It is the three types of core cell (blue), in the center of the retina, which gather the colours in light.*

Light arriving at the retina causes the pigment in the sensory cells to break down. This has the effect of setting off a nervous impulse that travels along the optic nerve to the visual areas (the visual cortex) at the back of the brain. Impulses from the right eye travel to the left side of the brain, while those from the left side travel to the right half of the brain. This means that the nerve fibers actually cross over, in a part of the brain called the optic chiasma.

Not all the light impulses received through our eyes are used solely for the purpose of sight, however. Nervous impulses from the eyes travel not only to the visual cortex of the brain but also

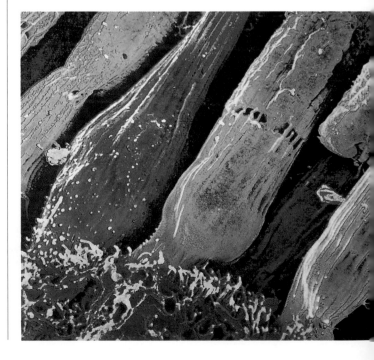

via the hypothalamus to the pituitary and pineal glands. Therefore, many body functions are stimulated or retarded by light, and different colours of light have specific effects on the brain and nervous system. The different-coloured rays also have effects on our energy system and the more subtle layers of our being.

FEELING COLOUR THROUGH THE SKIN

Light enters our body also through our skin. We have all experienced the warming and indeed burning rays of infrared light, when we have been out in the sun for too long. Even when we are clothed we still have a natural sensitivity to the colour wavelengths.

Often we are only aware of the effects of colour energy through our skin when we find some clothes uncomfortable to wear while others make us feel warm, relaxed, and confident. It is not only the texture of the fabric but also the different energies contained in the colours that affect us.

Although our sensitivity to colour through our skin is mostly unconscious, it is also possible to develop a sensitivity to colour energy through our fingertips and other parts of our

bodies. Many blind people are able to differentiate colours by passing their fingers or hands over an object and actually feel the quality of the colour. Some colours feel hot while others seem cool; often people with no sight also describe colours by their texture and feel.

In Russia, sighted people have also been taught to identify colours through their hands. It takes only a few weeks of instruction for anyone to learn to do this. Like riding a bicycle, this skill is never lost. Many healers working with colour are also sensitive to colour vibrations and can identify them within our bodies.

You can try an experiment in this yourself, by cutting out some brightly coloured paper or felt squares. Close your eyes and, holding your hands just above each square in turn, try to feel the quality of each colour. You will be surprised how easy it is to distinguish between warm and cool colours.

BLUE IS A COOL COLOUR AND HAS A CALMING, SOOTHING EFFECT ON THE WEARER

ABOVE *The energies in the colour of clothing affect us. This is why some clothes make us feel comfortable and relaxed.*

PLACE A VARIETY OF COLOURED PAPER OR FELT SQUARES ON A TABLE

HOLD YOUR HANDS OVER EACH SQUARE, CLOSE YOUR EYES AND TRY TO FEEL THE QUALITY OF EACH COLOUR

LEFT *Try this experiment to see if you can sense the different colour vibrations of the warm and cool colours.*

HOW DOES COLOUR AFFECT OUR BODIES?

The effect of colour does not end when we close our eyes. Light is required for our cells to function normally, and individual colours affect them by causing changes in growth and behavior. It therefore affects our system at a cellular level, and the vibrational patterns giving us life, hold us together. At death, these patterns are broken down and the body begins to decay.

ABOVE *In the summer we have abundant energy, which is stimulated by the full range of colours in sunlight.*

First, coloured light affects the pituitary gland, called the "master gland" of the endocrine system since it produces substances that regulate the hormones produced by the endocrine glands. These control many of our body functions including our patterns of growth and sleep, our temperature control, our sexual drive, and energy levels, our metabolic rate, and appetite.

The pineal gland located deep within the brain is also light sensitive. This gland acts as an internal body clock, producing a substance called melatonin, which regulates our daily sleep cycles and also inhibits sexual maturation. At night the lack of natural sunlight results in an increase in melatonin production, which aids sleep, while daylight suppresses its production.

The amount and quality of the light reaching the pineal also alter with the seasons. Changes in the proportions of the colours within sunlight according to season cause our body functions, like those of animals and plants, to mimic the energy of the seasons. So during the summer we feel full of vibrant energy, while during the winter we conserve energy by becoming less active.

RED

Red is the most physical of all colours and has the slowest vibratory rate and longest wavelength. It is the colour of blood and has a stimulating action on our heart and circulation; red light will raise the blood pressure. Our body system is fortified by red, which helps build up red blood cells. It also stimulates the adrenal glands, helping us become strong and building up our stamina.

Pink, which is a mixture of red to which white has been added, is more gentle in its stimulation than red and helps our muscles relax.

ORANGE

Orange stimulates the sexual organs and has a strong and beneficial effect on the digestive system. It also strengthens the immune system, including the spleen, and the lungs and pancreas. It has a releasing action on the body fluids.

YELLOW

Yellow wavelengths of light stimulate the brain, making you alert, clear-headed, and decisive. Yellow also strengthens the nervous system generally. It creates energy in the muscles by

[handwritten note in margin: Scientific proof Red lowers cortisol ∴ lowers stress also red has no effect on testosterone or aggression.]

activating motor nerves. It also activates the lymph system and cleanses the digestive tract. It has a sympathetic resonance with the pancreas, the liver, and the gall bladder.

ABOVE *The green of nature relaxes the body and mind and soothes the soul.*

GREEN

Green is good for the heart on a physical and emotional level. It brings physical equilibrium and relaxation. It has a balancing quality and helps regulate our circulation. It also stimulates the pituitary gland. It works through the sympathetic nervous system, relaxing the muscles in our chests to help us breathe more deeply and slowly.

BLUE

Blue is linked to the throat and thyroid gland and is very soothing, cooling, and calming. Blue light has been shown to lower blood pressure by calming the autonomic nervous system. It has a constrictive action and is anti-inflammatory.

Deep blue stimulates the pituitary gland, which regulates our sleep patterns. Dark blue has wonderful pain-healing properties. It also works on the skeleton, keeping bone marrow healthy.

Scientific proof Blue has no effect on cortisol + no effect on testosterone

TURQUOISE

Turquoise has a sympathetic resonance with the thymus gland; this gland performs a major role in warding off infections. If you suffer from frayed nerves and a weakened immune system, turquoise acts like a refreshing tonic. It also stimulates the thyroid gland and lungs.

INDIGO

Indigo has been found to have narcotic qualities, and some doctors in Texas have used indigo light to induce anesthesia for minor operations.

VIOLET

Violet affects the brain and nervous system and has a purifying and antiseptic effect. It cools the system and alleviates "hot" conditions such as heat rash and sunburn. Violet also suppresses hunger and balances the body's metabolism.

BELOW *Each of the systems in our body is associated with a different colour vibration. When the body is lacking one colour in the spectrum the system related to that colour suffers.*

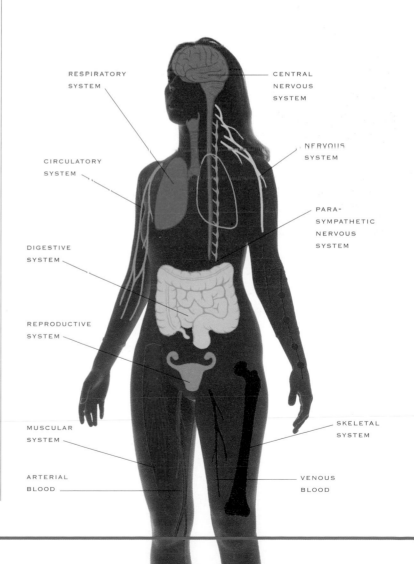

RESPIRATORY SYSTEM

CENTRAL NERVOUS SYSTEM

NERVOUS SYSTEM

CIRCULATORY SYSTEM

PARA-SYMPATHETIC NERVOUS SYSTEM

DIGESTIVE SYSTEM

REPRODUCTIVE SYSTEM

MUSCULAR SYSTEM

SKELETAL SYSTEM

ARTERIAL BLOOD

VENOUS BLOOD

THE PSYCHOLOGY OF COLOUR

We all know that colour can affect our moods. We find some colours uplifting and inspiring, and others depressing. We often use terms such as "feeling blue," "yellow-bellied," "green with envy," and "seeing red" without thinking of the meaning behind the words.

Our feelings and emotions are directly affected by the balance or imbalance of hormones in the body; since this is affected by colours (*see* p 16) they will also have a marked influence on our moods and feelings. Certain colours can calm our minds, while others stimulate mental activity. By restoring a balance of colour energy flowing to the pituitary, metabolic and emotional equilibrium can be restored. This can alleviate stress, tension, anxiety, and depression. Certain colours can help us deal with feelings of loneliness, frustration, and grief.

Using colour to alter emotional energy also results in changed perceptions of the world, and our experience of it. Since colour directly links to the subconscious mind we can use it to diagnose and treat a problem at a deep level.

RED

Red is a powerful colour that has always been associated with vitality and ambition. It can help overcome negative thoughts. However, it is also associated with anger; if we have too much red in our system, or around us, we may feel irritable, impatient, and uncomfortable.

Pink is emotionally soothing and calming, and gives a feeling of gentle warmth and nurturing. It lessens feelings of irritation and aggression, surrounding us with a sense of love and protection. It also alleviates loneliness, despondency, oversensitivity, and vulnerability. While red relates more to sexuality, pink is associated with unselfish love.

*ABOVE **Red is an energizing colour that can help combat negative thoughts and emotions.***

*RIGHT **Cheerful and optimistic, yellow is the colour of the sun. It can aid communication and self-expression.***

ORANGE

Orange is a joyous colour. It frees and releases emotions and alleviates feelings of self-pity, lack of self-worth, and unwillingness to forgive. It stimulates the mind, renewing interest in life; it is a wonderful antidepressant and lifts the spirits. Apricot/peach is good for nervous exhaustion.

YELLOW

Yellow is also a happy, bright, and uplifting colour, a celebration of sunny days. It is associated with the intellectual side of the mind, and the expression of thoughts. It therefore aids the powers of discernment and discrimination, memory and clear thinking, decision-making and good judgment. It also helps good organization, assimilation of new ideas, and the ability to see different points of view. It builds self-confidence and encourages an optimistic attitude. Conversely, dull yellow can be the colour of fear.

GREEN

Green has a strong affinity with nature, helping us connect with empathy to others and the natural world. We instinctively seek it out when under stress or experiencing emotional trauma. It creates a feeling of comfort, laziness and relaxation, calmness, and space, lessening stress, balancing and soothing the emotions. Dark green is helpful for emotional uncertainty.

But when green becomes muddy, dull, or olive, it indicates decay. Just like fallen leaves when they return to the Earth, muddy green represents the onset of death and is nondescript, unassertive, a negation of life and joy. Lime and olive-green can have a detrimental effect on both physical and emotional health since sickly yellow and green are associated with the emotions of envy, resentment, and possessiveness.

TURQUOISE

We associate blue-greens with the refreshing and cool ocean. It is therefore invigorating, cooling, and calming. Like green, turquoise is good for mental strain and tiredness or feeling washed-out. It is an elevating colour that encourages us to make a sparkling fresh start. Turquoise is also helpful for feelings of loneliness, since it heightens communication, sensitivity, and creativity.

BLUE

Blue is a cool, calming colour and is associated with a higher part of the mind than yellow. It represents the night, so makes us feel calm and relaxed as if we are being soothed by the deep blue of the night sky. Light and soft blue, make us feel quiet and protected from all the bustle and activity of the day, and alleviate insomnia. Blue inspires mental control, clarity, and creativity. Midnight blue has a strong sedative effect on the mind, allowing us to connect to our intuitive and feminine side. Too much dark blue can be depressing, however.

ABOVE *Green is a stress-relieving, calming colour. It creates a feeling of peace and security.*

LEFT *Blue is tranquil, soothing, and encourages creativity. Midnight blue has a particularly relaxing effect.*

INDIGO, VIOLET, AND PURPLE

Indigo, violet and purple have a deep affect on the psyche and have been used in psychiatric care to help calm and pacify patients suffering from a number of mental and nervous disorders. These colours balance the mind and also help transform obsessions and fears.

Indigo is a powerful, psychic colour associated with the right side of the brain, and stimulates intuition and imagination. It is also a strong sedative. Violet and purple are colours of transformation at a very deep level, bringing peace and combating shock or fear. They have a cleansing effect in emotional disturbances. They are also connected with artistic and musical impulses, mystery, and sensitivity to beauty and high ideals, stimulating creativity, inspiration, sensitivity, spirituality, and compassion. Violet can exert strong psychic influences, however, and a person attracted by it has to guard against living in a fantasy world. Purple is associated with psychic protection.

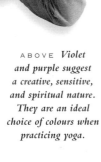

ABOVE *Violet and purple suggest a creative, sensitive, and spiritual nature. They are an ideal choice of colours when practicing yoga.*

MAGENTA

When we are feeling despondent and worried about our condition, or are feeling angry and frustrated, magenta draws us out of this attitude and lets our spirits soar. It is a spiritual colour but also with practical overtones, associated with a compassion, support, and kindness.

From a negative perspective, magenta, like violet, makes us desire to be lifted out of the demanding world and avoid challenges. It can also be too relaxing. So avoid magenta if you are chronically depressed or introverted.

WHITE

The colour of ultimate purity is white. It is an all-round colour of protection, bringing peace and comfort, alleviating emotional shock and despair, and helping inner cleansing of emotions, thoughts, and spirit. If you need time and space to reflect on your life, white can give you a feeling of freedom and uncluttered openness. Too much white, however, can be cold and isolating, because white separates us from other people.

BLACK

This colour is both comforting, protective, and mysterious. It is associated with silence, the infinite, and the feminine life force – passive, uncharted, and mysterious. Black can also prevent us from growing and changing. We often cloak ourselves in black to hide from the world.

GRAY

Associated with independence, self-reliance, self-control, gray acts as a shield from outside influence. However, gray generally has a negative feeling – thick gray clouds, fog, and smoke. Gray is the colour of evasion and noncommitment since it is neither black nor white. It relates to walling everything off, remaining separate, uncommitted, and uninvolved, inevitably leading to loneliness. It also denotes self-criticism.

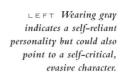

LEFT *Wearing gray indicates a self-reliant personality but could also point to a self-critical, evasive character.*

SILVER

Silver is the colour of the moon, which is ever-changing. It relates to the feminine principle and the emotional, sensitive aspect of the mind. It balances, harmonizes, and is mentally cleansing.

GOLD

Like yellow, gold is associated with the sun and is therefore related to abundance and power, higher ideals, wisdom, and understanding. It is mentally revitalizing, energizing, and inspiring, and helpful for fear, uncertainty, and lack of interest. Pale gold is excellent for depression and sharpens the mind.

BROWN

The colour of Mother Earth, brown brings a sense of stability, alleviating insecurity. However, it also relates to bottling up of emotion, a retreat from and a fear of the outside world, and also narrow-mindedness. This often results from a lack of self-worth.

LEFT *Brown clothing reflects a stable, secure nature – all characteristics associated with Mother Earth.*

PSYCHOLOGICAL ASSOCIATIONS OF COLOURS

RED: *vital, powerful, warm, cozy, sensual, determined, friendly, courageous, assertive, antidepressant, angry, impatient*

PINK: *emotionally soothing and calming, gently warming, nurturing, kind, considerate, unselfish loving*

ORANGE/PEACH: *warm, secure, glowing, creative, stimulating, fun, enlivening, uplifting, bringing laughter and joy, humorous, independent*

YELLOW: *uplifting, happy, light, bright, mentally stimulating, logical, intelligent, orderly, optimistic, clear thinking, fearful*

GREEN: *harmonizing, mental and physical relaxation, peaceful, natural, cooling, calming, balancing, sincere, secure, free, contented, sharing, self-control, generous*

TURQUOISE: *refreshing, cooling, mentally calming, youthful, strengthening concentration and control over speech, and powers of communication, confidence*

BLUE: *cooling, cleansing, relaxing, mentally calming, bringing peace, tranquillity, and wisdom, spacious like the sea and sky, sensitive, hopeful, faithful, trusting, flexible, reassuring, accepting*

INDIGO/VIOLET/PURPLE: *dramatic, spiritual, creative, intuitive, meditative, mystical, inspirational of beauty and art, protective, cleansing*

MAGENTA: *supportive, natural, yielding, compassionate, kind, considerate*

WHITE: *peaceful, purifying, cold, isolating, creating space to think*

BLACK: *comforting, mysterious, feminine, protective, restrictive*

GRAY: *independent, self-reliant, separating, lonely, self-critical*

SILVER: *changing, balancing and harmonizing, feminine, sensitive*

GOLD: *wisdom, understanding, powerful, high ideals, abundance*

BROWN: *nurturing, earthy, supportive, retreating, narrow-minded*

COLOUR IN THE PLANT AND ANIMAL WORLDS

The colour energies that plants and animals receive from natural sunlight help them to keep their patterns of growth and behavior in harmony with their environment, in tune with natural cycles of day and night and with seasonal changes.

ABOVE *Insects have a highly developed sense of colour, using it to identify their food.*

RIGHT *Foxes, like other night hunters, can see shorter wavelengths than humans, enabling them to see in the dark.*

BELOW *Fish are similar to insects in that they are colour-sighted. The colours red and black with yellow signal danger and help to ward off predators.*

Different colour wavelengths affect growth and flowering times in plants. The plant and animal kingdoms also use colour as a language among members of their group, and also for interspecies communication. Generally in nature the colour red, or the combination yellow-black, spells danger, and many plants, insects, fish, and other animals have this colouring to discourage other creatures from approaching them. Red can also be a sexual signal, aiding mating displays in animals, and in plants attracting pollinating insects.

COLOUR SENSE IN ANIMALS

The animal kingdom is governed by the same five senses that we have, but some of these are much more highly developed, all being closely linked. Human eyes see better than the eyes of lower animals simply because our brains are better able to interpret the messages coming from our sense organs. Most mammals except apes are virtually colourblind, but insects, birds, and fish all have colour vision. Many animals see better

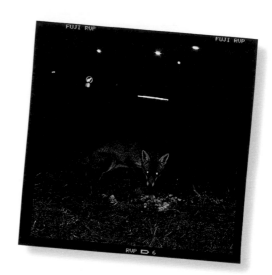

in the dark than human beings, although we see better in the daylight. Most warm-blooded creatures have no need to see colour although they are extremely sensitive to other types of electromagnetic information (*see below*). However, just because an animal's eyes are unable to see a certain colour frequency does not mean that they are not aware or affected by it. For instance, a bull cannot actually see the colour red, but this does not mean that it is not affected by the red colour vibration.

NIGHT HUNTERS

Those animals who need to see at night will see shorter light wavelengths, while those whose food is hidden often also have the capacity to sense red or infrared waves, which emit heat, or sound. For instance, cats can "see" infrared, and this is the reason why they always find the warmest spot in the house. Cats, foxes, owls, and

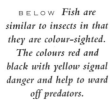

other night predators have a highly developed sense of sight and are able to see much longer wavelengths than we can. Many night hunters such as owls and cats have a third, additional eyelid known as the *tapetum*; this is a reflective translucent lid that is drawn across the eye in bright sunlight and acts like sunglasses, filtering the strong light.

BIRDS AND INSECTS

Colour is highly developed in birds and some insects; it is through colour messages that they are able to identify suitable food. The eyes of these animals are sensitive to different ranges of colours from infrared through to ultraviolet light. Birds, for example, are sensitive to longer wavelengths than we are, while many insects are able to see ultraviolet light.

In the insect world, mosquitoes have been shown to sense colour and prefer dark blue, red, and brown, while avoiding yellow, pink, and other light colours. Bees can see ultraviolet but not orange and red vibrations; a flower that appears a uniform yellow to the human eye may have ultraviolet pollen guides and patterns visible to the bee.

OTHER SENSES

The supersensitivity of animals to electromagnetic vibrations of all types makes them aware of many subtle changes in the environment long before we are. Many have a keen sense of hearing that extends well above or below our own range of sound; whales and elephants communicate by transmitting extremely low-frequency sounds, which travel great distances. Animals generally have a much keener sense of smell and taste than we do, or are sensitive to other types of electromagnetic vibrations such as the earth's magnetic field and the effect of the moon, heat, and electricity, while many appear to have a "sixth sense," which enables them to do seemingly strange and incredible things.

Not only are animals able to see and hear electromagnetic vibrations out of our visible range, they are also able to sense other types of vibrations that permeate the air. Many animals become extremely nervous and agitated just before a thunderstorm, and may hide away under a bed or their bodies may start to shake; they are sensing the change in electrical vibrations, for the air becomes charged with positive ions just before a storm. Their tension is then released when it actually rains because water releases negative ions into the atmosphere, balancing the positive ions.

ABOVE *Although this passion flower has a vibrant colour, it may be that it is ultraviolet pollen guides that attract bees.*

LEFT *The eyes of insects can pick up a wider range of colours than human eyes can, including ultraviolet light.*

COLOUR IN
SYMBOL AND RITUAL

*Humankind has always regarded colour as having great
symbolic and religious significance. To the first humans living
outdoors, the colours of day and night were all-important.*

ABOVE *Colour is
used symbolically in
religious rituals the
world over, such as the
Sing Sing ceremony in
Papua New Guinea.*

During daytime our ancestors were able to hunt and protect themselves from enemies, so the red Earth and the yellow sun came to symbolize life, while the blue-black of night related to passivity and quiet. Darkness was also frightening and dangerous, so black was associated with death. For some societies, certain colours acquired particular importance – for instance, the Maori distinguish many hues of red, while the Inuit perceive many shades of white. In our urban society, we have come to distinguish many grays.

Social respect and status were marked by a variety of colours in Ancient Greece. Natural scientists such as Empedocles and the Renais-

sance physician Paracelsus also considered colour the soul of life and the root of all existence; the four elements of Earth, Air, Fire, and Water (*see* p 198) were given the colours of yellow, black, red, and white respectively. Finally, many contemporary artists and philosophers have attributed spiritual qualities to colour. These extremely intense "subtle bodies" of colours cannot be seen with the eye, but only with the inner vision as the "third eye" opens. White is linked to intelligence, yellow to spirit, green to the soul, red to nature and the will, bright green to the imagination, and blue to intuition.

RED

According to Hebrew tradition, the name of Adam, the first man, means "red" or "alive," and still today, in some Slavic languages, red denotes "living" or "beautiful." To the Ancient Egyptians, red was the colour of Ra, the sun God, and later in Roman times it was linked to Mars, the God of War. To this day, red is still associated with war; red and black were adopted as the colours of the Russian Revolution and later in the 1930s by the Nazis in Germany.

ORANGE AND YELLOW

Orange is the colour of love and happiness to the Chinese and Japanese, while the orange robes of Buddhist monks represent humility. In some portrayals of the Garden of Eden, an orange rather than an apple is shown on the Tree of Knowledge. To the Hindus, and to Christians too, the colour yellow signifies Life and Truth.

GREEN

In both European and Chinese tradition, green is associated with spring and new growth. Green also represents the spirit and the fertility of nature, giving Northern Europe the mythology of the the Green Man, while to the Ancient Greeks it was the colour of Venus, the Goddess of Love. Islam also holds the colour green as sacred, for in its tradition Allah is present in nature

but never shown in human form; green was therefore the colour of the prophet. In Christianity, St. John accredited Jesus Christ with a rich emerald green, which is also the colour of the Trinity.

BLUE

This is the colour given to the Virgin Mary, known in popular European Catholicism as the "Queen of Heaven," who is often shown with a royal blue cloak. In Greek and Roman mythology, the sky gods Jupiter, Juno, and Mercury were associated with blue. In the Old Testament, God the Father was also represented by a deep blue. In Islam, blue or turquoise is the colour of the Islamic religion and community, and often decorates mosques. Blue also symbolizes peace, truth, and cooperation, and is used for the flag of the United Nations and the background of the European flag.

PURPLE

The rich hue of purple has always been associated with royalty and also spiritual authority. Kings, emperors, and priests are clothed in purple gowns. This is partly because in ancient cultures only the wealthiest could afford the expensive purple dyes for cloth. It was often the custom to wrap a newborn baby in purple cloth to encourage prosperity and success.

BLACK

Black is the colour of the planet Saturn, and the Roman God of Agriculture whose midwinter festival later became Christmas. In Ancient Egypt it was the colour of Isis, the Black Virgin Goddess who symbolized the fertile black earth of the Nile, so black cats were considered sacred in Ancient Egypt. This tradition was later brought to Europe.

WHITE

White is the colour of the moon, and in Imperial Rome, China, and India, it is also the colour of death. The custom of brides wearing white on their wedding day originated in Ancient Greece; the temple dedicated to the goddess Athena was created in white marble, so the colour white came to signify virginity.

ABOVE Black cats were seen as sacred in Ancient Egypt and are still the source of superstition today.

LEFT The Green Man, clothed in leaves, with the staff "from which he sprang," was an icon of fecundity and new life throughout Northern Europe.

LEFT White traditionally symbolizes purity and virginity, and is still predominantly worn by brides in Western countries.

PART TWO

COLOUR AND YOU

Before we can care for others and our environment we have to learn to care for ourselves. Our aim should be to work on ourselves from both within and without, eventually leading to perfect balance and harmony of mind and spirit. We are instinctively drawn to certain colours during our lives. Sometimes a colour will remain our favorite for our whole life but at other times we are drawn to colours fleetingly. These attractions can tell us a great deal about ourselves, often reflecting our general health. By introducing certain colours into our wardrobe, cosmetics, and jewelry we can enhance our natural character traits, building up our self-confidence so that we can be ourselves.

The colours we are attracted to are strongly linked to our personal colouring, in our hair, eyes, and skin. We naturally choose colours that harmonize with our own colour energy. If we find we are surrounded by colours that do not harmonize it will cause an energy imbalance in our system, with the result that we will feel lousy and have problems in different areas of our life. Colour can be very effective in remedying these imbalances; by introducing complementary colour energies we can restore peace and contentment.

Since we take in colour not only through our eyes but also through our skin, our clothing can be either beneficial or have an adverse affect on our health. Fabric acts as a light filter and the different colours of clothes we wear will allow different colour wavelengths to permeate.

Colour vibrations and aromas are closely linked. Our experience of many aromatic herbs and flowers is a combination of scent and colour. Essential oils and other aromatic plant-based beauty products contain light energy from the sun that have many therapeutic qualities. We can use these for body care and perfume to enhance our inner harmony and sense of well-being.

YOUR OWN PERSONAL COLOURING

We are all born with individual colouring. Our skins, eyes, and hair all have a particular colour and tone. This is not an accident; our genetic makeup sets the basic colour blueprint, while other environmental factors also influence it.

There is no way we can predict the exact colouring a child will have. However, according to genetic science it is likely that a child will have the colouring of one or both parents, whichever genes are strongest. It is not enough though just to look at your parents. I am one of those people whose colouring is quite different from both my parents. Instead of inheriting their brown hair and eyes (both qualities of which are dominant), I inherited the fair colouring of my grandparents. This means that each of my parents must have been carrying a gene for fair colouring. The genes for fair colouring are less "strong" than those for dark colouring (they are called "recessive"). Sometimes these genes can be carried hidden for several generations, before appearing in a newborn child.

But why is a particular child born with dark or fair colouring? I do not believe that this is a result of a cosmic roulette game. My mother tells me I was born with a mass of dark hair, which fell out and when it grew again it was auburn. The hair colour of many children changes as the child grows older and develops its personality.

Avicenna (980–1037), an Arabian disciple of Aristotle, believed that the innate temperament of people might be found written in the colour of the hair. So your natural colouring will give you strong clues as to the type of person you are. Perhaps my hair colouring changed from black to red so that it would be more in keeping with my particular personality!

FAIR HAIR HAS BEEN PASSED DOWN FROM THE GRANDMOTHER TO HER GRANDCHILD

EYE COLOURS

Scientists in the United States have now found a link between the eye colours of children and their personalities. Dark-eyed children were found to be more gregarious and outgoing than their blue-eyed peers.

THE DOMINANT DARK COLOURING OF THE PARENTS HAS BEEN OVERRIDDEN IN THEIR CHILD BY A FAIR GENE

RIGHT *Recessive genes can sometimes skip a generation, passing from grandparents to grandchildren.*

YOUR RULING COLOUR VIBRATION

We tend to have a particular colour that best expresses our personality type and makes us feel most comfortable or gives us extra vitality and inspiration. This colour is often the consequence of our physical colouring and body type.

FAIR-HAIRED PEOPLE ARE EXPECTED TO BE LIVELY AND FUN

RED-HAIRED PEOPLE ARE EXPECTED TO HAVE FIERY TEMPERS

DARK-HAIRED PEOPLE ARE OFTEN SEEN AS SERIOUS AND MORE STABLE THAN THOSE WITH LIGHTER HAIR

LEFT *We tend to assume that the different types of colouring are invested with very different personalities.*

Red-haired people, who generally have blue or green eyes, find they feel happy and comfortable in blue, turquoise, and green, and naturally look good in these colours. A person with a dark or sallow complexion, or dark hair and eyes, is likely to be attracted by bright, rich colours. People with pale complexions will generally feel more comfortable in clear softer pastels. Fair-haired people often have blue, gray, or green eyes; their preference is frequently for blue and green.

Our physical colouring, particularly our hair colour, can have a profound psychological effect on others. Dark-haired people are often perceived as vital and mysterious, while fair-haired people are usually expected to be fun-loving. Most of us expect red-haired people to be strong-willed and have fiery tempers. Recent research in Texas, US, and the University of Luton, UK, supports these connections, finding that fair-haired people are more outgoing than their more serious brunette counterparts, while red-haired people are more unpredictable and liable to mood changes.

Many people naturally choose colours in their clothes to complement their personalities without knowing why they have been attracted to those particular colours. Others believe they are choosing a colour for esthetic reasons alone, to complement their colouring. Carole Jackson, in her book *Colour Me Beautiful*, reminds us: "Nature is the best designer and we are born with definite colour preferences." Essentially we tend to know which colours we prefer for our own well-being. These colours usually harmonize perfectly with our natural colouring.

We all know intuitively what colour rules our lives. Say to yourself, "I am a... (colour) person."

DYEING HAIR

Many people strive to change their personal colouring by dyeing their hair or wearing coloured contact lenses. They may be subconsciously drawn to the personality popularly associated with certain colours, which they feel may be lacking.

FINDING YOUR SOUL COLOURS

The colours we are attracted to over long periods of time are linked to our personality type, our strengths and weaknesses, as well as indicating our potential in life.

These colour preferences, which often remain unchanged for our whole lives, are known as "soul colours." They indicate the intrinsic qualities and inner resources we have at our disposal and also the challenges we must face because of our deficiencies.

Look at the colours you wear most often and see what they reveal about you. The following analyses are based on various psychological tests including the Max Luscher Colour Test. This test was developed for use by psychiatrists, psychologists and physicians to provide them with accurate information about a person through his or her choice of colour. I have also used elements of Dorothee Mella's *Self-Image Colour Analysis* and the work of Theo Gimbel, Marie Louise Lacy, and Mary Anderson (*see* Further Reading, p 250).

ABOVE *If you wear red, you are an energetic and excitable person who likes to be the center of attention.*

IF YOU WEAR RED...

You are impulsive, excitable, and energetic. You are ambitious and like things to happen quickly when you want them to do so. You like to be the best in everything you do. You may be a bit insensitive to the feelings of other people, since you like to be the center of attraction. Learn to be a good listener. Red means vital force, with your nervous activity urging you to achieve results and be successful. If you make a habit of wearing red it may indicate that you place importance on sexual desire and eroticism. This energy can be best used in the form

RIGHT *Choosing to wear peach suggests you are caring toward others.*

of creative endeavor, leadership, and development and expansion. You are courageous and extroverted, but tend to become irritable and bad tempered if you do not get your own way. Learn patience. Maroon and brick reds show you are fun-loving, but be careful not to become resentful and feel victimized by others.

IF YOU WEAR PINK...

You have an affectionate, loving nature, which makes you sympathetic and understanding. You may lack willpower and show weakness when you cannot control affairs of the heart. You need a great deal of support from others and can be childlike in your behavior. You must learn to accept and love yourself. If you become more self-reliant you will attract and give out the feelings of warmth and love you desire.

IF YOU WEAR ORANGE, PEACH, OR APRICOT...

You are competent, action-oriented, and impatient. You are also independent, an organizer, and self-motivated. Orange is the colour of practicality and creativity. Your energy levels are high, and you are sometimes restless. You have a forceful will and tend to be active and competitive. You are also excitable and can seek domination over others. Bright orange and burnt orange can make you feel frustrated or blocked. Try wearing peach, which will direct your energy to others in a more caring way.

IF YOU WEAR YELLOW...

You have an interesting and stimulating personality. You like to be active and involved in whatever is going on. Lively and vital, you can cope well with life's challenges. Bright yellow represents spontaneity and communication. You are active, aspiring, and investigatory. There is a desire and hope of greater happiness, which implies some minor conflict in which release is needed. Yellow presses forward to the new, modern, the developing and unformed, and draws in ideas from the "higher mind."

IF YOU WEAR GREEN...

You are a cautious person and not inclined to trust others easily. You are an observer of life, but do not wish to get involved more than you have to. A quiet life suits you best. You are benevolent, humanistic, and service-oriented. If you wear blue-green you need a peaceful environment, wishing release from stress, and freedom from conflicts or disagreement. You take pains to control the situation and its problems by proceeding cautiously. You have sensitivity of feeling and a fine eye for detail. Try wearing pale yellow with your green to help you share yourself and develop an optimistic attitude.

IF YOU WEAR LIGHT BLUE...

You are creative, perceptive, and sensitive. You have a good imagination and practical approach to life. Your approach can be analytical and you are best advised to use your knowledge for problem solving. You like to do things in your own time and not be rushed. You need a secure and peaceful environment.

LEFT *Green is the colour of a cautious person, suited to a quiet life.*

BELOW *Light blue suggests a creative and sensitive nature. A tranquil environment suits you best.*

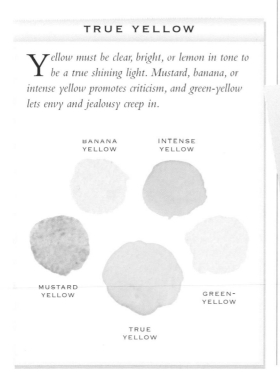

TRUE YELLOW

Y*ellow must be clear, bright, or lemon in tone to be a true shining light. Mustard, banana, or intense yellow promotes criticism, and green-yellow lets envy and jealousy creep in.*

BANANA YELLOW

INTENSE YELLOW

MUSTARD YELLOW

GREEN-YELLOW

TRUE YELLOW

RIGHT *Combining dark blue with green will encourage self-expression and help you to relax.*

FAR RIGHT *Those who wear gray may need to escape from everyday stress.*

BELOW *Wearing purple suggests you have high aspirations.*

IF YOU WEAR DARK BLUE...

You are intelligent, self-reliant, and have a great depth of feeling. You feel a responsibility for others and enjoy decision-making. You need tranquillity around you and must be surrounded with tenderness, love, and affection. Noisy people disturb you. You may suffer from mental stress owing to lack of play and relaxation. Try wearing some blue-greens or greens to help your self-expression and improve your health.

IF YOU WEAR VIOLET...

Yours is a sensitive, compassionate nature so you can be easily imposed upon and should be careful to pick friends who are as sensitive as you are yourself. To be happy, work where you feel needed. Try wearing lilac or magenta, a colour with more red in it. This will boost your self-confidence and provide your vulnerability with protection.

IF YOU WEAR PURPLE...

You are very intuitive and have deep feelings and high aspirations. You are interested in the best of everything, including your friends. Lesser mortals do not interest you or enter into your scheme of things except where necessary. Watch that you do not become arrogant – try to make more time for

listening. Orchid, violet, or grape can make you feel imposed upon by others' belief systems, rules, and regulations. Be sensitive to your personal and spiritual needs. Try yoga or meditation to release mind blocks.

IF YOU WEAR WHITE...

White contains all the other colours in the spectrum, showing that you have a positive, well-balanced, and optimistic personality. You are highly individual, a loner, and might even be lonely. You seek a simplified lifestyle free from outside pressures. You have chosen a simple and pure colour, but one that reaches out for recognition. You are probably going through a transition period with new ideas that have not yet taken form. Be open-minded and communicate, for with white all things are possible.

IF YOU WEAR GRAY...

You are very much an individual. Many people may get the impression you are self-sufficient as you have excellent self-control and prefer to remain uninvolved. Those who wear gray have a tendency to isolate themselves, which can lead to loneliness. You may be passive because you feel stressed and overburdened.

You need rest, relaxation, and freedom from daily stress. Maybe you need a good break – take in the blue of the ocean or green of the countryside. People who wear gray are often those who make judgments and may be good critics. Those who lack judgment and struggle to form opinions should wear gray.

IF YOU WEAR BROWN...

Brown clothing suggests an honest, down-to-earth person who likes a structured, supportive lifestyle. A lover of the best things life has to offer, you are a sensuous type, appreciating good food, drink, and company. Brown is the colour of Mother Earth. It is a protective colour, but you may be bottling up emotion or a secret that makes you retreat into your shell and fear the outside world; thus you feel protected by wearing brown or muddy colours. There is a desire to be emotionally secure and accepted by the outside world. You need to understand your self-worth and ward off narrow-mindedness.

IF YOU WEAR BLACK...

You are strong willed, opinionated, and disciplined. You may be too inflexible and too independent. Watch out that these are not defense tactics. You may really lack confidence in yourself and your own ability to handle life efficiently. It may be you have a little way to go to maturity and are using black to cloak yourself while you discover your true identity. Black represents renunciation – the ultimate surrender or relinquishment – and those who choose to wear black constantly want to renounce everything out of a stubborn protest. Black worn on certain occasions shows you have control of yourself in order to communicate an authoritative image.

LEFT *Black clothes suggest a an organized and independent character. However, they could also signal a lack of confidence.*

THE USES OF GREEN

If you are feeling vulnerable, introduce the balancing effect of green. This colour will draw out earthy brown and help you expand and relate to others without so much hesitation or fear. You need to encourage your imagination and branch out. Try wearing apple green to help you begin new projects, adventures, and opportunities that challenge you. Out of the brown earth grow the greens of life. You can also wear gold or golden yellow to complement your earthy vibrations.

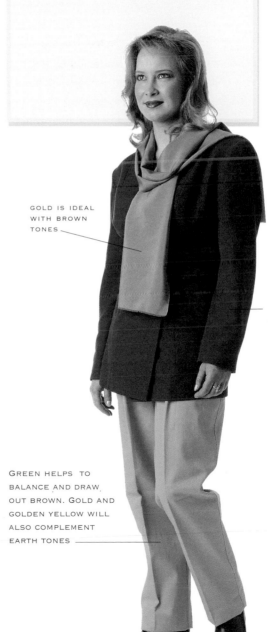

GOLD IS IDEAL WITH BROWN TONES

BROWN CAN BE A PROTECTIVE COLOUR, BUT TOO MUCH CAN SUGGEST A FEAR OF THE OUTSIDE WORLD

GREEN HELPS TO BALANCE AND DRAW OUT BROWN. GOLD AND GOLDEN YELLOW WILL ALSO COMPLEMENT EARTH TONES

SEASONAL COLOUR TYPES

If we study the natural world either scientifically or as an artist or philosopher we will discover that there is an underlying order in natural rhythms and cycles, which repeat themselves year after year.

Each season has its distinctive colours, feelings, sensations, and energy flow. We often forget we are part of this natural order, but our inner makeup fits into the rhythmic and colour patterns found in the seasonal cycles. Our personal colouring can also be classified into different groups that relate to seasonal colours.

Johannes Itten, a colour theorist working from the Bauhaus School of Art in Germany, observed that most of his art students wore and used colours in their artwork that complemented their natural colouring. He noticed that their personal colouring had many similarities to the colours of the four seasons, so he devised a method of colour analysis by grouping people into their seasonal colours. This method has been used very successfully in identifying colours in clothes that suit various natural colourings.

Each of us has a range of colours that suits our seasonal type. Not only do we find that our seasonal classification can give guidance to wearing colours that best suit our looks, but these colours will also best support and express our

personality. Choosing the colours that harmonize with our natural seasonal colouring help us to look good; they also feed our energy levels and boost our self-esteem. The seasonal types not only have distinct personal colouring but also display personality traits that complement their colours. When we dress in colours that suit us we feel good and let our positive qualities shine out.

Look at the following personality descriptions to discover which seasonal colour type you are. Then you can use your seasonal colours to create a wardrobe of colours that will best reflect your character and also provide you with the perfect support you need in many different situations in life. (Also look at p 121 to discover how to combine your best colours together.)

THE WINTER PERSONALITY

- **Skin:** *cool blue or blue-pink undertones, rose-beige, olive, brown*
- **Hair:** *dark brown, black, silvery-gray*
- **Eyes:** *clear whites, iris is black, brown, blue, green*

BELOW *Winter people generally have striking colouring, mirroring the darker, cooler colours and stark contrasts of winter.*

WINTER PEOPLE OFTEN HAVE DARK EYES AND CLEAR WHITE IRISES

SKIN COLOUR TENDS TO BE OLIVE OR DARK IN TONE

DARK HAIR IS CHARACTERISTIC OF THIS TYPE

A SELF-ASSURED CHARACTER IS SUGGESTED BY STRONG, STRIKING COLOURING

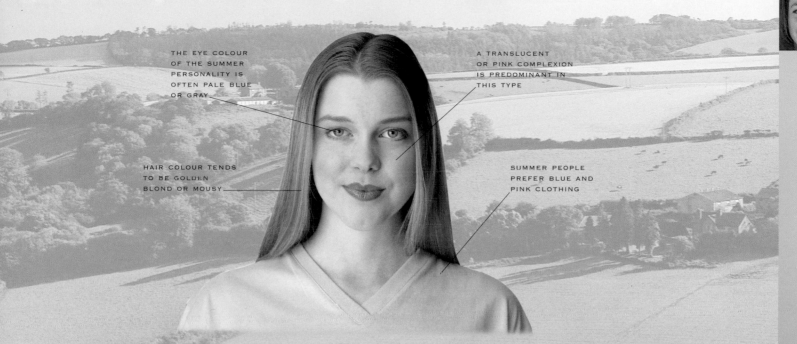

THE EYE COLOUR
OF THE SUMMER
PERSONALITY IS
OFTEN PALE BLUE
OR GRAY

A TRANSLUCENT
OR PINK COMPLEXION
IS PREDOMINANT IN
THIS TYPE

HAIR COLOUR TENDS
TO BE GOLDEN
BLOND OR MOUSY

SUMMER PEOPLE
PREFER BLUE AND
PINK CLOTHING

Winter is a time of darkness, coldness, and strong contrasts. Its signature colours are the dark silhouettes of trees and the white of winter snow. Winter people generally also have striking colouring, which makes them look strong, self-assured, and in control, but in fact they may be shy and prefer their own company. They are usually quite introverted and have a small circle of friends. Winter people appear cold and aloof, but if we take time to get to know them we will discover they have deep emotions lying below the surface. Winter people have strong minds, are deep thinkers, and often do well in business. They are also loyal, responsible, and reliable in a crisis. Quick at making decisions, they prove to be good organizers and often have positions of authority.

THE SUMMER PERSONALITY

- **Skin:** *pink, translucent, and smooth complexion, rose-beige or pale beige*
- **Hair:** *white, golden/ash blond, mousy brown*
- **Eyes:** *misty blue, blue-gray, hazel, gray-brown*

The colours of summer are the blues of the sky and sea, and warm deep hues of pink. These hues reflect the heat of the sun and a joyful summer energy. The pink and blue of summer symbolize the masculine and the feminine aspects within us. Both these colours are present in summer people, making them outgoing and adventurous but also gentle and sensitive. Their cooperative nature makes them good listeners, dependable, and good as part of a team. While they may be go-ahead, summer people are reluctant to acknowledge their talents and to give themselves credit. They also find it difficult to express their feelings. Summer people tend to be serious people but with a warm heart and need to build their self-esteem before they can reach their full potential.

ABOVE *The summer personality combines the energy of the sun with the softness and sensitivity of the sky.*

CONSERVATION AND REST

BLACK

WHITE

WINTER

SUMMER

PINK

BLUE

JOY AND ACTIVITY

LEFT *This chart compares and contrasts the winter and summer personalities.*

SPRING TYPES
OFTEN HAVE GREEN
OR HAZEL EYES

THE "PEACHES AND
CREAM" COMPLEXION
IS TYPICAL OF THE
SPRING PERSONALITY

GOLDEN BLOND
AND BROWN HAIR
IS COMMON

SOFT PINKS AND
PEACH CLOTHES SUIT
THIS TYPE BEST

ABOVE *Spring colouring combines the soft colours of blossom with the pale green of new spring growth.*

THE SPRING PERSONALITY

~ **Skin:** *ivory, peachy pink, golden beige, creamy complexion*

~ **Hair:** *flaxen and golden blond, golden dark brown hair, gray with yellow tone*

~ **Eyes:** *blue or green, blue-gray, hazel*

In the spring, as the sap rises, our spirits feel light and airy after the short dark days of winter. The light soft pastel colours of blossoms help to re-energize us slowly and happily. This season is also full of new life, and its predominant colours are the soft pinks and peaches of spring blossoms and light greens of young shoots and leaves. Spring people are lively, outgoing, gregarious, with soft vitality, laughter, and enthusiasm and full of new ideas. It is as if they cannot contain themselves and so are impetuous. This means that they tend to lack organization and routine in their lives. The natural enthusiasm spring people have for life often results in their trying to take on too many projects at the same time. Although they have boundless energy, they can easily become disorganized. If something particularly captures their imagination, however, they can persevere to reach a goal. They make friends easily and are good humored, with plenty of natural energy. Green relates to both the physical and emotional heart. Spring types certainly have an abundance of love to give, but they can also be superficial and fickle in their relationships.

THE FALL PERSONALITY

~ **Skin:** *golden skin tone, tan, golden-beige to deep copper or ivory*

~ **Hair:** *auburn to copper, strawberry blond to red*

~ **Eyes:** *green-brown, hazel, green*

Fall is a time of year when the leaves drop, our energy levels wind down, and we "return to earth," while colours deepen and become the rich oranges, golds, and russet browns of fallen leaves. Fall people are earthy characters – warm, loyal, and lovable. Like the unpredictable fall weather, they can change quickly from happy to pensive. Moody and unpredictable, one moment they are outgoing and fun-loving, the next they prefer seclusion and quiet. Fall is a time of movement and change and independent fall people do not like routine of any kind. They are also able to handle many projects at once.

FRESHNESS AND GROWTH

GREEN

GOLD

SPRING

FALL

PEACH

ORANGE

RESTLESSNESS AND GATHERING

RIGHT *The colours and characteristics of the spring and fall personalities.*

Knowing our seasonal colour type not only improves our appearance, but helps us select colours that benefit our health (see p 44). Within the colour ranges are warm colours: red, pink, orange, gold, and yellow, and magenta; and cool colours: shades of green, blue, and violet. We can use warm colours to energize us when we are down. Cooling colours help us relax when we are tired; these colours can also help us unwind after a day's work or when we feel emotionally drained. Summer people can wear pinks to warm and strengthen and sky blue for relaxation. Winter people can boost their energy with bright red and unwind in royal blue. Peach is nourishing for spring personalities, while soft greens are relaxing. For a fall colouring, gold and rust colours stimulate while blue-greens sedate. When we have a positive outlook on life we are more likely to be healthy; enthusiasm for life builds up our immune system.

BELOW *The fall personality is warm and friendly and their colouring is reminiscent of the golden leaves of trees and flowers.*

EYES ARE USUALLY GREEN, GREEN-BROWN, OR HAZEL.

FALL PEOPLE OFTEN HAVE AUBURN, COPPER, OR RED HAIR LIKE THE RICH GOLDS OF FALL LEAVES

AN IVORY OR GOLDEN COMPLEXION IS COMMON IN THIS TYPE, AS ARE FRECKLES

THE SEASONS IN TRADITIONAL CHINESE MEDICINE

According to the theory of Traditional Chinese Medicine (T.C.M.) certain tendencies to illness are linked with each season and element. Winter is linked to black, the element of Water, and coldness. The health weakness of winter types lies in the kidneys, the urinary system, and the bones. Summer is associated with red, the element of Fire, and heat; its body areas are the heart, small intestines, and the blood. Spring relates to green, the element of Wood, and the wind; spring people have to protect the liver and gall bladder, the tendons and muscles. Fall is related to white, the element of Metal, and dryness; its body areas are the lungs, large intestine, skin, and hair. Earth, the fifth Chinese element (which has no seasonal denomination and is shown at the center of the cycle of the seasons), is related to yellow, humidity, and the stomach and spleen.

ABOVE *The Chinese traditionally associate each season with a colour and element and these in turn are associated with the different body parts and organs.*

37

COLOUR MOODS

Although we may have favorite colours, there are also many colours to which we are drawn fleetingly, depending on our moods and emotions. These changes in colour preferences can give a helpful indication of changes in our energy levels, illnesses, and areas of life where an imbalance is developing that needs attention.

When we are at critical times in either our personal, social, or work lives we can be drawn to new colours. These colours may be very different from our usual preferred colours; we are drawn to them instinctively, and they may be used to get us through a difficult period or give us energy to make a needed change in our life.

When we wake up each morning we can usually sense which colour mood we are in. When you look in the closet in the morning and there is "nothing to wear" it is probably because the colour you need is not there.

COLOURS AND HEALTH CHANGES

In order to be healthy and feel our best, we require a balance of all the rainbow colours in our energetic system. If we are depleted in one colour energy, another may be too prominent, which will cause imbalance and disharmony. If you surround yourself with the wrong colours, your internal body "colour system" can go wrong, just as you may suffer indigestion by eating the wrong foods. By choosing colours whose "psychology" is sympathetic to your nature and needs, you can make sure you maintain optimum physical, emotional, and mental health.

When we are feeling depressed it is often reflected by wearing dark or dreary colours, and when we are tired or stressed then neutral, light colours are often our choice. Colours can also dictate our mood, rather like setting the stage of a play. We are often attracted by the colour energy we need, so if you suddenly go out and buy an orange T-shirt, it may be that you require a boost to your energy levels, or that some joy is lacking in your life (*see* Dressing for Health, p 44).

If we are drained, tired, and depressed, we may need to wear stimulating colours: reds, oranges, and yellows. As the stronger shades may be too harsh for us in times like these, try subtle, warm tones of apricot, peach, and lemon yellow for a more gentle and caring support.

COLOURS AND LIFE CHANGES

A new preference for green or white can reveal the need for personal space, independence that is free from conflict, and a need for time to breathe. An attraction to bright, warm colours shows a desire for energy, expansion, activity, and decision-making. Pay heed to such changes because they give us vital information coming from feelings deep inside us.

Have you ever wondered why you have suddenly become attracted to clothes of a different colour, and continue to choose clothing in a particular colour for a period of time? My wardrobe used to be predominantly brown and

ABOVE *We tend to dress to suit our moods: dark clothes when depressed; light clothes when tired; warm colours when feeling energized.*

RIGHT *We can suddenly become attracted to a new colour, signifying a change of direction in our lives.*

blue, but suddenly, a few years ago, I had an uncontrollable urge to have everything bright primrose yellow. This dramatic change in my colour preferences was not an accident. I had just completed my interior design training and had started my own small design company. At this point in my life, I obviously needed to be clear-thinking, energetic, and organized. Yellow is the colour of the mind. It is an analytical colour, and a colour that promotes concentration of thought. It is also the colour of the Sun.

COLOUR CHANGE

If you have gone through a change in colour taste, try to pinpoint the things that were going on in your life at the time. The colour you were attracted to probably had the qualities that you wished to attract into your life at that time.

COLOURS FOR PROTECTION

We can also wear colours to protect ourselves from outside influences. If you do not have the appropriate "protective" colour in your wardrobe, you could could "symbolize" this colour by wearing a scarf or necklace of that colour. You can make a selection of scarves yourself by choosing several important colours out of natural fabrics such as cotton, silk, or wool. Wearing certain colours of gemstones or keeping a crystal with you will also have the same effect. Hats of particular colours can also be effective.

Different emotions are frequently "felt" in different body areas:

- *Fear* is often felt in the belly
- *Anger* may "rise up" from the base of the spine
- *Love and jealousy* may be felt from around the heart.

RIGHT *Choose a scarf or gemstone in a "protective" colour. This will help to shield you from unwanted outside influences.*

You could also wear a scarf around your shoulders and torso, waist, or even hips to protect the part of you that you feel is the most vulnerable. Finally, use can be made of coloured handkerchiefs, which can be put in either a top pocket if you need to protect the upper part of your body, or a side pocket if you need to protect yourself from emotions relating to sex or anger.

VACATION COLOURS

Weather affects the clothes we choose and it is interesting how differently we dress when on vacation. We usually link vacations with bright fun colours that reflect our surroundings. Sunny vacations make us instinctively wear bright reds, yellows, greens and blues, cerise pinks and oranges, and larger patterns. Vacations on the water inspire us to dress in green, turquoise, blues, and white.

Perhaps we can learn something from our choice of these carefree colourful clothes. They promote feelings of energy, happiness, and relaxation. Why wait for your vacation to experience these feelings? Wear these colours on weekends or introduce them into your everyday wardrobe.

We all have times when we want to create a mood of peace and tranquillity, when we really do not want to be noticed and can fade into the background. Wearing softer neutrals with light colours will help you and the people around you relax, since colour can have the same calming effect on the beholder. After a hectic week you may want to relax in a cream, pale blue, or pale gray tracksuit or other loose-fitting clothes.

Mixing brighter colours into your wardrobe adds sparkle to your life. That does not mean you should rush out and buy an entire new wardrobe. Adding bright colours to neutrals promotes action – you'll feel you have more energy and attract active and bright people to you. Adding light to bright colours gives a softer more carefree feeling.

COLOUR DISLIKES

You can also find out a great deal about yourself by looking at the colours you dislike: these can reveal hidden weaknesses or areas of your self-image that need boosting. The colours you dislike will help you determine your vulnerabilities. For example, if you dislike pink, you hate being in situations where you feel dependent on others; if you dislike maroon, you may feel resentful of others.

Our dislike for certain colours also tells us about energy blocks in our system. There are many other reasons we may not like particular colours, usually because they hold certain associations for us. For instance, a colour may remind us of a person or place of which we have bad memories. We should try to discover what these bad associations are, so that we can start to put these memories behind us and bring this colour energy back into our life. The table opposite shows some broad associations.

Colours are neither good nor bad, for like everything in our universe they are made up of both positive and negative qualities. Generally speaking, however, clear bright or light colours reflect the positive aspects of a colour, while dark muddy versions of the colour reflect the negative side.

ACCEPTING COLOUR

*R*ather than force yourself to wear a certain colour you do not like, you need to find a form of the colour that is acceptable to you. Most colours have a wide range of hues, one of which will almost certainly attract you. For instance, if you have a dislike for the colour orange, you could try a subtler shade in the same colour family, such as peach or apricot.

COLOUR ENERGY ASSOCIATIONS

- **Red:** *suffered rejection, defeat, or physical illness*
- **Pink:** *unreconciled emotions with mother or father*
- **Orange:** *mental or physical exhaustion*
- **Gold:** *rejection of material or spiritual wealth*
- **Yellow:** *suffered disappointments and loss of personal power*
- **Green:** *loneliness, grief, rejection, or mental trauma*
- **Blue:** *fear of failure or loss of wealth, status, or position*
- **Turquoise:** *shutting off feelings, afraid of change, in a rut emotionally*
- **Dark blue:** *someone being disloyal or letting you down, loss of faith*
- **Purple:** *feeling trapped by someone else's authority, creative block*
- **Black:** *desire to control and not relinquish personal power*
- **White:** *need to come to a decision and make a clean break*
- **Brown:** *striving to become independent, change in attitude*
- **Gray:** *need of cooperation and support from friends and family*

LEFT *If you have negative associations with the colour pink, this may signify conflict or painful feelings around your mother and father.*

COLOUR BIORHYTHMS

If we are to create balance and harmony in our lives we need to appreciate the importance of giving our life natural rhythm. Understanding that life is not constant, and that our levels of activity and energy should change through the seasons, helps us be kind to ourselves and develop a sensitivity to nature and natural cycles once more.

ABOVE *Keep track of colour in your life by colouring each day in your diary.*

We live each day governed by an inner sense or mood that can be characterized by colour. The colours we choose to wear and have around us tell us if there is an area of imbalance that needs healing. Keep track of this ebb and flow of colour through your life by colouring each day of your diary. Try to set aside a time each day to do this, and quietly reflect on what "colour" you were feeling. Then refer to your colour biorhythms chart to track your biorhythms. Here are some points to look out for:

🌿 Look at the past two months of your life. Does one colour stand out? Perhaps there are two or three colours that predominate? Make a note of them.

🌿 If one colour predominates, then read the reflection for this colour only.

🌿 If you have many contrasting and diverse colours, this has been a period of mood changes and different energies coming into your life.

🌿 If your group of colours shows a close relationship – that is, they are neighboring colours (*see* p 48), e.g. red, orange, yellow (warm colours) or blue, green, violet (cool colours) – you will need to look at the qualities of the missing group in order to bring more balance into your life.

🌿 If the colours that predominate are two complementary colours (*see* p z13) – red/green, orange/blue, or yellow/violet – then these colour energies are working together.

SELF-HELP

Introduce the balancing colours into your diet, dress, home, and work environment or give yourself a colour-healing treatment, such as those described in the following section.

MONDAY	TUESDAY	WEDNESDAY	THURSDAY	FRIDAY	SATURDAY	SUNDAY
1	2	3	4	5	6	7
8	9	10	11	12	13	14
15	16	17	18	19	20	21
22	23	24	25	26	27	28
29	30	31				

LEFT *Keeping a monthly chart of your colour biorhythms will help you identify areas of colour imbalance that need healing.*

MISSING COLOUR VIBRATIONS

If we discover that certain colours are absent it is likely we will be missing this colour energy from our system.

Red

This colour has an association with irritation, anger, and physical force. In relationship to ill-health you may be suffering from exhaustion or lack of energy. It could be you are feeling tired and need to work on lifting your energy levels. You need to take action by improving your diet, making sure you get enough relaxation and exercise that is suitable for your capabilities.

Orange

A lack of orange in your system could indicate a worn-out immune system or problem relating to low self-image and esteem. Perhaps you should take up some form of dancing or movement, which will connect you to your body. Giving or receiving a therapeutic massage can be of great help. You need to bring more joy into your life.

Yellow

You may be nervous or tense regarding a decision that needs to be made in your life. You should introduce the golden-yellow of wisdom to help you think clearly and feed your nervous system. Yellow also relates to the ego, and you need to examine any problems you may have relating to your personal power.

Green

A rejection or insufficiency of green in your life will take its toll with stress and relationship problems. We all need green to be able to relax and to enable us to give and receive selfless love. Green can help us attract abundance into our lives both materially and spiritually.

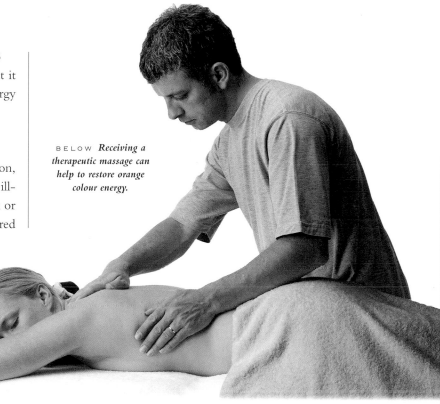

BELOW Receiving a therapeutic massage can help to restore orange colour energy.

Blue

Blue is the colour of the sky. It represents loyalty and trust, so if you are missing blue in your life it may indicate that you feel let down or rejected by someone you trust. Blue relaxes the "higher mind" and connects you to your intuition. When you tune in to this inner wisdom it will help you understand your situation and bring more peace and harmony into your life.

Violet

Should you find violet missing in your biorhythms, you may have lost connection with your inner being. Perhaps you are a creative person who is suffering from a block. Try to relax more by listening to soothing music or by reading a good book. Violet helps open the channels to our spiritual nature and enables us to connect with creative energy.

BELOW Our creativity and artistic nature can flourish only when we have a balance of colour in our lives. Violet is especially important for this.

DRESSING FOR HEALTH

The colours we wear can offer protection against many physical ailments and also give us emotional inspiration and protection. Of course clothing also protects us from the elements and is a form of self-expression. It shields us from the world and affects the way we feel and think.

ABOVE *Only the green vibration shines through green cloth.*

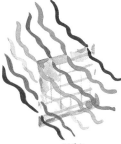

ABOVE *White fabric allows all the wavelengths of light to pass through.*

ABOVE *Black cloth reflects all light away from it.*

ABOVE CENTER *Choose colours to suit your mood. For example, wear red if you want to feel vivacious.*

Fabrics act as colour filters allowing certain colour waves to pass through our skin. This means, for instance, that in the case of a green cloth, it is green because the cloth absorbs all the wavelengths other than green. When natural light passes through the weave of the fabric, it picks up the green vibration, which is absorbed into our system. White clothes, on the other hand, allow all the wavelengths of light to pass through, thus nourishing us with equal amounts of different-coloured energy. This is why wearing white is often associated with cleansing and purifying our system. It can literally make us feel "lighter"! Conversely, black reflects all light away from us and this is why black clothes often form a protective cloak around us. Wearing black too often, attracts negative energy and can have a detrimental effect on our health because the body requires light energy in order to function normally as a living organism.

For many reasons, there is a strong relationship between the colours of our clothes and the effect their energy has on us. The colours we wear can offer protection against many physical ailments and also give us emotional support and provide mental inspiration. Choose the colours from the following list that harmonize with your seasonal colour type and relate to your present energy levels, your state of physical health, and your state of mind.

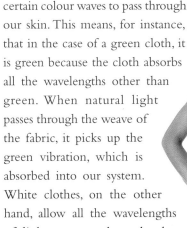

RED (PURE, CRIMSON, BURGUNDY, DEEP ROSE)

❦ WEAR

When you need a pick-me-up, or when you are tired and lethargic or need to encourage physical exercise and a competitive spirit. Red will help with positive progress and success, and to put your plans into action. Wear red when you want to feel sensuous and vivacious.

❦ AVOID

When you are easily tired, or are suffering from bad flu, ME (myalgic encephalomyelitis), infectious mononucleosis, or chronic fatigue syndrome. Do not wear if you have a ruddy complexion, high blood pressure, or are quick to anger. Avoid also if you are nervous or tense. Maroon can turn your feelings to victimization.

ABOVE *The colour red is best avoided if you have a ruddy complexion or high blood pressure.*

PINK (SALMON, PEACH, DEEP ROSE, PALE PINK)

✎ *WEAR*

If you are affectionate, loving, and need to be compassionate and sympathetic. Pink encourages self-nurturing and being kind to yourself. Shell pink and rose pink will promote the two-way flow of love. Salmon pink and deep rose will surround you with universal and selfless love. Shocking pink or maroon stimulates the more sensual pleasures, fun-loving and risk-taking.

✎ *AVOID*

If you are emotionally immature, need a father or mother figure, or are too dependent on others. You may be feeling overburdened by outside dependencies.

RIGHT *Orange is the colour of joy and can help alleviate depression and boost the immune system.*

ORANGE (BRIGHT RUST, APRICOT, PEACH)

✎ *WEAR*

When you are suffering from depression, or need to bring joy or lightness into your life. Orange relieves seriousness of thought and promotes laughter. It encourages independence of spirit and self-motivation, and will help release creativity and negative emotions related to a poor self-image. Orange is good if your adrenals are drained and you suffer from aches and pains – especially in your neck, arms, and joints.

✎ *AVOID*

When you feel confused, frustrated, or claustrophobic. Orange is not good if you feel sick or nauseous, because it will make you feel worse.

YELLOW (GOLDEN-YELLOW, LIGHT, OR LEMON)

✎ *WEAR*

When you wish to be alone so that you can become detached and impartial. Yellow promotes rational thought and reasoning, and can improve the memory. It aids communication, sharing, and self-expression. Yellow is a good colour for accessories when going for a job interview – perhaps combined with a dark blue or gray suit. Golden-yellow promotes sparkle and vitality and the ability to meet new challenges. Yellow is empowering and confidence-building.

✎ *AVOID*

If you are prone to criticism and suffer from a loss of anchorage and stability. Yellow can encourage egotism and is not good if you place too much importance on material wealth. Yellow can cause irritability and a feeling of nausea. Introduce gold rather than yellow, which will encourage you to find your inner wisdom.

YELLOW CAN BE COMBINED WITH FORMAL COLOURS FOR A BUSINESS MEETING

A HINT OF YELLOW PROMOTES SELF-ASSURANCE

LEFT *Yellow promotes good communication and is an excellent colour to accessorize with dark blue or gray when attending an interview.*

ABOVE *Green is the colour of health, happiness, and clear decisive thinking.*

GREEN (APPLE, GRASS, BLUE-GREEN, TEAL, EMERALD)

WEAR If you are hyperactive but find it difficult to make decisions or exercise clear judgment. Apple green promotes health, happiness, and innovation. Grass green gives you understanding and help to others, and encourages abundance in your life. Blue-green promotes optimism and faith in yourself and others.

AVOID When action is needed – green offers balance, but arrests movement. Green provides space and time when you do not want to make decisions, but can promote boredom, repression, and inactivity.

BLUE (DUCK EGG, SKY, KINGFISHER, MIDNIGHT, TURQUOISE)

WEAR If you need quiet and relaxation and want to unwind and are suffering from mental fatigue. Blue helps self-reliance, independence, and responsibility for others. Blue brings insight and wisdom, encourages decision-making, and helps you to link to your sense of intuition.

Turquoise is good for the tense and nervous; it makes you feel fresh and young. It also aids communication and strengthens your powers of speech.

AVOID If you are feeling depressed, since blue can make you feel worse. If you need to recharge, need energy, or are nervous, blue will not provide any support. If you are relying totally on your mental faculty

RIGHT *Blue is a soothing colour, but introduce complementary soft oranges if you need to recharge your energy and self-motivation.*

to provide solutions for your life, you may need to become more in touch with your emotions. Introduce some soft oranges into your wardrobe.

PURPLE/VIOLET (PURPLE, INDIGO, DEEP VIOLET)

WEAR If you want peace and love without anxiety, and authority without demand. Violet clothing provides peace and calm suitable for meditation and prayer, helping you become aware of your sensitivities and inner guidance. Wearing purple will help you to open your mind to higher forces thus making a channel for creative energy.

AVOID If you do not like silence or have feelings of invasion of personal privacy. Do not wear if you are feeling oversensitive and need to be socially accepted or you are feeling imposed upon by rules and regulations. Try wearing magenta since the red ray will help to build up your self-esteem and promote action.

MAUVE/LAVENDER (LILAC, MAUVE, LAVENDER, ORCHID)

WEAR If you want to promote sensitivity, a calmer and more gentle nature. Mauve induces a sense of reserve, yet is nurturing to others. It promotes listening to your intuitive side and using these insights to help others. Wear mauve whenever you need time for relaxation and meditation.

AVOID If you suffer from a lack or freedom or are around people who are not sensitive to your feelings. You require sensitive support from others, so wear more pink.

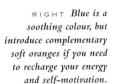

PURPLE WILL HELP TO INSPIRE YOU AND OTHERS

RIGHT *Wearing purple will help you to get in touch with your creativity and intuition.*

BLACK

⋘ WEAR

If you are self-sufficient, in authority and control, and are in a position to protect. If you need to be opinionated and not swayed by others' ideas, black will protect you. You have to be in control of your-self in order to communicate an authoritative image. Make sure you always wear black with highlights of a strong colour in order to counterbalance the negative effects. Diamond jewelry will inspire and protect you with a rainbow of colour; a scarf, belt, or shawl will not only look stunning but add vibrancy and life to the black.

⋘ AVOID

If you are depressed or despairing because of lack of self-recognition and self-denial. Black rejects help from others and promotes isolation.

DIAMOND JEWELRY IS INSPIRATIONAL AND PROVIDES THE FULL SPECTRUM OF COLOURS

A RED SCARF WILL PROVIDE POSITIVE, DYNAMIC ENERGY.

ABOVE *Black can promote an authoritative image. Insure you always wear bright-coloured accessories with black to counteract its negative aspect.*

WHITE

⋘ WEAR

If you need a greater awareness and insight in your life – you may be indulging in being separate from reality. Wear white if you need to be open-minded, clear, and receptive to new ideas and plans without action. White gives you time to stop and think, to reflect without decision-making.

⋘ AVOID

If you are feeling lonely, isolated, or cut off in any way, or if you need to participate, act, or make decisions. When you are ready you can use yellow to promote communication and sharing. Pink will bring love into your life. Blue will bring understanding, and orange can promote action.

COLOUR COMBINATIONS

One of the most difficult things to do well is to combine colours successfully. Not only do certain colours enhance each other or detract from one another, but also their effects on your body and your mental state will be altered by the combinations you choose.

ABOVE *As well as having visual appeal, neighboring colours strengthen each other's healing qualities.*

BELOW *The colours on opposites sides of the colour wheel are complementary.*

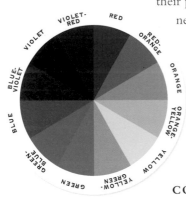

RIGHT
Complementary colours such as violet and yellow impart a balance of vibrational energy.

Different colour combinations will be appropriate depending on the situation: the colours you need to wear to help you when sitting an examination are different from those in which you would be comfortable spending a lazy day at home.

NEIGHBORING COLOURS

Colours from the same end of the spectrum work well together visually, but also mutually reinforce their particular healing action. Combining neighboring tones of cream, gold, tan, brown, orange, and red creates a harmonious effect while boosting your self-confidence and energy levels. You can vary the colours you wear by choosing tints and shades (*see* p 123) for subtle colour combinations.

COMPLEMENTARY COLOURS

Complementary colours are those on opposite sides of the colour wheel (*see* p 13). These also work well together because they provide a balance of vibrational energy and mutually enhance each other. So a green looks good with magenta, while a deep violet looks good with yellow. Red energy can be harmonized with tones of turquoise, cyan, or another blue-green.

The colours on either side of a complementary colour can also be used. These are known as bicomplementary colours. Therefore red can be balanced with green, but also with blue or turquoise. Red and green are complementary but you could also wear magenta or violet with green, while violet looks good with gold and green as well as yellow, and so on.

YELLOW AND VIOLET VIBRATIONS WILL HAVE A POSITIVE EFFECT

LIGHT AND DARK COMBINATIONS

Colour combinations in clothes look better when one of the colours is a paler tint, and the other darker. Navy trousers look good with a pale pink or lemon-coloured shirt. A deep rust suit skirt is good with a duck egg blue or fern green blouse. A burgundy coat could be enhanced with a cream or light blue scarf.

If we suffer from winter depression, we can use the light and brighter colours of spring and summer to counteract these symptoms. Fall is a time of movement and change, so if we wear fall shades we can encourage changes in our outlook, which is especially helpful if you feel you are in a rut. The strong rich colours of winter help us store energy but also bring us inspiration. Use rich darker shades in your range for celebrations and special occasions.

LIGHTER COLOURS ADD A SUMMERY FEEL TO WINTER CLOTHING

PINK LOOKS GOOD WITH NAVY BLUE

PINK SUITS A CREAMY SKIN TONE

WE WEAR DARKER COLOURS IN THE WINTER

SEASONAL COLOUR COMBINATIONS

We naturally tend to wear darker colours in the winter and lighter hues in the summer months. Our subconscious mind connects us to the rhythms of nature and we mimic the colours in the natural world. Spring fashions therefore usually feature light refreshing colours, while in the fall the stores are full of rich earthy tones. Wearing colours that tone in with the colours in the garden keeps us in tune with nature, but we can also use our knowledge of the type of energy associated with colours to improve our health.

COLOUR COMBINATIONS FOR DIFFERENT HAIR COLOUR AND SKIN TONE

Dark colouring or hair

LIGHT SKIN TONE

Cool whites, black, cool grays, navy, pale ice blue, true blue, royal blue, turquoise, cool aqua, true green, emerald green, icy green

DARK SKIN TONE

Natural white, cream, bronze, pewter, true red, scarlet, orange, true yellow, gold, royal blue, turquoise, pale blue, true green, emerald, pale green, pale pink, cerise, orchid, magenta

Fair colouring or hair

PINK SKIN TONE

Soft white, camel, rose-beige, blue-gray or warm gray (depending on skin tone), red-brown, sky blue, duck egg blue, powder blue, medium blue, aquamarine, blue-green, navy, pastel green, fern green, pastel pink, deep rose pink, cool pink, raspberry, burgundy, maroon, plum, mauve, orchid, lavender, blue-violet

CREAMY SKIN TONE

Ivory, cream, beige, camel, warm gray, golden brown, tan, light navy, royal blue, periwinkle blue, peachy-pink, apricot, coral, rust, golden yellow, violet

Red hair

Oyster white, camel, golden beige, dark brown, tan, coffee, bronze, gold, deep blues, turquoise, earth greens, jade, forest green, yellow-green, peach, orange, salmon, rust, terra-cotta, tomato red, orange-red

LEFT *When combining colours, make sure you choose a darker colour with a paler tint, for example, navy and pink.*

NATURAL AND ARTIFICIAL COLOURS AND FABRICS

The body is a living organism that reflects the softness and texture of a natural form. The beauty of our subtle and natural-looking colouring can be lost if it is surrounded by harsh artificial colours and materials.

HEALTHIER NATURAL FIBERS ARE BECOMING MORE POPULAR

PIGMENT DYES TEND TO BE SOFTER COLOURS AND ARE BETTER FOR THE ENVIRONMENT

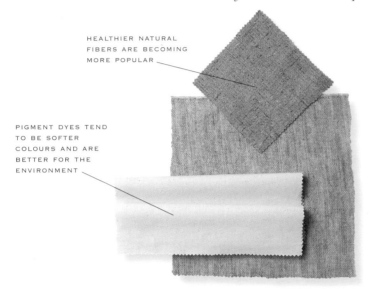

ABOVE *Fabric manufactured from organically grown plant material is now more widespread.*

None of the natural fibers that are used to weave cloth have a brilliant white colouring. This is obtained by bleaching cloth in harsh chemicals. Although most of the bleach is washed away, traces of the chemicals are absorbed into the fibers of the cloth and the waste water is often released back into rivers and streams, doing untold damage. If we wish to wear neutral hues, it is much better to wear clothing made from undyed cloth; the subtle variations of soft whites, beiges and creams are much more flattering than bleached whites when worn next to the skin.

With the vast choice in fabric types available to us these days it is not surprising that most of us have clothes made from artificial fibers. Unfortunately, although these fabrics are easy to wash and often cheaper than natural fibers, they can also have an adverse affect on our health.

NATURAL AND ARTIFICIAL COLOURS

Many clothing manufacturers and fashion houses are now offering garments made from organically grown plant materials that are not bleached in the manufacturing process. These natural fibers are pigment dyed, producing softer colours more in keeping with those seen in nature, which harmonize with our skin tones.

BELOW *If you wish to wear neutral tones, natural fibers are softer and more flattering.*

With the use of synthetics, manufacturers are now able to produce an astounding array of aniline dyes; these tend to be out of tune with our natural colouring. Synthetic colours, such as electric green and orange, can make us appear pale and ill. Often artificial fabrics also have patterns with bright clashing colours and strong geometric designs, giving off conflicting vibrations that are not in tune with any of our bodily organs or functions and can contribute to behavioral problems.

NATURAL AND ARTIFICIAL FABRICS

It is not only the colouring of the fabric itself that can set up harmonious patterns in our clothing, but the texture and type of fabric also alter the way the light waves affect us. Natural cloth has similar vibrations to our own, so will be harmonious to our health; while synthetic fabrics emit their own vibrations that will interfere with any light vibrations, so distorting their vibratory rate. Such materials interfere with our natural body electricity (*see* p 220). This is particularly the case with leisure and sports clothing, which is frequently made with nylon. Wearing nylon does not allow the skin to breathe and produces a lot of static electricity. Other synthetic fabrics include acrylics and polyesters, the manufacture of which is not environmentally friendly.

Natural fibers, on the other hand, have a positive effect on the body – cotton, wool, silk, and even a 50 percent cotton/polyester mix, allow the skin to breathe and natural sunlight to penetrate.

Silk

Silk has a very fast vibration; it is able to absorb and hold light energy for a long period of time, setting up positive vibratory patterns in the body. This is revealed in the fineness of its texture and its ability to reflect deep rich colours. The interplay of light on silk makes it one of the most beautiful and luxurious of fabrics and has the added bonus of being soft next to the skin.

Cotton

Cotton is also a wonderful natural material that has been used for thousands of years to produce strong and serviceable clothing. Because of its coarser weave, cotton allows our skin to breathe, while allowing air and light to enter.

Wool

Wool is a natural product that keeps us warm by trapping a layer of our body heat. It also lets light and air penetrate, keeping us healthy. Its texture absorbs natural dyes so easily that it is possible to obtain thousands of subtle colour variations.

TIRED CLOTHES

Start each day with a clean set of clothes. Clothes pick up dust and dirt and become "tired" when worn. Wearing them again will only make you feel tired too! Clothing also picks up the wearer's vibrations, which is why many Indian and Oriental people believe that you should never wear someone else's clothes. This is especially true of footwear. According to tradition, energy exits from the feet. This is why footwear is often removed when entering a place of worship.

BELOW *An extraordinary natural fabric, silk has been valued for centuries.*

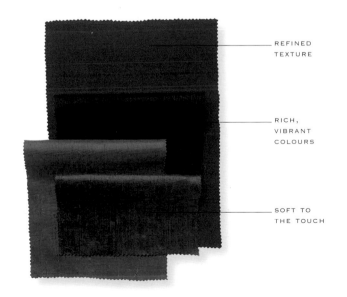

REFINED TEXTURE

RICH, VIBRANT COLOURS

SOFT TO THE TOUCH

DRESSING FOR YOURSELF

Does your style of clothes suit you, or do you dress for others?
We should dress for our own well-being and not just for the
external impression we want to create.

If we feel happy and comfortable in ourselves we will be naturally attractive to other people. We should surround ourselves with the colours we need, especially if we live alone.

Make sure you wear what expresses you and avoid slavishly following fashion trends in colours. There are always fashion styles that you can wear, without your having to squeeze into short or tight jackets and skirts that don't suit you; or wearing high heels or pointed-toed shoes that deform and numb your feet.

Living with a partner obviously means we have to take the moods of that person into consideration. Your partner may have different soul colours from you, but his or her colours should complement yours. It may be that the soul colours of your partner are those that you need, and this is often the reason why you are attracted to that person in the first place. For example, a timid and sensitive person may be drawn to a dynamic and confident person who becomes the decision- maker for both people. However, such unequal relationships can become destructive to your health. I am sure most people have experienced being with a person who seems to sap your energy, and we all do this from time to time in varying degrees. It is only when two people have a balanced energy system that a stable and long-term relationship will develop.

BELOW *We may be attracted to a partner with different soul colours, but for a relationship to endure they should complement your own soul colours.*

DO THE COLOURS YOU WEAR COMPLEMENT OR CONTRAST WITH YOUR PARTNER'S PERSONALITY TYPE?

BALANCED COLOUR ENERGY WILL HELP TO SUSTAIN A RELATIONSHIP

ABOVE *If you are depressed, dark-coloured clothes will reinforce your mood.*

DRESSING CHILDREN

Traditionally we have dressed infants in pastel colours: blue for boys and pink for girls. Pink is the colour of love and nurturing, associated with femininity, but it is also a warming colour linked to Mother Earth. Blue is the colour of the sky and sea, and associated with movement.

INFANTS

Infants are very sensitive to their surroundings, and experience the world through all their senses simultaneously. A young baby will not only look at a toy, but will taste and smell it. Colours have a profound effect on babies. Light colours are more gentle; all pale colours give off soft vibrations that are more in keeping with the skin and sensitivity of a young child. It is a good idea to clothe a baby in natural colours or soft pastels.

Pink, peach, and warm earthy tones mimic the colour of the mother's skin and give off supporting and loving vibrations to boys and girls equally. Light blue and green are cooling and sedating and it would be a particularly good idea to clothe a child in such colours if he or she is hyperactive or has a skin rash.

OLDER CHILDREN

As a child grows, its needs change. Like adults, some children are quiet and sensitive, while others are active and outgoing. Parents and designers should pay attention to these differences, rather than foisting their own colour preferences or fashion trends on children. We all have past experiences that hold colour associations for us – colours worn at school, uniforms, colours associated with relatives and their houses.

Until very recently children, and boys especially, were dressed in sensible colours that did not show dirt so obviously. However, most children – if left to choose their own clothes – will choose brightly coloured garments. They need to dress for energy and fun, for laughter and excitement. They sometimes mix and match strange and shocking colour combinations, but this is perfectly natural. They are experimenting with how to use colour in much the same way as they experiment in other forms of play. Gentle guidance will help them understand the nature of colour and discover their own colour preferences.

LEFT *Colour has a profound effect on young children. Light colours are more gentle and subtle.*

BRIGHT COLOURS DENOTE ENERGY AND ZEST FOR LIFE

STRIPES OF BRIGHT COLOUR ARE FUN

ALLOW YOUR CHILD TO EXPERIMENT WITH VARIOUS COLOUR COMBINATIONS

RED IS THE COLOUR OF ACTION

LEFT *Children prefer bright colours reflecting their boundless energy and sense of fun.*

DRESSING FOR WORK

*Until the 1960s, drab and restricted colours were usually worn for most jobs
where a uniform wasn't required. Workers had to be seen as upright,
responsible, hard-working citizens, and dark, restrained colours not
only helped give this impression but if worn frequently they
also keep our true personalities under wraps.*

ABOVE *A dark-coloured suit is considered appropriate for business people around the world.*

We often use colour in our work clothes to alter the way people see us and feel about us at work and to promote image and status in the world, rather than to suit individual needs.

BUSINESS SUITS

A dark suit is recognized internationally as appropriate for business. Black worn in business denotes power. Going into a meeting in a black or charcoal suit gives out the message that you are a force to be reckoned with and that you are there to give orders. Red with black indicates that you consider yourself to dynamic, action-oriented, and a leader. Yellow used with black conveys mental superiority, and a preference for persuading by using logic and reason. Pink worn with black shows superior social standing. Green is seldom worn with black; its soothing vibrations would cancel out the dominance and power conveyed by black.

If your business approach is always one of cooperation and negotiation, a navy or dark blue outfit would be more appropriate than black. Dark blue promotes authority, but also sends out the message that the wearer possesses fairness and integrity. Light neutrals of beige or tan tones indicate approachability and are better worn by those who work in a people-oriented field.

Someone with a quiet or introverted personality could be overpowered by dark gray or black. If so, try wearing a suit of deep, rich blue or golden brown and see how it affects you.

USING ACCENT COLOURS

Brighter colours can be used as accents in your accessories. This allows you to keep an expression of your own identity and personality while conforming to work requirements. Dynamic colours are exciting and ideal to wear for giving lectures and presentations – the brighter the colour, the more attention grabbing. Turquoise aids communication, while a golden-yellow helps clear logical thinking. If we are talking to large audiences in person or in front of a camera, striking rich colours hold their attention, whereas wearing light or dark neutrals in a lecture hall would result in your fading into the background.

RED ADDS A
DYNAMIC TOUCH

BLACK
DENOTES
POWER

NEUTRAL TONES
ARE LESS
INTIMIDATING

SOFT COLOURS
INDICATE
UNDERSTANDING

DYNAMIC COLOURS
ARE BEST FOR
PUBLIC SPEAKING

RICH COLOURS
HOLD ATTENTION

COLOURS FOR DIFFERENT OCCUPATIONS

Here are some colour guidelines for different occupations. If you cannot wear these colours at work, find an object of the colour to keep by you.

≪ *Fine artists and designers* should wear inspirational lavender tones. They should also use beautiful orange tones to aid their creativity and green for insight and intuition.

≪ *Writers, journalists, and media people* will find inspiration by the use of clear blue. They will have their creativity and self-expression enhanced by golden-yellow tones.

≪ *Teachers, scientists, physicians, nurses, and healers* will be strengthened by deep blue, which imbues power with understanding in the service of others. They will be strengthened by using soft pure violet, gold, and orange. Lilac, lavender, orchid, cream, apricot, and peach are all colours that reflect either the violet or orange ray.

≪ *Mothers and babysitters and nursery teachers* will be greatly aided by pinks and greens.

≪ *Chefs, dietitians, naturopaths, herbalists, guards, and police* will be helped by magenta, together with a clear healing violet and pure orange.

≪ *Ministers, lawyers, people in public office, and politicians* will enhance their powers of service and benevolence by use of rich blues and pure purple.

≪ *Engineers, architects, and interior designers* will have their practical skills and attention to detail enhanced with oranges.

≪ *Accountants, statisticians, and storekeepers* will find their business acumen improved by blue-green.

≪ *Athletes, soldiers, farmers, gardeners, and people who work outdoors* will increase their energy and endurance by the use of clear reds.

≪ *Pregnant mothers* should use mist like green and silver tones during their pregnancy.

ABOVE *A dark suit worn with red will help you appear more forceful; a soft neutral tone indicates approachability; a less commonly worn colour will be eye-catching.*

CLOTHES FOR AFTER WORK

In our leisure time it is a good idea to choose clothing to promote freedom from the constraints of dark work colours. People who have to wear a business suit of dark or neutral colours often come home and change into comfortable clothes of a softer colour with soothing qualities. These softer tones help you to relax and ease away the stresses of the day. Choose blues and greens, neutrals, or pastels if you wish to be let down gently and calmed. On the other hand, if you are going out after work you may wish to wear a rich or warm-coloured outfit, for instance in red or orange, to give you more energy and dynamism for the evening. Only wear black at night if you are feeling in optimum health, otherwise you will not only looked pale and drained, but you will also tend to be introverted and withdraw into your "black cloak."

With the shift in modern psychology, it is becoming acceptable for men as well as women to express their individuality and emotions, and we have seen a sudden explosion of wonderfully coloured clothes. Men especially have at last been set free and now revel in wearing colour in their leisure- and sportswear.

MESSAGES

Men often use their clothing to show that they belong to a distinct group – whether at work or at play. Logos and team scarves, hats and club ties are very popular. Sportswear and leisurewear for men demonstrate the use of the energetic and activity-generating colours. The strength of the messages these colours give out, together with their effects on bodies and emotions, means that they must be worn with discretion. Combining colours such as bright green and cerise pink, purple and orange, or red and black results in conflicting vibrations that can promote feelings of aggression, confusion, discord, and even fear in the beholder.

RIGHT *Rich or warm colours will re-energize you for an evening out.*

RIGHT *Softer colours are soothing and will help you to unwind after a day at work in dark business clothes.*

PALE COLOURS PROMOTE RELAXATION

WEARING TRANQUIL BLUES HELPS TO BANISH THE STRESSES AND STRAINS OF THE WORKING DAY

UNIFORMS

Many large businesses have a corporate identity, incorporating the company logo and colours into their staff uniforms. It is of utmost importance that designers of corporate colours are sympathetic and knowledgeable about the psychology of colour, both from the point of view of the client as well as from that of the employee. Great care must be taken when using company colours in a decoration scheme to make sure the colours are suitable for the building, workspace, type of work, and general well-being of the people who are to be surrounded by them. It is better to consult the workers when designing a uniform, and if possible their views on colours for their workplace should be given consideration.

CORPORATE COLOURS

The following guidelines outline the messages different colours convey when used for corporate identity, decor, and uniforms.

- **Red:** *speed, movement, travel, strength, stamina, action-oriented*
- **Orange:** *building, healthy, energetic, practical, motivated, sociable*
- **Yellow:** *communicative, happy, bright, sunny, clever, new ideas*
- **Green:** *natural, peaceful, harmonious, fresh, clean, relaxing, understanding*
- **Blue:** *loyal, trustworthy, peaceful, clean, caring, authoritative, healing*
- **Violet:** *special, luxurious, creative, royal, powerful, inspirational, spiritual*

Uniforms should, where possible, be designed around a neutral colour. Distinctive strong colours can be added to the accessories – such as the tie, scarf, buttons, or hat. This will allow for the wide variety of shapes, sizes, and colouring of the staff who will be wearing the uniforms, and any strong colours will have to

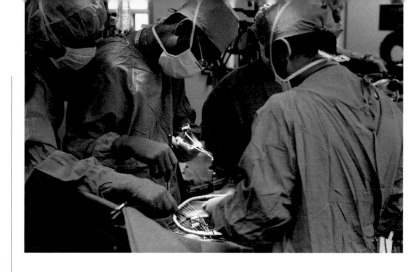

be tolerated only in small doses. Directors should remember that although a uniform is a good idea in places where staff identification is required, the attitude of staff will be even more important. You cannot hide sour-faced, unhappy people behind the mask of a uniform. If staff are discontented, the uniform will reinforce the connection between your business and bad service.

ABOVE *Surgeons and hospital staff wear blue – a colour that communicates trust, cleanliness, care, and healing.*

BALANCING COLOUR

If you find yourself obliged to wear a uniform whose colour makes you feel uncomfortable, wear a piece of jewelry or carry a gem in your soul colour. This will allow you to balance the colours of the uniform that conflict with your personality and inner vibrations.

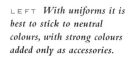

A UNIFORM SHOULD BE UNOBTRUSIVE WITH DISTINCTIVE COLOURS USED ONLY AS ACCENTS

LEFT *With uniforms it is best to stick to neutral colours, with strong colours added only as accessories.*

SKINCARE
AND COSMETICS

The makeup and cosmetics we use should always complement and enhance our intrinsic colouring. Choose makeup derived from natural materials; the colours will be in harmony with your skin, eyes, and hair.

MIX YOUR TREATMENT AT HOME

CUCUMBER IS A NATURAL DIURETIC

DRINK PLENTY OF WATER

YOGURT TO NOURISH

LEMON WILL LIGHTEN HAIR AND REDUCE OIL

OATMEAL MAKES A GREAT FACIAL SCRUB

RIGHT *Wholesome, natural ingredients can benefit your skin either when eaten or when applied as a face pack or other skin treatment.*

The skin is the largest organ in the body, covering an area of approximately one and a half square yards (1.5 sq. m.). It secretes sebum, which oils the hair; the sweat glands eliminate waste products. The skin also acts as a sense organ. Our skin is both light and sound sensitive and through it we absorb colours and substances such as essential oils. Light penetrates our cells and causes complex chemical changes to occur; sunlight provides the only means by which our bodies can naturally produce vitamin D.

The huge cosmetic industry encourages us to paint ourselves – our faces, nails, and hair – in as many different colours as can be invented for its products. But painting on colour does not give beauty, but rather this appears when you are healthy and your eyes shine, your skin glows and your hair glistens with colours.

We may, however, need to add extra colour to our faces if we have been living in a cold climate or are looking pale from stress and overwork. Fair-haired people or those with hair that has turned gray or white also need to introduce colour to avoid looking washed out and ill. Wearing bright colours will make you look even paler if you do not counterbalance the colours with a brighter lipstick, blusher, some eyeshadow, or nail polish.

Facial cosmetics

Formerly most women wore thick foundation. However, in recent decades a shift to a more

RIGHT *A healthy diet will insure that your skin is clear and smooth.*

SMOOTH COMPLEXION

healthy lifestyle and diet has meant our complexions are becoming clearer. Most of us now use the minimum of face makeup.

Rather than covering your skin with foundations and base, it is much better to work from within, so that your skin develops a naturally smooth and glowing tone. The amount of water you drink has a direct bearing on the condition of your skin. Dry, wrinkled skin is crying out for hydration and, although you may spend a fortune on moisturizing creams, it is much better to hydrate yourself from within. Cleansing and toning with face masks and mud packs have also been used for centuries to improve the complexion.

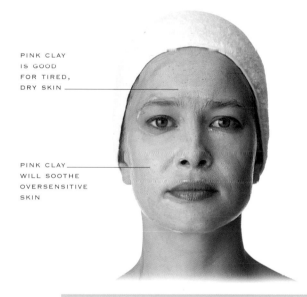

PINK CLAY IS GOOD FOR TIRED, DRY SKIN

PINK CLAY WILL SOOTHE OVERSENSITIVE SKIN

TRADITIONAL MAKEUP

Makeup is the oldest and most personal art form. Painting ourselves is also a social activity that we have performed throughout time. Men and women have always decorated their bodies with paints and oils made from minerals and plants. Egyptian and Middle Eastern cosmetics included tubes of kohl; and lipstick, applied with a brush, was probably made from crushed red ocher. Young girls from African tribes today plaster their faces with yellow ocher to protect themselves from the sun and to keep their skin smooth and soft.

SKIN SENSE

Since the skin promotes a two-way flow of electrical vibrations – including colour and aroma – it is important you should not block it with lotions and creams. You should use only creams that are readily absorbed and do not remain on the surface.

Clays

Coloured earth or clay has absorbed minerals and plants from the Earth and energy from the sun over millions of years, and as a result contains many healing qualities. The Chinese treated summer diarrhea and cholera with it; kaolin is named after a mountain in China where it was first extracted. Europe and North America too have a long tradition of using it for digestive, joint, and infectious problems.

There are red, yellow, black, green, white, and brown clays. These combine beautifully with essential oils to make face and body treatments, as well as being the base for many cosmetics and face powders. Face powders and face packs today are also made from crushed rocks, such as fine chalk.

The following coloured clays can be used as face packs to cleanse and improve the texture of our skin.

⟳ **Red clay** is a useful tonic for the skin because of its iron content.

⟳ **White kaolin** is milder, astringent, and good for sensitive skin; it removes impurities.

⟳ **Pink clay,** which is a mixture of red and white, is popular for tired, dry, and very sensitive skins.

⟳ **Fuller's earth,** a soft brown clay, has a very stimulating effect on the skin because it removes the top layer of dead cells, leaving the skin silky smooth and clean.

⟳ **Green clay** is rich in minerals and has a rejuvenating and nourishing effect, stimulating the circulation of oxygen.

ABOVE *For glowing skin you need to cleanse from the inside out with the right foods and plenty of water.*

LEFT *Pink clay can help remoisturize and calm the skin.*

ABOVE *Darker lipsticks look good on brunettes, especially true red.*

ABOVE *Brick red and orange lip colours complement those with auburn or red hair.*

ABOVE *Peach and coral toned lips are ideal for fair-haired people. Mix different shades together until you get a colour you like.*

LIPS AND NAILS

Synthetically coloured lipsticks and nail polishes send out conflicting vibrations. There are natural alternatives to both that can be used to make lips and nails more attractive.

Nails

Everyone would like strong healthy nails, and a plentiful intake of calcium promotes healthy teeth, hair, bones, and nails. Ridges or white marks on the nails usually indicate stress or a mineral or vitamin deficiency. Try to use more of the colour orange in your life in order to assist in the formation of calcium.

If you wish to paint your nails, it is better to use a naturally coloured polish for everyday use and only use a brighter more fun colour for a special night out. Buffing nails makes them look as shiny as clear polish does, with the bonus that they won't chip and there's no drying time.

Lips

The condition of our lips often reflects our state of health internally. Dry cracked lips can indicate a deficiency of vitamin B2, or be a symptom of oral thrush or allergy to lipstick or cream. Cold sores often develop as a response to overexposure to sun, stress, or just being run-down. Blue-tinged lips can show that you are not getting enough oxygen into your blood; this may mean that your heart is not pumping efficiently or that you have a lung problem. Red energy stimulates the heart and raises blood pressure, so use this colour to improve your circulation.

In the summer, when your skin has more colour, select a slightly darker lipstick. Modify lip colours by mixing shades together; beige will tone down a bright colour, while light pink will make any shade of lipstick prettier and more pastel. The exact tone will depend on your skin colouring and clothing, but here is a guide.

- **Dark hair:** *true red, pinks, plums, burgundy, raisin, blackberry*
- **Brown or auburn hair:** *brick red, orange, coral, peach, rust*
- **Blond or light hair:** *peach, warm pink, coral*

Lip balms are extremely useful in dry or windy weather and are available in many delicious aromatic scents and tastes. Again, try to use ones made with natural flavorings and not based on animal products.

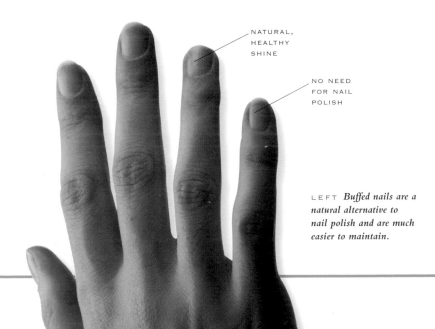

NATURAL, HEALTHY SHINE

NO NEED FOR NAIL POLISH

LEFT *Buffed nails are a natural alternative to nail polish and are much easier to maintain.*

EYES

When we talk about the colour of our eyes, we are usually referring to the overall effect. In reality the iris is made up of many varieties of subtle shades, all of which blend together to create a general eye colour. It is well worth looking in a mirror to pick out the tonal flecks in your eyes, around which you can base your eye makeup.

Try to stick to colours that either contrast or harmonize with your own eye colour. The principles of colour show that colours look more intense and striking when set off against complementary shades, while similar colours create a much softer look.

Enhancing your eyes with colour is like painting a beautiful land- or seascape. Colours should blend subtly together so that there are no harsh lines. Think of different moods created by the sea or sky for your inspiration and link these to your personality and colouring.

Eye makeup for blue eyes

Blue-eyed people should not use blue eyeshadow. If you have blue eyes they will appear much clearer and brighter when highlighted by a contrasting beige, cream, gold, or gray. If you wish to use blue, select a shade that is different from that of your eyes.

Eye makeup for brown eyes

Brown eyes can be complemented with shades and tints of brown, soft mauves or violet, green, or pinky-beige.

Eye makeup for hazel and green eyes

People with hazel and green eyes look better using shades and tints of pink, bronze, and gold.

Mascara and eyeliner

Dark-haired people or those with gray or white hair with brown, green, or blue eyes should use black or black-brown mascara with black or charcoal liner. If you have brown, auburn, or golden hair and green or brown eyes then use brown or light brown mascara with brown or green-brown liner. Brunettes or fair people with blue or gray eyes should wear gray mascara, with teal or gray liner.

EYESHADOW

Your eyeshadow should be paler than your eye colour or your lids will appear heavy and half-closed. Use a dark neutral in the orbital bone to create a shadow and a pale highlighter such as off-white, silver, or beige under the brow.

BELOW *Choose tones of eye makeup to complement the colour of your eyes.*

GOLD ENHANCES BLUE EYES

SOFT BEIGE OR GRAY EYELINER IS BEST

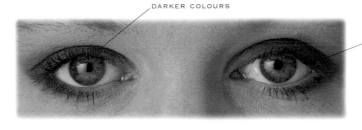

BROWN EYES TAKE DARKER COLOURS

SOFT MAUVE OR VIOLET WORK WELL

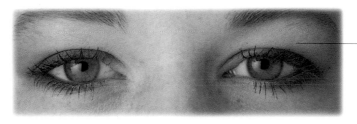

PINK IS PERFECT FOR HAZEL EYES

THE COSMETIC COLOUR WHEEL

*Sensitive use of makeup is not only decorative, but therapeutic too.
It can help us enhance our self-image especially at times when we feel tired,
ill, or depressed. Caring for yourself when you feel low gives you a
psychological lift, boosting self-confidence.*

Like the colours of our clothes, our makeup gives off subtle vibrations that can have a beneficial effect. If you select cosmetics made of natural pigments and ingredients, these energies will be in harmony with our own and their healing effect will be greater. Knowing you look good will not only send this message to other people, but will be reflected back to you.

RIGHT **The Colour Cosmetic Wheel.**

WINTER – COOL TONES
Eye-shadow: *gray, silver, plum, mauve, smoky blue, soft turquoise.*
Lip colour: *bright pink, pastel pink, magenta, fuchsia, burgundy, true red*

SUMMER – COOL TONES
Eye-shadow: *off-white, smoky gray, soft pink, mauve, soft turquoise.*
Lip colour: *pale pink, deep rose, cool red, raspberry, orchid*

FALL – WARM TONES
Eye-shadow: *beige, apricot, muted green, brown, blue, aqua.*
Lip colour: *orange, orange-red, tomato red, apricot, salmon*

SPRING – WARM TONES
Eye-shadow: *ivory, golden-brown, apricot, blue, turquoise.*
Lip colour: *peach, salmon, coral, orange-red, warm pink*

SUMMER TYPE

SPRING TYPE

FALL TYPE

WINTER TYPE

ABOVE *Spring colouring. Eye tones for spring have a warm undertone – warm beige, tan, honey, various blues, and turquoise. Lip colourings are best with a peachy apricot tone.*

ABOVE *Summer colouring. Makeup for eyes should reflect sea and sky tones – aquamarine, lavender, mauve, and gray-blue. Lipsticks are best kept in the cool range, pale or rose-pink, and cool red but not orange.*

ABOVE *Winter colouring. Eye makeup for winter people can include many frosty cool shades – ice green, aqua, blue, or violet. Silver tones and burgundies work well for darker skin tones. Lipsticks should have a cool undertone – true red, magenta, deep pink, or fuchsia.*

ABOVE *Fall colouring. Shades of beige, apricot, soft greens, blues, and brown for eye makeup. Lips can complement this with strong, warm shades of orange, tomato-red, and apricot.*

COLOUR TO ENHANCE CHARACTER

We can use our clothing and makeup to enhance our natural colouring and also to balance our personality traits and health weaknesses. Spring and fall people will have an excess of warm energy in their system, which can be balanced with cool colours. Summer and winter people, on the other hand, have predominantly cool natures which need warming up.

Our basic wardrobe is best made up of neutral colours that reflect our seasonal type. Spring and fall people should have warm neutrals while summer and winter people are best clothed in neutrals with a cool bias. Introduce accent colours in other items of clothing, accessories, and makeup to balance your seasonal colour energy. You can select the colours you need for these to suit your moods and health requirements on a daily basis. If you use makeup that is in tune with your personal hair, eye, and skin tone, these will enhance the effects of your clothes, whatever these may be. Change the colour of your lipstick to reflect the tones in your outfit.

ABOVE *Choosing makeup that suits your own hair, eye, and skin tone will enhance the effects of your personal basic wardrobe colours.*

Winter colours

Although winter people usually have a striking appearance and colouring, their coolness of character often makes it difficult for them to relax and express their emotions easily. Winter people are more controlled and their strong mind gives an orderly and logical approach to life. Your basic wardrobe colours should be strong neutrals of black, white, gray, and navy, but you need to introduce some warming colours such as true red or lemon yellow, or emerald green to give you emotional strength. True blue will help you relax so you can express yourself more openly.

Spring colours

The boundless enthusiasm of spring people often means they lead an untidy and disorganized lifestyle. Their personality colours are peach and green, which create a natural balance between the heart and the solar plexus which can become over-excited. These colours are best worn in makeup and as accent colours in dress. Their basic wardrobe best

LEFT *True blue will help the winter person relax and express their emotions.*

RIGHT *The spring person's basic wardrobe should be made up of neutral colours. Add a cooling blue if you wish to feel calm.*

reflects the neutrals of ivory, cream, and tan. Spring people can use cooling tones such as mauve blue and light turquoise or aquamarine for its calming and soothing qualities.

Summer colours

The summer personality is soft and gentle and their basic wardrobe best reflects off-whites and rosy brown tones. Summer people need to be drawn out of themselves with soft, warm shades. Use raspberry or rose pink to develop confidence and boost self-esteem or lavender or sky blue to support intuition and creativity.

Fall colours

The changeable nature of fall people reflects the natural movement of late summer. Like the fall leaves, sometimes they are up in the air while at other times they are right down in the dumps. Fall energy is warm with rich, earthy tones and the basic neutrals for fall people are oyster white, camel, tan, gold, or dark brown. The accent colours of golden yellows and orange will give fall people both stability and focus when they need to be grounded, while turquoise and jade green will lift them when they are feeling down.

RIGHT *Soft, warm shades and off-whites help to boost the confidence of the gentle summer personality.*

RIGHT *Dark brown is one of the basic neutrals for fall people.*

RIGHT *Winter people can make a striking impact if they team dark colours with pale "icy" shades.*

BELOW *Rich, earthy tones are ideal colours for the fall personality.*

LAVENDER

JUNIPER

ORANGE PEEL

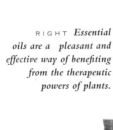

SANDALWOOD

ABOVE *Each plant relates to a different colour with a range of healing qualities.*

ESSENTIAL OILS FOR BEAUTY TREATMENTS

All plants utilize sunlight for their life and growth, locking up the life energy derived from its component rays, so plants offer a unique way of absorbing colour vibrations into our system.

Essential oils are natural organic substances produced by the dissemination of minute particles of the flowering plant. They embody the very essence or "spirit" of the plant, hence the name. Unlike synthetic substances, which have no vital force contained in them, essential oils are filled with living, pulsating vibrations. This is why aromatherapy, like colour therapy, forms a part of "vibrational medicine" – a form of medicine that utilizes the powerful vibrations of the electromagnetic spectrum.

Properly preserved plant essences can have a powerful effect on us at all levels. When applied to the skin these essences regulate the activity of the capillaries and restore vitality to the tissues. However, note that not only can these essential oils benefit you, but, incorrectly used, some can also be harmful, being concentrated essences of powerful medicinal herbs. Only a few oils can be applied neat to the skin; the others should be blended in oils or creams.

Whether you use essential oils in massage or in an aromatic bath, you are using the colour frequencies that relate to their qualities and therapeutic actions.

☙ Lavender and juniper utilize the properties and power of the violet ray, which has a purifying effect. While lavender helps rejuvenation of a mature skin, juniper is a treatment for acne.

☙ Sandalwood and tea tree, related to the blue ray, have cleansing and astringent properties and can be used neat on spots and boils.

☙ Yellow-related oils, such as lemon and camphor, are cleansing and toning.

☙ Orange and red ray oils, such as neroli and black pepper, are stimulating and act as tonics.

Many oils combine the characteristics of more than one colour vibration – usually a complementary colour pair such as yellow and violet, or pink and green (*see* p 13). You can use colour as a guide to using essential oils, by mixing those with similar or complementary colours. Essential oils are an ideal form in which to use plants for skincare because they can easily be incorporated into base creams, lotions, ointments, gels, toilet waters, perfumes, and bath oils.

INVISIBLE COLOURS

It is becoming more evident that odors give off vibrations that fit into the invisible part of the electromagnetic spectrum (see p 12). A good way of describing scents, therefore, is as "invisible colours." Since the skin is such a sensitive detector of electromagnetic vibrations, we should not underestimate its receptivity to sensations of odors and the colour rays.

RIGHT *Essential oils are a pleasant and effective way of benefiting from the therapeutic powers of plants.*

TREATMENTS

ORANGE SKIN TONIC

Put 1 drop of orange essential oil and 1 drop of neroli into 1/2 cup/4fl oz/100ml orange flower water. Use as a cleanser, as required.

YELLOW HEALING BALM FOR ACNE AND SPOTS

Mix 1 drop each of lemon, camphor, and lavender oil with 6 drops of evening primrose oil. Spread onto the affected area morning and evening.

VIOLET TONIC FOR BLEMISHED SKIN

Put 1 drop of lavender and 1 drop of juniper oil into 1/2 cup/4fl oz/100ml of lavender water, and use to cleanse the affected area.

PINK/GREEN TREATMENT FOR BROKEN CAPILLARIES

Mix into 2tbsp/30ml almond oil 20 drops of parsley, 10 drops of geranium, and 5 drops of cypress oil. Use in the bath, or gently massage into the area around the broken capillaries. Never massage directly over the affected area.

VIOLET/YELLOW CELLULITE BATH MIX

Mix into 2tbsp/30ml of almond oil 10 drops of juniper, 10 drops of lemon, and 12 drops of grapefruit oil. Add to the bath as required.

ESSENTIAL OILS AND THEIR RELATED COLOUR WAVELENGTH

ESSENTIAL OIL	RELATED COLOUR	BEAUTY CARE
Black pepper	red	warming • stimulating to the circulation
Palma rosa	pink	gently stimulating • antistress
Orange	orange	normal to oily skin
Sandalwood	orange	softens dry skin
Carrot	orange	for broken capillaries • protects lips
Neroli	orange	normal to oily skin
Patchouli	gold	mature or dry skin
Evening primrose	yellow	skin complaints • eczema
Lemon	yellow	acne • oily skin • cellulite
Camphor	yellow	acne and spots
Lemon grass	yellow	oily skin • breasts
Basil	green	astringent for oily skin
Peppermint	green	astringent and stimulating tonic for skin
Geranium	green	dry skin • for combination skin add to night moisturizer • also for broken capillaries
Camomile	blue	soothing for sensitive skin
Tea tree	blue	acne, use neat on boils and spots
Lavender	violet	rejuvenation of mature skin • oily skin • flabby arms • dry lips
Violet leaf	violet	cleansing and healing • use to close pores after steaming to prevent blackheads
Juniper	violet	acne • oily skin
Clary sage	magenta	all skin types, overhydrated
Rosemary	red/violet	stimulating tonic • anticellulite
Rose	pink/green	skin • cellulite • breasts

ABOVE *Your skin betrays your life: a face aged by happiness and joy is always beautiful.*

HOW OUR EMOTIONS AFFECT OUR SKIN

The state of your body is affected by the state of your mind, and your skin is no exception. In fact, your facial skin is probably the clearest reflection of your state of mind – both past and present. Your face is a mirror of your past life. There is a world of difference between an aged face that has happiness etched on it and one that shows a life of trouble and unhappiness. Inner peace and happiness give even the most plain face a lively glow that no amount of makeup can produce. Just as the skin needs protection from the atmospheric pollution it also needs protection from pollution within. Because the skin is an eliminative organ, your body gets rid of toxins through its surface, resulting in such conditions as acne. If the body is undernourished, the skin will almost certainly reflect that.

Using essential oils can improve the quality of the skin and although the aging process cannot in itself be reversed it can be slowed down, and we can regain lost health. We can also use essential oils in colour baths for healing (*see* p 204).

COMPLEXION

We can tell a lot about our health and personality by looking at the underlying colour and texture of our skin. A ruddy complexion often indicates high blood pressure or an excitable personality. A yellow appearance usually goes with an oily skin and a melancholic nature.

Redness and inflammation

Excessive grief can cause redness or inflammation of the capillaries on the skin's surface, and the condition of the heart and blood vessels affects the redness and blueness of the skin. Oils of neroli, lavender, and sandalwood can be used to apply to the skin or taken internally when prescribed by a professional aromatherapist. These will soothe the hot, red skin and cool it, thus reducing the puffiness and inflammation. Placing slices of cool green cucumber on the eyes and drinking peppermint tea will also balance the redness and cool and clean the insides.

Dry skin

Anger and frustration affect the liver and inhibit its multiple function. The result is the poor assimilation of food, no matter how much you eat. This often leads to a dry skin. Rose, ylang-ylang, and rosemary will help to correct this

MAKING PEPPERMINT TEA

ABOVE *Make peppermint tea using ½oz (12g) peppermint leaves and 1pt (500ml) water. You can also add the juice of 1 lemon. Drink hot or chilled (cool in the refrigerator and then add ice and a sprig of fresh mint).*

PEPPERMINT

imbalance of the mind and body; while rose, camomile, and sandalwood will help the skin more directly. The tell-tale yellowness of a jaundiced person can be reduced by drinking plenty of parsley tea.

Dehydrated skin is most associated with fear, which correlates to the malfunctioning of the kidneys and bladder. Sage, geranium, and sandalwood can be used to combat this problem. Environmental conditions, such as the sun and wind, can also cause dehydration. Dehydration is also due to congestion in the lymphatic system and spleen, and links to the emotions of wonder or compassion. People who are congested in this way are often slow and gullible, and tend to display an overconcern with the care of others. The use of lavender, rosemary, and juniper oil is indicated for this type.

Chronic congestion of the skin (oiliness, pallor, blackheads) leads to an excess of toxins in the cells of the lower layer of the skin. This causes an inefficient, unhealthy skin, and the general aging of the skin is speeded up. The antitoxic, antiseptic and tonic properties of essences are of great value, in preventing or clearing skin congestion.

Oily skin

Oily skin is related to worry and – physically – to the large intestine. Everyone worries, but those who worry excessively are prone to eat the wrong foods, too. They often also become constipated, and a change in diet is the only real way to get any results. Notice that problem foods, such as chocolate and coffee, are dark brown, and greasy foods are often muddy, oily green-brown. These are thick, earthy colours, which clog the body. Try eating light-coloured green and blue foods whose astringent qualities clean internally and freshen the blood.

Astringents made from lemon, or diluted witch hazel, combat the oil secreted by the skin with acid. Cypress and frankincense aid healing when the skin is broken, such as in acne, and discourage the secretion of sebum in oily skin. For acne, the antiseptic properties of bergamot, lavender and cypress are useful. Also linked with oily skin is puffiness caused by water retention (edema).

BELOW *Light-coloured, green, and blue foods reflect their purifying and cleansing qualities.*

LEFT *As their colouring indicates, brown, muddy-coloured foods are heavy and result in a sluggish digestive system.*

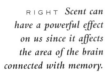
PERFUMES

The vibrations we receive through our senses of sight, hearing, and smell are so closely linked that we often associate different sounds with certain colours, while some colours invoke certain scents.

RIGHT *Scent can have a powerful effect on us since it affects the area of the brain connected with memory.*

Most people are unaware of the strong links between odor and colour, even though they experience distinct preferences for scents that are related to their visible colouring. For instance, popular aromas include rose, lilac, pine, lily of the valley, violet, balsam, cedar, wintergreen, orange, lemon, and vanilla. These also are substances that all possess clear, bright colours. We tend to dislike the smell of lard, rubber, kerosene, fish, vinegar, and onions – these are all odors of substances that tend to have a drab or muddy colour. Pink, lavender, pale yellow, and green are the "best-smelling" odors, while gray, brown, black, and dark shades in general are the least appealing.

It was not until the late 18th century that body odor came to be considered unpleasant and antisocial. Obsessed by personal hygiene, we now try to scrub away every trace of human scent, and then add perfumes containing the sexual scents of other plants and animals, such as musk. When applying other scents, stick to those derived from flowers and barks, since these are in keeping with our natural energy system.

PERFUME "NOTES"

The best perfume makers mix their perfumes with delicacy and flair in the same way as painters mix their colours or composers arrange their notes. Perfumes are dynamic and change with time; they also interact with the skin and the vibrations of each person. Perfumes evaporate at different speeds: the fast-evaporating ones are called the "top notes," the medium-fast ones the "middle notes," and the slowest the "base notes."

The base notes have the densest vibrations, which means that they come from the orange/red end of the spectrum, the middle notes coincide with the the yellows and greens in the middle of the spectrum, while the top notes are the highest vibrations correlating to the blue/violet end of the spectrum. The harmonious blending of the volatility of all three notes makes the best perfumes. Floral essences are classified into Yin (feminine) or Yang (masculine) scents. (*See* p 76 for a detailed explanation.)

BENZOIN   ORANGE PEEL

THE PERFUMES OF BASE NOTES ARE SLOW TO EMERGE AND LONGER LASTING

MASCULINE AND FEMININE OILS

Yin – feminine oils

BASE NOTES (RED/ORANGE RAYS)

Balsam de peru, benzoin, cedarwood, cinnamon, frankincense, melliot, myrrh, oakmoss, patchouli, sandalwood, tonka bean, vanilla

MIDDLE NOTES (YELLOW/GREEN RAYS)

Carnation, cedarwood, cinnamon, clary sage, frankincense, geranium, ginger, heliotrope, hyacinth, jasmine, jonquil, lemongrass, lime (linden), marjoram, mimosa, myrrh, orchid, oriental rose, patchouli, pine needle, rose, rosewood, sandalwood, thyme, violet, ylang-ylang

TOP NOTES (BLUE/VIOLET RAYS)

Bay, cassis, clary sage, hyacinth, marjoram, mimosa, neroli, nutmeg, rosewood, thyme

Yang – masculine oils

BASE NOTES (INFRARED/RED/ORANGE RAYS)

Bay, benzoin, cedarwood, cinnamon, frankincense, moss, myrrh, oakmoss, sandalwood, vanilla, vetiver

MIDDLE NOTES (YELLOW/GREEN RAYS)

Angelica, anise, basil, caraway, cardamom, carnation, clary sage, clove, coriander, cumin, geranium, ginger, jasmine, juniper, lavender, mandarin, marjoram, neroli, nutmeg, oregano, patchouli, peppermint, pine, rose, rosemary, rosewood, tarragon, thyme, ylang-ylang

TOP NOTES
(BLUE/VIOLET/ULTRAVIOLET RAYS)

Anise, artemisia, bergamot, cedar leaf, cumin, juniper, lemon, lemon grass, lime, mandarin, neroli, peppermint, sage, verbena

LEFT **The notes of oils can vary, depending on origin and processing.**

MIXING YOUR OWN PERFUMES

When mixing your own perfumes from floral essences, start with your base note or notes, then add your middle notes and finally your high notes. You can do this by choosing notes sympathetic to your own unique "soul" colour. Add your essential oils to a base of alcohol and distilled water. Swill it around gently daily for 4 to 6 weeks, out of the sunlight, before filtering through fine cheesecloth or filter paper, and bottling.

BODY MISTS

You can also make wonderful body mists in the following way. Place distilled water in a glass bottle adding several drops of essential oils – not more than 10 drops per 4 fluid ounces (100ml). Shake well and decant the mixture into an atomizer spray or bottle with a pump-action top. You can also put a body mist spray in a coloured glass bottle so that it becomes energized with that particular colour energy.

BELOW **Scents possess the qualities of either Yang (masculine) or Yin (feminine) and are classified according to the speed at which they evaporate.**

LEMONGRASS

CORIANDER

THYME

CLARY SAGE

LAVENDER

SCENTS WITH A MIDDLE NOTE EVAPORATE AT A MEDIUM RATE

TOP NOTES ARE FAST-EVAPORATING

PART THREE

COLOUR AND FOOD

Nearly everyone is sensitive to the colour of foods. Appetite is stimulated or dampened in almost direct relation to the observer's reaction to colour. Since food is one of the most important ways we can take colour energy into our systems, we should take pride and care in obtaining, preparing, and eating food. Colour and food are so closely linked that you expect a red apple to be sweet, a golden-yellow fish to have a lovely smoky taste, and red meat to be juicy and tender. This is why a meal that has well-balanced colours looks appetizing and gets our mouths watering.

Next time you have a meal, look at the colours on your plate. Do you have a range of colours including red or orange, gold or brown, and green? These are the colours of fresh natural foods, which nature imbued with goodness to keep us in perfect health. If the colours you see in front of you are bright and synthetic these are probably the result of artificial colouring, which is often used to make unhealthy food appealing.

The natural colours of foods are nature's way of telling us what nutrients they contain. When we learn to understand this language, we can identify the healing powers of different-coloured foods. Each colour has a specific quality and therapeutic action that affects the behavior and growth of all our cells and tissues. Energy imbalances can be corrected by choosing foods containing certain colour frequencies that will aid the free flow of vital energy around the body. This section of the book will help you to use food colours for good health.

COLOUR AND HOLISTIC NUTRITION

In order to be healthy we require a balance of colour energy in our system. Through choosing the right foods, colour can work every day in our lives to help improve health and clear-thinking.

If you eat a varied and balanced diet, whether you are a vegetarian or meat eater, you are probably using colour naturally to enhance the value of the food. You can then supplement this by choosing meals where one colour predominates, depending on the weather, atmosphere, or time of day. If a member of your family is unwell or you are feeling tired or run-down, you can tailor the colours in the food to suit specific needs.

The colour-care rainbow diet described here emphasizes the prevention of illness and the promotion of good general health. It is based on moderation and balance rather than restriction and elimination. It is a diet using colourful and aromatic food that suits your own needs rather than a standard diet program. By eating freely in harmony with natural rhythms, better health and the maintenance of an optimum body weight will automatically follow.

The colour-care diet is designed to be a quick and easy guide to make sure you are getting a balanced diet whether you are a vegetarian or a meat eater. It aims to ensure that you are extracting and utilizing the maximum amount of energy and nutrients from the food, keeping the need for vitamin and mineral supplements to a minimum.

The key to a healthy diet is variety and balance even if limited foodstuffs are available. One should eat regularly, choosing at least half of your foods in the middle of the colour spectrum (green to golden-brown). These are the natural colours of grains, pulses, fresh fruit such as apricots, peaches, and nectarines, as well as dark green leafy vegetables. These foods are all rich in beta carotene, providing the body with vitamin A; they also contain vitamins B and C.

The remainder of the diet should be made up of natural red and blue food, particularly from vegetables. Red foods are full of Yang energy (*see* p 76) and rich in minerals. Vegetables corresponding to the red ray provide the body with

BELOW *A healthy diet should consist of natural foods in the green, yellow, golden-brown, red, and blue colour ranges.*

YELLOW LEGUMES

ORANGE VEGETABLES

GOLDEN-BROWN GRAINS

DARK GREEN LEAFY VEGETABLES

YELLOW AND ORANGE FRUIT

EGGS ARE YANG AND A RED FOOD

RED VEGETABLES

BLUE FRUIT, BERRIES, AND LEGUMES

RED FRUIT

iron and help counteract poor circulation; they must be eaten regularly, although not necessarily daily. Animal products such as eggs, white meat, and red meat also fall under the red ray, but are high in cholesterol.

Meat also takes a great deal of the energy to digest, leaving little spare to utilize as body energy. If you are used to eating a meal of meat, two vegetables, and potatoes, it is a simple matter to redistribute the proportions on your plate to provide a meal that is in keeping with a modern lifestyle. All you have to do is shift the emphasis, basing your dinner around a complex carbohydrate such as potatoes, rice, or pasta. Serve it with a variety of fresh vegetables and a small quantity

AN EXCESS OF PROTEIN
AND TOO FEW VEGETABLES

A BETTER BALANCE OF
VEGETABLES TO PROTEIN

of fish, lean meat, legumes, or pulses. Delicious and nutritious snacks and lunches can be centered around baked potatoes or wholewheat bread.

Many people stick to familiar eating routines because they think their children will not like a diet based on vegetables and carbohydrates. In fact, children respond instinctively to colour and if they are encouraged from an early age to look for colours on their plate they will soon develop a taste for good natural food.

The old and infirm also need the energy and protection from good food. Rather than feed them pale lifeless dinners, prepare colourful drinks of pure fruit and vegetable juices. Stewed fruit and lightly cooked vegetables can also give a tasty nutritional boost.

ABOVE *For optimum nutrition we should insure that we eat the correct balance of carbohydrates, fats, protein, and fresh vegetables.*

BALANCED DIET

There are differences among commonly recommended diets, some allowing fresh fruit, milk products, or animal products, and others not. However, all these reveal that the healthiest people follow three simple principles.

1 Half of their food comprises starch and complex carbohydrates. Most modern nutritionists agree that the major part of protein should come from pulses, nuts, seeds, and complex carbohydrates such as grains, rice, bread, potatoes, and pasta. These foods are highly nutritious and easily digested.

2 They eat at least five portions of fruit and fresh vegetables a day.

3 They eat little saturated fats, preferring monounsaturates such as olive oil, or polyunsaturates such as oily fish; and have low salt intake.

RIGHT *Freshly made juices are colourful and enticing and will help to increase your vitamin intake.*

LEFT *Lightly steaming vegetables preserves the vitamin content and a good colour; overcooking (far left) results in unappealing food.*

CHOOSING FOOD COLOURS FOR HEALTH

Before we can consciously use the healing and balancing qualities of various colours in our diet we should understand their individual actions and qualities.

ABOVE *Some red foods improve the immune system.*

RIGHT *Red foods are energizing and include red-stemmed leafy vegetables, meat, and seafood as well as red fruit and vegetables.*

Each food contains the energy of one or more colours of cosmic rays, depending on its natural colouring, and contains corresponding groups of nutrients and other substances essential for health. Thus red, orange, and yellow foods have an energizing and stimulating effect, while green, blue, and purple foods are cooling and pacifying. If you are constantly eating food of one particular colour, your body may be craving something contained in that particular food. Look at any physical symptoms you may have, because these might indicate what the problem is.

RED FOOD – ENERGY

People with lots of red energy in their system will be physically active, tend to be lean and muscular in build, speak and move quickly. The benefit derived from this activity develops their stamina and influences their general outlook on life their body functions will be well tuned, they will glow with good health, and their immune system functioning will be optimal. People with plenty of red energy work tirelessly and hard to achieve their goals.

The pigment that makes tomatoes red – lycopene – is even more powerful than beta-carotene in fighting certain toxins that may trigger cancer cells. Cherries, raspberries, and strawberries are rich in vitamin C, which is thought to play a role in blocking the formation of some carcinogens. Red cherries and strawberries eaten on an empty stomach or between meals are also effective in lowering uric acid levels in the blood.

However, too much food at the infrared and red end of the spectrum, such as red meat and eggs, and stimulants such as coffee and tea, and salt, can cause hostility, irritability, impatience, and anger.

RED FOODS

strawberries • red cherries • asparagus leafy green vegetables containing iron • red plums watermelon • rhubarb • raspberries • red apples beet • tomatoes • red bell peppers • radishes red lentils • red kidney beans • meat • seafood • food made from animal products

ORANGE FOODS

oranges • mangoes • pawpaws (papayas)
apricots • peaches • nectarines • carrots • oranges
peppers • pumpkin • butternut squash
swedes • egg yolks • ginger

ORANGE FOOD – GOOD APPETITE

The colour orange is particularly good at stimulating the appetite and aiding digestion, and a person with plenty of orange energy will have a good appetite, strong digestion, and good immune system. They will be happy and joyous and have a healthy sex drive. They would also enjoy choosing and eating food, and have a balanced and varied diet. They should be able to eat most foods without any ill-effects or allergic reactions. They will be able to assimilate the goodness from the food and eliminate waste products before harmful toxins build up.

The orange pigment beta carotene, which is found in all brightly coloured fruits and vegetables, is a powerful antioxidant that helps protect against damaging effects of air pollution. It is particularly beneficial to those who spend a lot of time sunbathing, because it helps protect against potentially harmful and aging effects of ultraviolet radiation.

YELLOW FOOD – HAPPINESS AND CHEERFULNESS

The golden-yellow of the sun is the colour that symbolizes this radiant source of life. It is the colour of strength enriched with intelligence. So people with abundant yellow energy will be full of enthusiasm for new ideas, and be able to communicate these to others. They are happy and cheerful, and greet each day with enthusiasm and a positive outlook. Their positive thoughts help them stay healthy and radiate a protective force.

Golden and yellow foods lift the spirits, and help to cultivate a positive and happy attitude and encourage good humor. They also boost the nervous system and feed the brain, helping to stimulate mental faculties and improve memory. Pale yellow camomile tea is known to soothe and calm the mind. Yellow energy also has a purgative action on the liver, gall bladder, pancreas, and spleen. Bromelin, contained in pineapples, is an excellent tonic for the pancreas, and both pineapples and bananas are rich in nutrients essential for the brain and nervous system.

LEFT *Stimulating to the appetite, orange foods also aid digestion.*

LEFT *Golden and yellow foods boost the nervous system and the brain and encourage a positive outlook on life.*

GOLDEN AND YELLOW FOODS

wholegrains • rice • mung dahl • yellow lentils
nuts • seeds • pears • bananas • pineapples
melons • grapefruits • butter • corn and other yellow
vegetable oils • dark honey

ABOVE *Green foods increase resistance to illness and the effects of ageing.*

GREEN FOODS

green bell peppers • green grapes • kiwi fruit figs • lemons • limes • green lentils • lettuce broccoli • okra • celery • cucumber • cabbage • peas green beans • zucchini (courgettes) • cauliflower milk curds • live yogurt • olive oil • milk

GREEN – CALMNESS AND LOVE

Green is found in the middle of the spectrum and is nature's own balancing and harmonizing force. Balance in all areas of our life is essential to good health, and people with plenty of green energy are able to enjoy a balance between home and work, care for the Earth and other people, and exude an aura of love and harmony. They also have an abundance of good health and love.

Green vegetables and plants have an alkalizing function on the body and are a good source of bulk and natural fiber. Their juice cleanses and detoxifies the body, washing out potentially harmful waste materials. Green foods stabilize the blood pressure and the acid and alkaline levels in the body. Green herbs have been used for thousands of years for their healing properties.

RIGHT *Blue foods are soothing and relaxing, helping us to unwind and sleep soundly.*

Most naturally white-coloured food, especially milk and milk products such as live yogurt, contain green energy, which is the colour of the grass from which they are derived. If it is processed or salt is added, however, it loses its vitality.

BLUE AND INDIGO FOOD – GOOD SLEEP

People with an abundance of blue and indigo energy are cool, calm, and composed. They obtain the deep and good sleep they need in order to function at optimum level. Very few of us seem to get a restful night's sleep and when we do our sleep is often fraught with dreams and nightmares. We are full of fears, tensions, and frustrations from the day, during which our minds have often been overstimulated and our bodies understimulated.

Blue/indigo food is soothing and tends to be cooling. It is made-up mainly of blue- and black-coloured berries (bilberries, blueberries, blackcurrants, and plums), but also includes yeast, seaweed, and some white-fleshed fish.

BLUE AND INDIGO FOODS

blueberries • blue plums • bilberries • blackberries boysenberries • seaweed • chicory flowers • black cherries • black soybeans • brewer's yeast • vanilla beans • wild mushrooms • olives • juniper berries raisins • prunes • some freshwater fish

MACKEREL IS BOTH CALMING
AND STIMULATING

PURPLE-SKINNED
POTATOES, ONIONS,
AND PURPLE KIDNEY
BEANS ARE PERFECTLY
BALANCED FOODS

PURPLE AND VIOLET FOODS

*purple grapes • eggplant
(aubergine) • purple plums
purple broccoli • purple
onions • turnips
artichoke • purple sage
thyme • purple bell peppers
purple cabbage
radicchio • beetroot*

LEFT *Purple foods
contain both blue and
red colours, creating a
balance of Yin and
Yang energy.*

PURPLE AND VIOLET FOOD – CREATIVITY AND CONTENTMENT

Violet or purple has a very fast vibration, and people with an abundance of this colour energy easily connect to their spiritual side and allow creative energy to be channeled throughout their bodies into some form of expression. Being able to express themselves creatively helps them to connect with their intuition and inner wisdom, both of which help restore peace of mind and equilibrium in the body and soul. It is a shame that so many people strive for happiness in their lives, when happiness is such a transient feeling. It is impossible to be happy for any length of time, for we can only experience happy times in relation to unhappy ones. Instead, we should be searching for this peace of mind and contentment that the purple and violet colours signify.

Purple food has both the calming effect of the colour blue and the warming and stimulating effect of red; this makes purple food both uplifting and inspirational. For instance, many fish have a blue tinge to their scales but (because fish is an animal product) they also possess some red energy. Similarly, in the plant kingdom, many purple root crops contain Yang energy (*see* p 76)

ABOVE *Purple
foods tend to be very
nourishing, but they
do not overstimulate
the body.*

while also displaying blue in their colouring. Purple onions, purple kidney beans, and purple-skinned potatoes all contain a balance of both red and blue energy. As a result they are extremely nourishing without being overstimulating.

Synthetic drugs, some natural drugs, and sugar fall into the colour category of ultraviolet and violet. When consumed, foods falling at this end of the spectrum can cause extreme emotional thinking in certain individuals, typified by fear, suspicion, deceit, and jealousy.

COLOUR ENERGIES

- *Red and orange foods are stimulating and generally warming to our system.*

- *Orange and golden foods stimulate the immune system and the brain.*

- *Yellow foods are less stimulating and act more like a tonic.*

- *Green is the balancing and harmonizing force between the two extremes and this is why a green grape diet has become so popular. Grapes are packed with energy from sunlight, and the green ray, which they reflect, balances the acid and alkaline levels in the blood.*

- *Blue food is soothing and generally cooling owing to its water content and is often rich in iodine, which feeds the thyroid gland.*

The recipes on pp 86–100 give you some ideas on how to use different-coloured foods in your diet. You can use particular colours in foods to bring the qualities related to particular food colours into your life, to remove imbalances and deficiencies within your body, and to help in the treatment of common problems (*see* p 83 for more details on this).

LEFT *Without the right nutritional colour balance you will feel run-down.*

Underlying the view of the universe embodied by Traditional Chinese Medicine (T.C.M.) are two primal forces known as Yin and Yang, which represent the fundamental polarity underlying the structure of the entire universe: darkness and light, feminine and masculine, white and black, and so on. These are present in differing proportions in all things. Although opposite, they are also complementary; one cannot exist without the other. In the colour spectrum, Yin is linked to the colour blue, and Yang is linked to the colour red.

Neither total light nor total darkness is a balanced state, however; it is only when a third harmonizing force comes into play that harmony is created. In colour terms this is the colour green, nature's healing colour. In colour theory we refer to them as the three primary colours – red, blue-violet, and green.

SALTY   SWEET

SALTY   SWEET

We tend to eat a great deal of Yang foods such as red meat, eggs, and salt. Plants are predominately green, the colour of nature. Blue foods include sea vegetables, some freshwater fish, and other watery and cooling food.

Just as magnets are attracted, as Yang animals we often crave Yin foods such as sugar, yeast, alcohol, and synthetic drugs. When you eat too much Yin food, however, you become attracted to foods of the opposite side of the spectrum. You can prove this to yourself by eating a package of salty snacks. You will instantly have a craving for a sweet drink. You are like a constantly moving state seeking balance between two opposed but attracting forces.

ABOVE *The body is constantly seeking balance: when you eat salty Yang foods you will crave sweet Yin foods.*

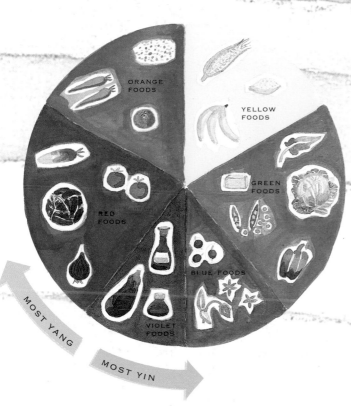

ORANGE FOODS

YELLOW FOODS

GREEN FOODS

RED FOODS

BLUE FOODS

VIOLET FOODS

MOST YANG

MOST YIN

ABOVE *Yin and Yang foods from the plant kingdom include red/brown crops, red/orange fruit and vegetables, grains, legumes, green fruit and vegetables, seaweed and kelp, blue berries, and flowers.*

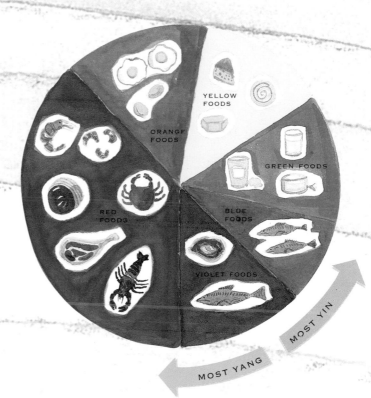

YELLOW FOODS

ORANGE FOODS

GREEN FOODS

RED FOODS

BLUE FOODS

VIOLET FOODS

MOST YANG

MOST YIN

ABOVE *Yin and Yang foods from the animal kingdom include red meat, oysters, crayfish, shrimp, crab, salty cheese, white meat, eggs, soft cheese, yogurt, milk, white fish (indigo), oily fish (violet).*

ABOVE *Eating plenty of green vegetables and fruits will help to balance your diet and prevent cravings.*

In T.C.M., illness is viewed as a fundamental imbalance of Yin and Yang. Too much Yin will result in cold, and weepy, depressive symptoms. A Yin condition is equivalent to an excess of blue. A Yang imbalance would be characterized by problems accompanied by a high temperature, and dry and hot symptoms. An excess of red energy is related to a Yang condition.

Just as Yin and Yang are attracted, colour energies in food also have opposing but attractive forces. So although our natural physiological tendency as animals is in the red to yellow end of the spectrum, we can balance this by eating green foods (fruits and green vegetables) and also a few blue foods (oil, yeast, honey, grains, and legumes). The foods in the middle of the spectrum contain their own Yin–Yang balance, so should form the bulk of the diet.

CHOOSING FOODS FOR DIFFERENT CLIMATES

With the increase in our ability to travel the world, the colours and flavors we reflect in our food may have an international flavor. Many exotic fruits and vegetables are now available in our stores, and we tend to add them to our diet purely on the basis of whether we like the taste, but we should also understand how different foods may be suited to different climates.

ABOVE *In some countries, it is customary to buy food daily from the local market.*

HOT CONDITIONS

People who live in hot climates tend to purchase their food fresh from a local market on a daily basis. This is not only because food does not keep well in the heat, but also because the quality and taste of foods such as bread or salad ingredients rapidly deteriorate.

In hot conditions, yellow, orange, and red/brown predominate in the environment. Also, our skin is flushed red or brown and our blood is hot. We need to be cooled. Travelers tend to do this by drinking lots of iced drinks, eating ice cream, etc. However, those people who live in hot temperatures have developed a knowledge of which foods are heating and which are

RIGHT *Traditional Japanese meal of fish balanced by green tea.*

cooling in their effect on the body. You can use more of the cooling colours of food such as blue foods in your cooking as well as the more cooling, Yin foods, which include tea, tofu, raw green vegetables, and sea vegetables, and fermentations such as marinades.

If fresh food is difficult to come by in hot, arid regions, the diet is often based on dried legumes, and breads, which are an excellent source of protein and complex carbohydrates. The refreshing juice from fruits such as cucumber or watermelon provides the cleansing, cooling, and hydrating nourishment needed in these extreme conditions.

In tropical areas and more temperate zones, we need less salt, fish, and grains, and more water, nuts, and fruits. If we do eat a lot of fish in a warmer climate, we need more raw vegetables or fruit to balance our diet. Fish corresponds approximately to the blue/violet wavelength, and needs to be balanced by green. The traditional Japanese diet is carefully balanced by drinking green tea with every meal, which counteracts the effect of salty fish. Barely cooked vegetables also form a large proportion of the typical Eastern diet, and it is interesting to note that many serious illnesses were almost unheard of before elements of a Western diet and lifestyle were adopted.

ICE CREAM CONSISTS MAINLY OF FAT AND SUGAR

HAMBURGERS CONTAIN SATURATED FATS

FRENCH FRIES ARE HIGH IN FAT

SWEET DRINKS ARE HIGH IN SUGAR

CHIPS CONTAIN FAT AND USUALLY ARTIFICIAL FLAVORINGS

COLD CONDITIONS

By contrast, people living in cold, dark conditions have developed a cuisine based on high protein and carbohydrate intake. This diet corresponds to the warming, invigorating, and stimulating colours of orange, red, purple, and brown, such as a bowl of pumpkin or carrot soup. Seasonal fruits grown locally provide all the vitamins needed to ward off winter colds and flu. In cold climates, the diet has been developed around meat, fish and eggs and foods high in cholesterol, so to maintain a balance we need to eat more grains and vegetables.

HEATING AND COOLING FOODS

In the Chinese tradition, warming foods contain the Fire element, which is also linked to the bitter taste. Warming foods contain red energy and they warm the blood and improve circulation. Many of these foods must be avoided if you have high blood pressure, heart problems, or suffer from any hot conditions such as skin rashes. However, some heating foods (e.g. cayenne) are used to induce a healing fever in cases of acute infection. A list of traditional warming and cooling foods is given in the table opposite.

Cooling foods contain the Water element; in the Chinese tradition this is linked to the salty taste. Cooling food is generally associated with the colours blue, green, and white. Some purple foods are also cooling.

WARMING FOODS

VEGETABLES

≼ asparagus ≼ red bell peppers ≼ chilis ≼ leeks ≼ chives and green onions ≼ chicory ≼ endive ≼ kale ≼ root vegetables ≼ squash ≼ chestnuts ≼ walnuts ≼ pinekernels ≼ ginger

FRUITS

≼ rhubarb ≼ apricots ≼ peaches ≼ guavas ≼ kumquats ≼ raspberries ≼ cherries ≼ dates ≼ lychees

COOLING FOODS

VEGETABLES

≼ barley ≼ wholewheat ≼ buckwheat ≼ millet ≼ kelp ≼ kombu ≼ eggplant (aubergine) ≼ mushrooms ≼ nori ≼ radicchio ≼ wakame ≼ water chestnuts ≼ bamboo shoots ≼ soy sauce ≼ cucumber ≼ iceberg lettuce ≼ celery ≼ celeriac ≼ chinese cabbage ≼ cauliflower ≼ cabbage ≼ mung beans and sprouts ≼ tofu

FRUITS

≼ pears ≼ blackberries ≼ blueberries ≼ bilberries ≼ cranberries ≼ apples ≼ watermelons ≼ bananas ≼ mangos ≼ grapefruits ≼ tangerines ≼ loquats ≼ persimmons

ABOVE *Soups made from butternut squash and pumpkin are warming; perfect for cooler climates.*

COLOUR DIETS TO IMPROVE HEALTH

Colours are effective as a cure for disease, and carefully selecting your foods may add years to your life. If you are making a meal that is restricted to one colour only, you can use the quality of the colour in the food to maintain balance in your body's systems.

COLOUR COOKING

*C*olour cooking is totally safe and adds another dimension to cooking for health and beauty. It provides a complementary therapy, helping to create a balance in the body and mind.

RED KIDNEY
BEAN CURRY

PEACH
SLICES TO
GARNISH

YELLOW BELL
PEPPERS ADD
COLOUR

ABOVE *Try an energizing meal of red and orange colours, such as this red kidney bean curry.*

ABOVE RIGHT *A plate of green and purple food will have a cooling effect.*

You may want to make a meal to stimulate and warm yourself on a cold winter day. A meal based on orange or red works wonders and will also help with bad circulation or depression. If you need to cool the body or calm the nerves, try making a meal of soothing greens and purples. To aid the mental faculties for work or study, make sure you eat a heartening yellow supper. The recipes on the following pages should give you some ideas on using colour cooking.

RADICCHIO

SLICED RADISHES

WATERCRESS
AND SPINACH

PURPLE
SPROUTING
BROCCOLI

BEETS

FOOD COMBINING

If you wish to food combine according to the Hay system, you can easily do so using the colour-care diet. Simply remember to base your meal either on a complex carbohydrate, such as rice or pasta, or on a protein such as fish, cheese, or lentils. Make a meal with orange, yellow, and green vegetables and accompany it with either a protein (red or purple) or a complex carbohydrate (red-gold). Alternatively, you could create a red and purple winter salad and combine it with a baked potato covered with yellow corn.

PROTEINS

VEGETABLES
AND GREENS
(FIBER)

CARBOHYDRATES

VEGETABLES
AND GREENS
(FIBER)

LEFT *When food combining make sure that your protein or carbohydrate meal is accompanied by orange, yellow, and green vegetables for colour balance.*

CORRECTING IMBALANCES

Colour diets can also help correct imbalances, give a boost to the immune system and can help fight off specific ailments. The body under stress or in any weak condition always gives at the weakest point and in times of stress this system will malfunction. We must, therefore, identify our weak points and work toward building up these areas. We can do this by taking into our system foods of specific colours in order to replenish our diminished energy reserves. Remember that you are only eating food of a particular colour to boost that colour energy in the energy centers in your body. Once you have regenerated that colour center, you can reduce the proportion of that colour food in the meal, returning to a plate with a variety of colours in it.

Also, it often happens that when one of our energy centers is depleted another will become overenergized, creating an excess of a certain colour energy in our system. If these energy imbalances are left unattended, they will also eventually manifest as physical illness and disease.

COLOURS AND THE INTERNAL ORGANS

Our internal organs vibrate at different rates corresponding to the vibratory rate of various colours; the heart is linked to the colour green, while the liver is linked to yellow. Each colour feeds and nourishes a certain part of the body or body system. Primarily, each colour affects that part of the system, which will have a follow-on effect on our mental and emotional state of health. By introducing the colour needed to correct any blockage, the organ will then return it to health, allowing the natural free-flow of energies around the body. Let us now look at the colours and the organs to which they are linked, and see which foods help the action of each ray and how it takes effect.

LEFT *The vital organs of our body correspond to and are affected by various colour vibrations.*

HOW COLOUR AFFECTS THE BODY				
COLOUR	GLANDS	ORGANS	BODY SYSTEM	THERAPEUTIC ACTION
red	adrenals	kidney, bladder, lower limbs	muscular	stimulating, strengthening, warming
orange	sex organs	spleen, legs, stomach	circulatory, lymphatic	freeing action, tonic, antidepressant
yellow	pancreas	liver, gall bladder, stomach	nervous	cleansing, laxative, mental stimulant
green	thymus	heart, lower lungs, ears, arms, breasts	digestive	relaxing, promotes harmony in cells, antistress, balancing
blue	thyroid	throat, mouth, upper arms, upper lungs	respiratory	healing, calming, pain relief, antibacterial, antiseptic
indigo	pineal	lower brain, left eye, nose	skeletal	astringent, depressant, calming, stimulates parathyroid
violet	pituitary	upper brain, scalp and hair	endocrine, central nervous	relaxing to the mind, hypnotic, narcotic, antibacterial

LEFT *This chart shows you the positive effects of certain colours on particular glands, organs, and body systems.*

USING THE COLOURS OF FOOD IN HEALING RECIPES

When we know a particular colour energy is missing from our food, it is important to find a way of reintroducing it into our diet. This section will provide you with a range of healthful recipes in every colour group to rebalance and rejuvenate your body, mind, and spirit.

RED – WARMING AND STIMULATING

Eating red food stimulates the base of the spine and reproductive center, promotes heat and body temperature, stimulates the circulation of the blood, and the release of epinephrine (adrenaline), increasing energy and vitality. It disperses feelings of tiredness and inertia, as well as chronic chills and colds. Psychologically, red foods stimulate and uplift feelings, giving confidence and initiative. They also alleviate depression, and increase willpower and courage.

Eat the following if you suffer from anemia, paralysis, poor circulation, or blood disorders, or are chilled and cold.

CHILIES

CAYENNE PEPPER

BEETS

RED PLUMS

RED FOODS

✦ *red cabbage* ✦ *beets* ✦ *red bell peppers*
(also chilies) ✦ *red plums* ✦ *rhubarb*
✦ *raspberries* ✦ *cherries* ✦ *currants*
✦ *cress and leafy green vegetables containing iron*
✦ *red meat and all animal products also fall into
this part of the spectrum, but should be eaten
sparingly since most are high in cholesterol.*

HERBS AND SPICES

✦ *black and white pepper* ✦ *ginger*
✦ *cayenne pepper* ✦ *rosemary (red/violet)*
✦ *wild sage* ✦ *nettles* ✦ *watercress*
(red/green) ✦ *hibiscus flower*

RHUBARB

Chilled red vegetable soup

INGREDIENTS

- *4 cups/32fl oz/1l tomato juice*
- *½ cup/4fl oz/125ml white wine (or vinegar)*
- *1 clove garlic*
- *2tsp/10ml sugar*
- *1 large red bell pepper, chopped finely*
- *1 medium red onion, chopped finely*
- *1lb/500g tomatoes, chopped finely*
- *1 bunch radishes, sliced*
- *salt and pepper*
- *crushed pink peppercorns (optional)*

METHOD

1. Into a large bowl combine tomato juice, wine (or vinegar), the garlic and sugar. Add the chopped bell pepper, onion, tomatoes, and radishes.

2. Season to taste.

3. Chill for 4 hours. Serve with ice cubes.

RED CABBAGE

Red kidney bean curry

INGREDIENTS

- 1½ cups/8oz/225g dried kidney beans, washed and soaked overnight in sufficient water to cover them
- 2 medium onions
- 3tbsp/45ml oil
- 1 bay leaf
- 1in/2cm cinnamon stick
- 6 cloves
- 6 small cardamoms
- 3 cloves garlic
- 1in/2cm fresh root ginger
- ½ tsp/2.5ml chili powder
- ¼ tsp/1.25ml turmeric
- ½ tsp/2.5ml ground coriander
- 1tsp/5ml ground cumin
- 15oz/500g can peeled tomatoes
- salt
- sprigs of fresh coriander leaves, chopped
- 2 green chilies

METHOD

1. Either pressure cook the beans for 15–20 minutes, or cook for 45–50 minutes until soft. Remove from heat and allow to stand covered.

2. Fry onions in oil until tender. Add bay leaf, cinnamon, cloves, and cardamoms and fry for 1 minute. Add the chilies, garlic, and ginger, and fry until golden. Sprinkle with chili powder, turmeric, ground coriander, and cumin; stir in the mixture to blend. Be careful it does not burn.

3. Add tomatoes and season with salt. Cover and simmer for 2–3 minutes. Add beans to tomato mixture, stirring gently, and cook for 1 minute. Add chopped coriander leaves. Serve with boiled rice or wholewheat naan bread.

RASPBERRIES

GINGER

LEFT *Chilled red vegetable soup, garnished with sliced radishes, is warming and stimulating to the system.*

Spinach umbuto

INGREDIENTS

- several handfuls of wild spinach
- 1 onion
- 1 potato, peeled and chopped
- butter
- salt and pepper

METHOD

1. Wash spinach under running water.

2. Lightly fry chopped onion, add chopped potato and cook until soft.

3. Add spinach and cook quickly.

4. Add butter, salt, and ground black pepper. Mash and serve.

Ricotta cheese and red cherries

INGREDIENTS

- 1¼ cups/9oz/250g ricotta cheese
- ¼ cup/2fl oz/60ml heavy cream
- ½ tsp/2.5ml cinnamon
- 2tbsp/30ml confectionery sugar
- Italian cherries in syrup or canned black cherries

METHOD

1. Beat the cheese with cream, cinnamon, and sugar until smooth. Pack into a small dish and chill covered.

2. Serve with cherries.

ORANGE – WARMING, RELEASING, DIGESTIVE TONIC

Orange foods act as a powerful tonic, giving us both physical energy and mental stimulation. They also aid the digestion. We can use orange foods to treat disorders and infections of the spleen and kidney diseases as well as gall stones, bronchitis and other chest troubles. They can also help gout and rheumatism. They are wonderful for removing inhibitions, any repression and feelings of being in a rut or fear of change, and give emotional strength. Above all, they act as a wonderful antidepressant. The writer D. H. Lawrence (1885–1930) wrote how he would make beautiful orange marmalade when he was depressed. Placing the bottles of marmalade on a shelf so that the light shone through immediately raised his spirits!

ORANGE FOODS

❧ most orange-skinned vegetables and fruits ❧ oranges ❧ tangerines ❧ apricots ❧ mangoes ❧ pawpaws (papayas) ❧ peaches ❧ melons ❧ carrots ❧ swedes ❧ pumpkins and squashes ❧ egg yolks

HERBS AND SPICES

❧ coriander ❧ cumin ❧ paprika ❧ ginger

PAWPAW (PAPAYA)

BUTTERNUT SQUASH

ORANGE

CUMIN

Pumpkin pecan pie

INGREDIENTS
- 1½ cups / 6oz / 175g flour
- ½ cup / 4fl oz / 100g frozen butter
- 1oz / 25g crushed pecan nuts
- 1oz / 25g granulated sugar
- 4tbsp / 60ml cold water

FILLING
- 1lb / 500g pumpkin flesh
- ½ cup / 4¼oz / 120g granulated sugar
- ½ tsp / 2.5ml freshly grated nutmeg
- ½ tsp / 2.5ml grated ginger
- 1¼ cups / 10fl oz / 300ml whipping cream
- 3 eggs

TO FINISH
- ½ cup / 4¼oz / 120g brown sugar
- 2oz / 50g butter
- 2tbsp / 30ml cream
- 1lb / 500g whole pecan nuts

METHOD
1. Sift flour into a bowl. Grate frozen butter into the flour.
2. Using a fork work the mixture together, then add nuts and sugar. Add cold water and continue working until you have a dough.
3. Press pastry into a 9in/23cm pie pan and leave to rest for 10 minutes.
4. Line pastry with tin foil and scatter a handful of rice to keep the foil weighed down.
5. Bake the empty pie shell at 400°F/200°C/gas mark 6 for 10 minutes. Remove rice and foil and bake for another 5 minutes.
6. Cook and purée pumpkin and allow to cool. Stir in the nutmeg, ginger, and cream.
7. Whisk eggs and sugar together until light and fluffy and fold into the mixture.
8. Pour into the pastry shell and bake at 375°F/190°C/gas mark 5 for 40–45 minutes.
9. Mix topping ingredients together, spread over the cooked pie and glaze under a hot broiler.

LEFT *Orange fruit salad – the perfect tonic if you are feeling low.*

PAPRIKA

TANGERINE

CORIANDER

EGG YOLK

GUAVA

Orange fruit salad

INGREDIENTS

• *oranges*
• *mango*
• *pawpaw (papaya)*
• *peaches or nectarines*
• *pink melon*
• *handful of orange geranium flowers*

METHOD

1. Cut all fruit into bite-sized pieces.
2. Soak in orange juice and chill.
3. Sprinkle with orange geranium flowers.

Baked butternut squash and banana

INGREDIENTS

• *2 medium butternut squashes*
• *1 ripe banana*
• *½ cup/4fl oz/125ml mayonnaise or yogurt*
• *1tbsp/15ml grenadilla/passion fruit pulp*
• *honey to taste*
• *pinch ground cinnamon*
• *1oz/25g chopped nuts*

METHOD

1. Bake butternut squashes until soft.
2. Cool, peel, remove pits, and slice.
3. For dressing, blend all ingredients.
4. Pour dressing over the squashes and serve.

Guava oat crisp

A coarsely textured crispy topping is perfect with the orange-flavored and spiced guavas.

INGREDIENTS

• *8 guavas (or peaches or nectarines)*
• *grated rind of 1 orange*
• *2 sticks cinnamon*
• *1 small piece fresh ginger, crushed*
• *grating of nutmeg*
• *½ cup/4fl oz/125ml soft brown sugar*
• *¾ cup/6fl oz/200ml rolled porridge oats*
• *¼ cup/2fl oz/60ml all-purpose flour*
• *¼ cup/2fl oz/60ml wholewheat flour*
• *¼ cup/2fl oz/60ml chopped pecans*
• *pinch salt*
• *¼ tsp/1.25ml ground cinnamon*
• *¼ tsp/1.25ml ground nutmeg*
• *½ cup/5oz/125g unsalted butter*

METHOD

1. Arrange guava halves cut side down in a single layer in a buttered baking dish.
2. Sprinkle orange rind over the fruit. Tuck in cinnamon sticks and smear the tops of the guavas with crushed ginger.
3. Grate over nutmeg and sprinkle with 2tbsp /30 ml of brown sugar.
4. Mix oats, flours, nuts, salt, remaining sugar, and spices. Cut in butter lightly and rub with the fingertips until sticky.
5. Crumble evenly over the fruit. Bake at 400F/200C/gas mark 6 for 30 minutes until brown and crisp.
6. Serve warm with light cream or yogurt.

CANTALOUPE
MELON

CARROT

COUSCOUS

GRAPEFRUIT

CASHEWS

VEGETABLE OIL

YELLOW
LENTILS

YELLOW FOODS

- yellow-skinned vegetables and fruits
- lemons - bananas - grapefruit
- pineapples - melons - corn
- yellow lentils - mung dahl
- yellow oils - butter - nuts
- seeds - wholegrains - rice

HERBS AND SPICES

- saffron - camomile
- cinnamon - lemon grass - dandelion
- evening primrose - marigold - bergamot
- dill - caraway - anise

YELLOW – CLEANSING, EMPOWERING, MIND FOOD, NERVE AND STOMACH TONIC, DIGESTIVE

Yellow is associated with the solar plexus, a very important center for the whole nervous system. This is why, when we are nervous, we often get butterflies in our stomachs and a feeling of constriction and pain in our chest and abdomen. Yellow also affects our digestive processes, especially the liver and intestines. The liver is the organ that eliminates blood toxins, so it is our body purifier. When we have jaundice or hepatitis the skin turns yellow from waste products accumulating in the blood, indicating that we have a block in our eliminating process. Eating foods containing yellow purifies the blood and is particularly good for the skin.

Yellow is also the colour associated with the mentality, and yellow foods will stimulate the intellectual faculties. So while studying or undertaking any mental or scientific study we should try to eat as much yellow food as possible in order to focus our minds and concentration.

Golden-yellow is the colour we associate with the rays of the sun and daylight, it raises our spirits if we are feeling low and brings a harmonious and optimistic attitude to life. Eating

yellow foods can be helpful in cases of nervous exhaustion, skin troubles, indigestion, constipation, liver troubles, and diabetes.

Parsnip and butternut cassoulet

INGREDIENTS

- 2 large onions, chopped
- 2tbsp/30ml olive oil
- 500g/1lb/2oz butternut or other yellow squash
- 500g/1lb/2oz parsnips, diced
- 3 cloves garlic, crushed
- 2 x 16oz/425g cans mixed beans
- 4 freshly chopped tomatoes or 780g can tomatoes
- 1¼ cups/10fl oz/30ml pint vegetable stock
- 2 sprigs fresh thyme
- seasoning
- 1¼ cups/75g/4oz fresh brown breadcrumbs
- ¼ cup/25g/1oz Parmesan (grated)

METHOD

1. Preheat oven to 180°C/350°F/gas mark 4. Heat oil in a skillet or wok.
2. Add onions and fry for 5 minutes until golden-brown.
3. Add butternut squash, parsnips, and garlic and cook for a further 3 minutes.
4. Stir in chopped tomatoes, stock, thyme, seasoning and bring to a boil. Add beans and stir in.
5. Transfer to a large casserole dish, making sure the vegetables are covered with liquid.
6. Sprinkle with breadcrumbs and grated Parmesan.
7. Cover and cook for 40 minutes. Stir well and cook for another 40 minutes.
8. Serve with garlic bread.

Corn loaf

INGREDIENTS

- 4 eggs
- ½ cup/4fl oz/125ml milk
- ½ cup/4 oz/125g sugar
- 1 cup/8 oz/250g corn meal (mealie meal)
- 5tsp/25g all-purpose flour
- 1tsp/5ml cake flour
- 1tsp/5ml baking soda
- pinch salt
- 1 can creamed corn
- 1 can whole corn kernels
  (or fresh from the cob if available)
- 1fl oz/25ml cooking oil
- paprika

METHOD

1. Beat eggs, milk, and sugar together.
2. Sift the dry ingredients and fold into the egg mixture.
3. Add creamed corn, kernels, and oil and mix well.
4. Pour into an oiled loaf pan sprinkle with paprika, and bake for 1 hour at 350°F/180°C/gas mark 4.
5. Remove from oven and allow to stand for 10 minutes before turning out.

Golden kedgeree

INGREDIENTS

- 1 cup/8oz/225g brown rice
- ½ cup/4oz/100g butter
- 1 medium onion
- ½ tsp/2.5ml fresh ginger root
- 1 clove garlic, crushed
- 1in/2.5cm piece cinnamon stick
- 6 cloves
- 1tsp/5ml ground coriander
- ¼ tsp/1.25ml turmeric
- salt to taste
- 2 green chilies, cut lengthways
- 2½ cups/20fl oz/550ml tepid water

METHOD

1. Heat butter in large pan, add onion and fry for 2–3 minutes.
2. Add the ginger, garlic, cinnamon, and cloves and fry for 1 minute.
3. Add the rice and coriander, turmeric, salt, and green chilies. Stir for 2–3 minutes.
4. Add water and bring to a boil, reduce heat and simmer until all water has been absorbed.
5. Serve with vegetable curry.

BUTTERNUT SQUASH

BANANAS

YELLOW *Corn loaf*

Yellow rice

INGREDIENTS

- 2 cups/1lb/500ml long-grained rice
- 4 cups/32fl oz/1l water
- 2 sticks cinnamon
- 3 cardamom pods
- 1tsp/5ml turmeric
- 1oz/25ml butter
- salt to taste

METHOD

1. Place all the ingredients in a saucepan, bring to a boil.
2. Reduce the heat and simmer until all the water is absorbed, add salt to taste.
3. Serve with curries.

PINEAPPLE

ABOVE Green pasta and asparagus salad. This delicious combination will calm and soothe.

GREEN – CLEANSING, PURIFYING, BALANCING, DIGESTIVE STIMULANT

Green is the colour of nature, bringing peace, balance, and harmony. It strongly influences the heart, lowers blood pressure, and soothes the nerves. Green is nature's healing colour and is refreshing and restorative. It can aid in neutralizing disharmony where there are malignant cells, cysts, tumors, and cancers. Green psychologically relieves stress, emotional problems and tension-related problems such as headaches.

Foods to help this action are the green fruits and vegetables, which contain a balance of Yin and Yang energy.

GREEN FOODS

≤ lettuce ≤ green cabbage ≤ cucumber ≤ green bell peppers ≤ zucchini (courgettes) ≤ olive oil ≤ green grapes ≤ kiwi ≤ limes ≤ celery ≤ artichokes ≤ green beans ≤ peas ≤ green lentils ≤ broccoli ≤ also neutral foods including natural yogurt, tofu, and curds.

HERBS AND SPICES

≤ peppermint ≤ parsley ≤ tarragon ≤ garlic ≤ fennel ≤ comfrey ≤ nettles ≤ alfalfa ≤ oregano ≤ aloe vera

GREEN PEAS

Green pasta and asparagus salad

INGREDIENTS

- *2 cups/18oz/450g green pasta shapes*
- *2tsp/10ml olive oil*
- *8oz/225g fresh asparagus*
- *2tbsp/30ml corn oil*
- *1tsp/5ml rich soy sauce*
- *Seasoning to taste*

METHOD

1. Add green pasta shapes to boiling salted water. Stir and cook for 8 minutes, then drain.
2. Toss in a bowl with olive oil and cool.
3. Meanwhile trim then slice the fresh asparagus on the slant.
4. Add to corn oil in a skillet and stir-fry for 2 minutes until bright green and tender crisp.
5. Add contents of the skillet to the pasta with soy sauce and a seasoning of salt and freshly milled pepper.

Avocado dip with chicory

INGREDIENTS

- *2 ripe avocados*
- *2tbsp/30ml lemon juice*
- *½ cup/4fl oz/125ml smooth cottage cheese*
- *¼ cup/2fl oz/60ml mayonnaise or yogurt*
- *1 clove garlic, crushed*
- *salt and pepper*

METHOD

1. Whip ingredients together to form a smooth thick paste. Pack into a dish, cover with plastic wrap, and refrigerate until serving.
2. Place on a large plate surrounding it with strips of green bell pepper, endive leaves, sticks of cucumber and celery.

KIWI FRUIT

LETTUCE

Stir-fried green vegetable sauce

These quickly cooked, bright green vegetables make a good base for a pasta sauce. Serve with spinach pasta for an exceptionally green meal.

INGREDIENTS

- *9oz/250g baby marrows*
- *9oz/250g broccoli*
- *9oz/250g slim green beans or asparagus*
- *¼ cup/2fl oz/60ml sunflower oil*
- *4oz/100g butter*
- *1 clove garlic, crushed*
- *2tbsp/30g chopped parsley*
- *2tbsp/30g chopped chives*
- *salt and pepper to taste*
- *grated Parmesan cheese*

METHOD

1. Rinse vegetables and dry well.

2. Trim the baby marrows and cut into strips. Break broccoli into florets. Slice beans diagonally.

3. Stir-fry the vegetables in a hot oil in a heavy skillet or wok until tender and bright green. Season to taste.

4. Add freshly cooked hot pasta to pan and mix well together.

5. Meanwhile whip the butter until fluffy and add the garlic, parsley, and chives. Season to taste.

6. Dish out the pasta giving each person a knob of herb butter, and some Parmesan cheese and a little of black pepper.

Lemon and zucchini quiche

INGREDIENTS

- *1 cup/8oz/250g all purpose flour*
- *½ cup/5oz/125g butter*
- *pinch salt*
- *1 egg yolk*
- *ice cold water*
- *4 zucchini*
- *1tsp/5ml dry mustard*
- *2tsp/10g chopped chives*
- *3tsp/15g chopped parsley*
- *rind of 1 lemon*
- *1 cup/8 oz/250g grated cheddar cheese*
- *½ cup/4 oz/125g fresh breadcrumbs*
- *½ cup/4fl oz/125g milk*
- *1 cup/8fl oz/350ml cream*
- *4 eggs*

METHOD

1. Rub the flour into the butter until it resembles fine breadcrumbs. Lift all the time to ensure there is plenty of air in the pastry.

2. Add salt.

3. Make a well in the center, add egg yolk and a few drops of water at a time and stir with a knife until all is incorporated. Gradually add enough water to bind pastry.

4. Place in refrigerator to rest then roll out and line a large quiche pan. Return to refrigerator while preparing filling.

5. Grate zucchini, then add mustard, chives, parsley, lemon rind, and cheese.

6. Soak breadcrumbs in the milk.

7. Beat cream and eggs together.

8. Combine all the mixtures well, place in the pastry shell and bake in a preheated oven at 325°F/180°C/gas mark 4 for 45 minutes or until golden and set.

PARSLEY

BEANS

GREEN APPLE

PEAR

CUCUMBER

GREEN CABBAGE

BLUE – SEDATIVE, ANTISEPTIC, ANTIFUNGAL, BACTERICIDAL

The colour blue is associated with the thyroid gland and throat. Its action is opposite to that of red (which is expansive and energizing), tending to cool, contract, and restrict. Blue foods help in infectious diseases where there is a rise in temperature; they tend to be antiseptic and have astringent qualities. They can be useful for treating throat troubles, inflammations, spasms, stings, sunburn, shock, insomnia, period pains, itching, fevers, children's ailments such as measles and mumps, inflammation, spasm, the effects of shock, and headaches.

The colour blue can bring peace and quiet of mind especially where there has been a state of overexcitement or mental torture. It can be relaxing and calming although too much blue can become depressing. While green foods bring calm to the physical and emotional side of us, blue foods bring stillness to the mind. The ocean, rivers, lakes, and sky are all quieting to the mind. Blue aids speech and self-expression.

Too much blue can become depressing, however, so it should be used in conjunction with the complementary colour orange to have the desired calming effect. If you serve a plate of blue foods, serve them either accompanied by orange food or on an orange plate.

BLUEBERRIES

BLUE FOODS

- blue plums
- bilberries
- blueberries
- sea vegetables
- dried fruits such as prunes

HERBS AND SPICES

- valerian
- marjoram
- kelp
- garlic
- Irish sea moss
- catmint
- yarrow
- blue sage
- caraway(blue/orange)
- chicory flowers
- borage flowers
- juniper berries

BILBERRIES

Sea vegetable salad

Use dried wakame, alaria, kombu, or dulse sold in packages or jars.

This salad tastes especially good with an Asian-inspired dressing made with ginger, plum, or sesame oil. The seaweed creates an interesting mix of textures and delivers a nutritious dose of vitamins A and C, potassium, and fiber.

INGREDIENTS

- ½ cup/4oz/125g of dried sea vegetables
- 4tbsp/2oz/50g dried dulse or pickled kombu
- 3 small carrots, peeled and sliced thin
- ½ cup/4oz/125g broccoli florets, blanched
- ½ cup/4oz/125g cauliflower florets, blanched
- 1 bag of mixed salad greens
- 4tbsp/60ml of salad dressing

METHOD

1. Soak the seaweed in water for 5 minutes, them remove and blot on paper towel.

2. Toss ingredients together and top with dressing.

Boysenberry and blueberry smoothie

INGREDIENTS

- 1½ cups/12oz/375g of boysenberry- or blackberry-flavored juice
- 1 cup blackberries or boysenberries
- 1 cup blueberries

METHOD

1. Blend ingredients together until smooth. Drink chilled.

2. For extra creaminess add half a cup of soy milk or yogurt.

PRUNES

Cabbage with garlic and juniper berries

INGREDIENTS

- 2tbsp/30g olive oil
- ½ medium onion, finely chopped
- 6 juniper berries
- 1 clove garlic, crushed
- 1lb/16oz/450g of cabbage, washed and shredded
- salt and freshly ground black pepper

METHOD

1. Heat the olive oil in a flameproof casserole or heavy saucepan and soften the onion for 5 minutes.
2. Crush the juniper berries and add them and the garlic to the onion.
3. Fry for about another half a minute, then add the shredded cabbage.
4. Stir until it is all covered with oil, season with salt and pepper, then cover with lid and let it cook in its own juice for 10 minutes, stirring once or twice.

Blueberry griddlecakes

INGREDIENTS

- 3oz/75g blueberries
- 1 cup/6oz/150g all-purpose flour
- 1¼ tsp/7g baking soda
- ½ tsp salt
- ¼ cup/1½oz/40g sugar
- 1 egg
- 7fl oz/200ml milk
- 3tbsp/1½oz/40g butter, melted
- brown sugar or honey

METHOD

1. Sift flour, baking powder and salt and mix together. Stir in sugar, egg, milk and melted butter. Beat to a creamy batter.
2. Mix in the blueberries. Heat and grease griddle or heavy skillet. Drop the mixture on in spoonfuls. Cook until golden brown on both sides.
3. Sprinkle with brown sugar or honey.

BELOW *Blueberry griddlecakes, served with fresh blueberries.*

Fruit punch with borage flowers

INGREDIENTS

- 1 cup/8fl oz/250ml of pineapple juice, chilled
- 1 cup/8fl oz/250ml of orange juice, chilled
- 1¼ cups/10fl oz/600ml sparkling mineral water, chilled
- juice of two lemons
- a handful of blue borage flowers

METHOD

1. Mix all the ingredients in a large glass bowl. Serve immediately in tall glasses.

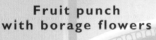

KELP

ABOVE *Fresh fig and raisin compote. This dish can be served with chilled, live yogurt.*

INDIGO – SEDATIVE, DIGESTIVE, STIMULATES VENOUS BLOOD

Indigo is associated with the brow area just between our eyes, and relates to the pineal gland. This gland controls the nervous, mental, and psychic potential, including the organs of sight and hearing. So, psychologically, indigo foods have a purifying and stabilizing effect, especially in cases where fears and repressions have produced serious mental problems. Indigo foods also help to broaden the mind and free it of the psychological burden of fear and inhibition.

Indigo food can be used to treat diseases of the eyes, ears, and nose, and diseases of the lungs, asthma, and dyspepsia. Foods in this group are similar to blue foods but tend to be have a black colouring; they include the following:

INDIGO FOODS

❧ black soybeans ❧ black beans
❧ soy sauce ❧ black olives ❧ blackberries
❧ boysenberries ❧ black cherries
❧ dried raisins and currants ❧ vanilla beans
❧ wild mushrooms

Fresh fig and raisin compote

INGREDIENTS

- 1lb/2oz/500g fresh figs
- 4oz/100g raisins
- 1oz/50g almonds with skin
- 2 thinly pared strips of lemon peel
- 1 bay leaf
- yogurt to serve

SYRUP

- 2 cups/14oz/400g brown sugar
- 2½ cups/600ml water or 1¼ cups/300ml water and an equal amount of red grape juice

METHOD

1. First make the syrup by dissolving the sugar in the water and grape juice over a low heat.
2. Add the figs, raisins, almonds, lemon peel, and bay leaf to the hot syrup. Bring to a boil and simmer gently for 12–15 minutes.
3. Serve with cold yogurt.

Wild mushroom spread

Try to serve this with granary bread, because the yeast in the bread is associated with the blue ray.

INGREDIENTS

- 3 cups/8oz/250g chopped large flat mushrooms
- 1tbsp/15ml chopped onion
- ½ cup/4fl oz/125ml butter
- 6tbsp/3oz/75g soft, low fat cream cheese
- dash of Worcester sauce
- lemon juice, salt, and pepper

METHOD

1. Fry the mushrooms and onion in butter for 2–3 minutes.
2. Liquidize or blend the mixture with the cheese, Worcester sauce, lemon juice, salt, and pepper until smooth.
3. Press into a pâté dish and chill until set.

Olive pâté

INGREDIENTS

- *handful of green or black olives*
- *garlic to taste*
- *lemon juice to taste*
- *fresh parsley to garnish*

METHOD

1. Pit the olives and purée in a blender. Add garlic and lemon juice as required.
2. Serve in a ramekin garnished with fresh parsley.

Black bean tortillas

You can use dried or canned beans, canned or frozen corn. Soy yogurt makes a great nondairy stand-in for sour cream.

INGREDIENTS

- *1 can of black beans or dried beans prepared by soaking and boiling until tender*
- *1 can corn kernels or 1 cup/8oz/250g of frozen corn*
- *1tsp/5g ground cumin*
- *1 small red onion diced*
- *2 tomatoes cut into small pieces*
- *⅓ cup chopped fresh coriander leaves*
- *sea salt and chili powder to taste*
- *4 corn or wheat tortillas*
- *1 cup/8oz/250g grated cheese (you can also use soy cheese)*
- *4tbsp/60ml soy yogurt or sour cream*
- *salsa*

METHOD

1. Pit beans and corn into a bowl. Stir in cumin, onion, tomatoes, and coriander. Season with salt and chili powder to taste.
2. Pile into tortillas, sprinkle with soy cheese, and heat in oven until cheese is melted.
3. Top with salsa and soy yogurt or sour cream.

Pasta with black bean sauce

INGREDIENTS

- *10oz/300g pasta (swirls or shells)*
- *a 2in/5cm piece of ginger root (peeled and grated)*
- *1tbsp/30ml black bean sauce*
- *6fl oz/175ml vegetable stock*
- *2 garlic gloves, crushed*
- *zest of half lemon*
- *3tbsp sesame oil*
- *6oz/175g button mushrooms*
- *4oz/125g bean sprouts*
- *soy sauce*

METHOD

1. Cook the pasta in plenty of boiling water for about 10 minutes, until cooked but still firm.
2. In another dish mix together ginger, black bean sauce, soy sauce, stock, garlic and lemon zest.
3. Heat the sesame oil, add mushrooms and stir-fry until well coated in oil for a few minutes.
4. Add bean sprouts, and increase heat so that they are cooked but still crisp.
5. Pour over sauce and mix thoroughly. Drain pasta and transfer to warm plates and cover with sauce. Serve immediately.

Blackberry leaf tea

In herbal medicine, blackberry leaf tea is used as a remedy for diarrhea, as a decongestant and a stomach tonic. Mrs Grieve in *A Modern Herbal* (1931) suggests adding 1oz/25g dried leaves to 2½ cups/600ml boiling water.

BLACK OLIVES

BLACK BEANS

CURRANTS

SOY SAUCE

RAISINS

VIOLET/PURPLE – PURIFYING, SEDATIVE, DIURETIC, PROTECTIVE

Violet is the colour associated with intuition and spiritual understanding; it is linked to the pituitary gland and the crown of the head. Psychologically, this colour has the most wonderful healing effect on all forms of neurosis and neurotic manifestations, so violet/purple foods are helpful in nervous and mental disorders, neuralgia, sciatica, and diseases of the scalp. They also act as a soothing tranquilizer on frayed nerves and for those of a highly strung disposition. Artists, actors, and musicians often suffer from anxiety disorders and would find these foods useful to restore peace and calm.

Physically, violet foods can be used to treat rheumatism, concussion, epilepsy, tumors, cerebrospinal meningitis, kidney and bladder diseases. According to Roland Hunt, violet is also a purifier of the blood and helps stop the growth of tumors. Ultraviolet light is used quite extensively in orthodox medicine.

VIOLET FOODS

- eggplant (aubergine)
- purple grapes - purple plums
- purple broccoli - purple onions - globe artichokes
- purple bell peppers
- purple cabbage
- radicchio - beets

HERBS

- purple sage - thyme - feverfew
- lavender

LONG, THIN EGGPLANT (AUBERGINE)

Warm salad of purple vegetables

INGREDIENTS
- olive oil
- 1 large clove garlic
- medium red onion, peeled and chopped
- 1 eggplant (aubergine) cut into cubes
- 1 cup of radicchio, cut into strips through roots
- 2oz/50g shredded purple cabbage
- 2oz/50g cooked beet
- salt and pepper

METHOD
1. Heat oil in a large skillet or wok, add the garlic and onion, and stir-fry for 3–4 minutes, or until the onion is soft.
2. Add eggplant (aubergine) and fry for another 3–4 minutes.
3. Add radicchio, cabbage, and beet and stir-fry for 2–3 minutes more. Season well and serve.

Eggplant (aubergine) purée

INGREDIENTS
- 3 medium or 2 large eggplant (aubergine)
- salt
- 1 clove garlic
- ½ small onion
- lime or lemon juice to taste
- 2tsp/10ml olive oil
- 2tsp/10g chopped parsley

METHOD
1. Wash and dry eggplant (aubergines). Put under the broiler. Turn frequently until they soften.
2. Then turn up the heat until the skin is charred all over and broken in places.
3. Remove and place in a blender with the other ingredients and blend to form a stiff mixture.
4. Serve with pitta bread.

Glazed baby beets

INGREDIENTS
- 16oz/450g baby beets
- 1oz/25g butter
- 1tbsp/15ml fresh orange juice

METHOD
1. Peel beets retaining 1in/2cm of the stems.
2. Boil gently until tender and drain.
3. Melt butter, add juice and bring to boil.
4. Add beets and toss gently until well coated and heated.

RED CABBAGE

GLOBE ARTICHOKE

ROUND EGGPLANT (AUBERGINE)

Purple plum pie

INGREDIENTS

- *1 ready-made pastry base (or make your own, see below)*
- *8oz/200g cream cheese*
- *3tbsp/45ml sugar*
- *1tbsp/15ml grated lemon rind*
- *2tbsp/30ml lemon juice*
- *2 peaches*
- *6 7 small purple plums*
- *fresh blackberries*
- *4–5tbsp/60–70ml blackberry jelly or jam*
- *additional fresh fruit*

PASTRY

- *4tbsp/2oz/50g butter*
- *½ cup/4oz/100g all-purpose flour*
- *1 whole egg*
- *2 egg yolks*
- *¼ cup/1oz/25g sugar*
- *pinch of salt*

METHOD

1. If making your own pastry, cut butter into flour until the mixture resembles sand.

2. Mix together egg, egg yolks, salt, and sugar, and combine with flour mixture. Place in the refrigerator to rest for at least 1 hour.

3. To line pie pan, press it into the form with fingertips. Prick bottom with holes and bake at 400°F/200°C/gas mark 6 for 5 minutes only.

4. Beat together the softened cream cheese, sugar, lemon juice and grated rind until smooth and creamy. Spread the mixture over the pie crust.

5. Cut the peaches and plums in half and take out the stones.

6. Arrange with the blackberries across the pastry in rows. Finally, melt the jelly and brush it over the fruit to give it a jewel-like glaze.

7. Chill well before serving.

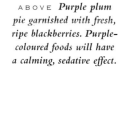

ABOVE *Purple plum pie garnished with fresh, ripe blackberries. Purple-coloured foods will have a calming, sedative effect.*

Purple broccoli salad

INGREDIENTS

- *1lb/450g purple broccoli*
- *4oz/100g raw mushrooms*
- *1tbsp/15ml red wine vinegar*
- *1tsp/5ml dried tarragon*

DRESSING

- *5tbsp/60ml sunflower oil*
- *2tbsp/30ml lemon juice*
- *½ clove garlic, crushed*
- *½ tsp/2.5ml mustard*
- *sea salt*

METHOD

1. Blanch broccoli for 3 minutes, drain. Place on a serving plate.

2. Combine the mushrooms with the vinegar and tarragon and sprinkle over the broccoli.

3. Combine all the dressing ingredients and pour over the salad.

PURPLE
BROCCOLI

PURPLE
GRAPES

RED ONION

FLOWERS IN COOKING

*To make food all the more delicious, and provide extra colour,
simply add flowers. Salads and sandwiches, soups, stews, and desserts can
all be enhanced very simply and cheaply when garnished with flowers and
greenery. A bowl of fruit, tea with a slice of lemon, red anemones,
and strawberries all add a visual feast to a summer tea
in which red and white predominate.*

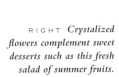

ABOVE *Rose petals
and mint make an
attractive and unusual
garnish for sandwiches.*

Many herbs have edible flowers, which not only look attractive, but also when used in conjunction with their leaves bring a wonderful aroma and taste to the meal. Bergamot leaves and flowers can be added to green salads, while nasturtium flowers and leaves impart both vivid colour and a peppery flavor to a salad.

Here are a few ideas for using flowers in food.

⋐ A plate of sandwiches decorated with fresh herbs, zinnias, mint, and rose petals adds to the effect of colour. A colourful plate of reds, oranges, and yellow can be set off by pale green lettuce and glowing nasturtium flowers, marigolds, and dandelions. A walnut oil dressing completes a visual and gastronomic feast.

⋐ Serve a plate of freshly baked scones on a bed of lavender flowers.

⋐ Curly-edged, pinky-russet endive has a slightly bitter taste but blends well with the flavor of little sprigs of aromatic thyme flowers, sweet violet, or delicate-flavored pink rose petals and tiny white flowers of camomile. This is particularly delicious made with a mustard dressing.

⋐ Crystalized flowers are easy to prepare and look beautiful decorating a special cake or dessert; but bear in mind that white sugar is not healthy, so do not use crystalized flowers with a rich, sweet dessert. Rather, try to use them to enhance homemade yogurt or fruit salad.

⋐ Float a handful of pretty pink chive flowers on a summer soup to which you have added finely chopped chives.

⋐ Add blue borage flowers and young leaves to a summer salad or fruit punch.

Remember that the perfume of the flower will also enhance its visual and vibrational effect on us. Different-coloured flowers give off different perfumes according to their type and colour. Red flowers give off a deep rich perfume, pink and white a light fragrance, yellow and orange a more sweet and pungent perfume, and dark yellow and brown a more woody and exotic flavor. The aroma of flowers can enhance flavors, as well as improving our ability to digest food.

RIGHT *Crystalized
flowers complement sweet
desserts such as this fresh
salad of summer fruits.*

CRYSTALIZED FLOWERS

Violets, primroses, rose petals, narcissus, mint, and melissa (lemon balm) all crystalize well. If you do want to make crystalized soft flower petals or herbs, dip them into stiff egg white to which you can add one drop of essential oil. Put them on a wire tray to dry and sprinkle with plenty of granulated sugar.

1. Whisk a cup of egg whites until stiff, add a drop of essential oil and then carefully dip your chosen flower and coat it with the egg white.

2. Once coated with the mixture, lay the flowers gently on a wire tray.

3. Sprinkle the flowers with granulated sugar and leave to dry.

USING FLOWERS IN FOOD PRESENTATION

Flowers on your dining table will enhance the colour and general flavor of the meal. Use a light bright display for a summer supper, or a rich dark arrangement using fruit and berries for a warming winter dinner. Even the breakfast tray is enhanced with a few fresh orange and yellow flowers in a vase or loose on a tray. This will cheer you and wake you up – enhancing the energizing qualities needed for the day.

Many herbs have delicate flowers, which we can appreciate only if we look at them closely. Leave a bowl of fresh cut herbs and their flowers on the table during the day. They not only cleanse the air but give out a refreshing aroma when you walk past. You will be able to appreciate the delicacy and colour of the flowers when you sit down to eat.

We can learn from the Japanese tradition of creating a simple flower arrangement on the table, which could be appreciated and act as a subject for discussion during a meal. They believe that we should discuss only happy topics at the dinner table, because heated debates instill negative vibrations into the food.

FLORAL HONEY

A good alternative to crystalizing flowers is to prepare floral honey. Preserve beautifully fragrant honeysuckle flowers in honey for the winter by filling a jar full of flowers and pouring over enough honey to cover them fully. Use this aromatic honey to flavor tea or to soothe sore throats.

YELLOW FLOWERS ARE REJUVENATING, ESPECIALLY AT THE START OF THE DAY

LIGHT GREEN WILL HELP CALM THE NERVES, THEREBY AIDING DIGESTION

LEFT *A flower decoration enhances the pleasure of eating.*

ESSENTIAL OILS IN COOKING

Essential oils made from different flowers have been used extremely beneficially as massage oils and in aromatherapy, and some essential oils, and flower essences such as the Bach flower remedies (see p 210), can be taken internally.

ABOVE *Try adding essential oils to enhance the flavor of your food – rice pudding is transformed by palma rosa oil.*

ABOVE *A drop of lemon essential oil is a wonderfully aromatic addition to a fish or chicken dish.*

In many countries, fruit is cooked with meat to enhance the flavor and aid the digestion. The same effect can be achieved with a few drops of essential oils added to the stock or sauce. Use orange or lemon essential oil with chicken and fish. Alternatively you can add a couple of drops of either oil to peppercorns or herb salt.

Hot desserts too can be transformed with essential oil of flowers. These desserts will have added benefits when served to those who are ill or weak. Rice pudding will taste delicious with the addition of palma rosa; custard is improved with oil of tangerine, mandarin, or orange; chocolate mousse can have lemon, lime, or peppermint added. Crêpes, custards, and soufflés can also be transformed with the addition of a few drops of floral essence.

Most spices are warming and have a pungent aroma. They are related to the warm end of the spectrum and when ground are often bright red, orange, or gold in colour. The essential oils made from these spices are wonderful added to spicy party punches and warming winter casseroles and puddings. Try adding a drop of essential oil of clove, cinnamon, nutmeg, coriander, or cardamom to spice up a winter soup or stew.

CINNAMON STICKS

CLOVES

NUTMEG

SPICES SUCH AS CLOVES, CINNAMON, AND NUTMEG ARE RELATED TO THE WARMING, RED END OF THE COLOUR SPECTRUM

ABOVE *A winter punch is warmed up by the addition of aromatic and stimulating spices.*

Citrus oils are associated with the orange and yellow colour rays. They have a sharp, refreshing aroma and include lemon, lime, mandarin, orange, tangerine, and grapefruit. Adding a couple of drops of citrus oils to cold or warm drinks, sauces and soups can create a wonderful taste that cleans the palate and aids digestion when you have eaten a heavy meal or oily food. Other oils good for digestion are ginger, peppermint, fennel, and coriander.

Floral essential oils such as geranium, melissa, verbena, rose, and neroli contain pink and green colour energy. These can be used to flavor eggs, cheese, and rice dishes. Desserts, cakes, and ices can also be enhanced by the addition of rose, melissa, or geranium oil, giving them a subtle aroma and adding to the "feel good" factor.

ADDING OILS

*A*dding essential oils to food brings out their lovely aroma, as well as capturing the essence of the vital light force within the plant. For instance, you can add a few drops of essential oil to ice cream recipes, ices or frozen yogurt. Fragrant flower jams can be made using orange or rose flower water and a couple of drops of essential oil.

RIGHT *Jams and jellies, especially those made from flowers, such as rose petal jam, are made extra-special with essential oils.*

SOLARIZED HERB VINEGAR

*N*atural sunlight can energize many natural foods. Try solarizing herb-flavored vinegars; the sun's rays will bring out the full flavor and healing qualities of the herbs they contain. Herb vinegars can be used to enhance salads and savory dishes and they also look stunning on a kitchen shelf.

There are many herbs suitable for herb vinegar, each with its own special flavor and use. Try basil, rosemary, dill, celery, chives, elderflowers, mint, marjoram, sage, tarragon, or oregano. You can also add cloves of garlic.

To make herb vinegar, fill a glass bottle with vinegar and leave it in a sunny spot for 5 days. Each day remove and replace the herbs, varying this according to the flavor required. Finally strain the vinegar through some cheesecloth and place a fresh sprig of herb into the bottle for identification.

To further the therapeutic qualities, decant the vinegar into a coloured glass bottle. The sunlight will be filtered through, the rays helping to energize the contents with that particular colour vibration.

Another method of bringing colour into the vinegar is to make a delicious raspberry-flavored vinegar in the same way, but afterward remove the raspberries altogether because they will ferment if left in the bottle. You can then add some herbs into the rich wine-coloured liquid.

The double purple flowers of hollyhocks can be dried and used to colour wine and herb vinegar. Place a couple of flowers in a bottle and place this in a sunny place for 3 days. Strain and pour into clear glass bottles so you can enjoy the lavender colour and lovely aroma.

1. To make a herb vinegar, fill a glass bottle with vinegar and leave in a sunny spot for 5 days.

3. After 5 days, strain the vinegar through some cheesecloth and decant into a fresh glass bottle.

2. Each day place fresh herbs in the vinegar; you can vary your choice of herbs according to taste.

4. In order to identify the flavor of your herb vinegar, place a fresh sprig of the herb into the bottle.

USING COLOUR IN FOOD PREPARATION AND SERVING

Colour has an important role to play in the presentation of a meal. Passing a festive dinner table of decorative trays stimulates our senses as we anticipate the food to come. The visual feast of a colourful meal can be set off against contrasting tableware and attractive tableware.

ABOVE *Vibrant ingredients are set off against white tableware.*

ABOVE *Sliced oranges glow against a midnight blue plate.*

ABOVE *A colourful stir-fry contrasts well with white, while the rice is balanced by the green.*

The colour of your tableware can greatly influence your perception of a meal and can enhance the colours on your plate. Colourful food looks perfect against a pure white plate, but a pale soup or stew looks much more appetizing when served in a richly coloured bowl.

If you are making a dish that has a predominant colour, try to find a serving bowl in a contrasting colour. A bowl of stewed peaches would look wonderful in a green or blue glass bowl, while stuffed green peppers would look more appetizing if presented in a terra-cotta casserole.

Red food particularly should not be served in earthenware pottery, but rather blue or green tableware to allow the colour to have its full effect. If you have only earthenware plates, however, you can balance colours by garnishing and combining one colour food with another. A red bean curry, for example, can quite easily be served on rice in the brown pottery plate; as the pale colour of the rice will contrast with the beans and so enhance the action of the red ray.

Peach colours arouse hunger. This colour has been shown in tests conducted by cafeterias and restaurants to be the most appetizing hue for eating places. Other wall colours that are effective are turquoise blue, light coral, and light yellow-cream (*see* p 146). So we see that colour has a great effect on our subconscious. For instance, there was a cafeteria chain that wanted to improve its salad sales and did so by replacing the usual white tableware with pale green plates. The sales went up 100 percent!

Cream, yellow, and gold aid the digestion, and are revitalizing and rejuvenating. Orange is also good for the digestion, and is a joyous, light colour, helping us to relax and to ease the body.

Presentation is as important to children as it is to adults. Children love bright colours on the table, which is an attraction in itself. Try cutting vegetables and fruit into appealing shapes or putting rice or potatoes into jelly molds to make the food more attractive. Colourful plates make the food look more appetizing and tasty and this encourages a child to try out new food.

Our midday meal is often the one that is eaten with haste although it is the most important meal nutritionally. This meal should be eaten in as much natural light and relaxing surroundings as possible in order to feed our energy levels. If you are at work, take time off to find a park or green space where you can eat your lunch. At home find a quiet place where you won't be disturbed. You don't need to spend a long time laying out a table; a colourful table mat and napkin are quick and easy to set up.

YOU WILL ENJOY YOUR MEAL MUCH MORE IF YOU TAKE CARE WITH THE LOOK OF THE TABLE

SIMPLE FLOWERS PROVIDE A FOCAL POINT AT THE TABLE

TABLE SETTINGS SHOULD BE IN A SIMILAR OR COMPLEMENTARY COLOUR AS THE FLOWERS

LIGHTING

The quality of the natural or artificial lighting found in the room where you eat can have a profound effect on your enjoyment of the meal and ultimately on your ability to assimilate goodness and nourishment from your food.

Natural sunlight in the morning has the effect of stimulating chemicals in the brain that wake up our body organs. So breakfast should be eaten in the room that catches the morning sunlight. The light coming into the room will stimulate our metabolism and enhance our energy levels.

Lighting also affects our perception of food colours. For example, one railway company found that blue fluorescent lighting in its dining cars was making the coffee look weak and gray, and the diners didn't like it. They were tasting the coffee with their eyes! Once the blue lights were removed from the dining cars, passengers reported that the quality of the coffee was much improved.

Serving an evening meal by candlelight has been found to have the effect of making us eat more slowly. Candlelight creates a warm and intimate ambience, which is conducive to conversation. I am sure that if more meals were eaten by candlelight, communication would improve and mealtimes would once again become a special time to share with your family.

ABOVE *A joyful, relaxing colour, orange is wonderful for flower arrangements and table settings.*

LEFT *Soft lighting or candlelight makes mealtimes special by providing an intimate, ambient setting, and encourages us to relax and eat more slowly.*

PART FOUR

COLOUR AND INTERIORS

THE MOST FORTUNATE OF MEN,
BE HE A KING OR A COMMONER,
IS HE WHOSE WELFARE IS ASSURED IN HIS OWN HOME.
GOETHE, *Iphigenia in Tauris*, 1787

*W*e all need to create a healing and peaceful atmosphere around ourselves. The colours in our homes and surroundings affect our physical, emotional, and mental health. By carefully choosing the colours that surround us, we are indirectly caring for ourselves in prosperous and hard times. In stressful times, or when we are going through a period of illness or depression, it is easy to neglect ourselves. These are the times when the good vibrations from the colours in our home can reflect back to us as positive radiations.

The best way to learn about the effect of colours is to look at those we choose in our home environment. These give many clues to our personalities and inner feelings. Carefully chosen colours can build our self-image, so that we are better able to cope with the stresses of modern life and improve our relationship with others. Colour preferences coincide with major changes in our lives, and a change in attitude or physical state is often accompanied by a change in our colour preference.

Colour is the most important single ingredient in preparing a scheme for your house, and in itself costs nothing. Attractive colours cost no more than drab ones and a holistic design does not have to be outdated in style. If you understand the therapeutic actions of different colours you can blend these with your colour personality and ideas relating to general fashion trends.

SOUL COLOURS
IN THE HOME

*The colours in your home will give out messages about your
personality and who you are. So show yourself and your home off to the fullest
and most colourful, making sure you use colours sympathetic to your character.*

BLUE AND PINK
PAINTWORK ENLIVENS
AND ENERGIZES AN
OTHERWISE PLAIN,
WHITE ROOM

INSTEAD OF DECIDING
ON ONE DOMINANT
COLOUR, TRY ADDING
CUSHIONS AND THROWS
IN BRIGHT COLOURS TO
A NEUTRAL ROOM

THE DETAILS AND
ACCESSORIES STAMP
THE OCCUPIER'S
PERSONALITY ON
THIS ROOM

Imagine coming into your home for the
first time, wondering what type of person lives
there. Starting at your front door, walk into each
room in your home, paying attention to the
atmosphere and feeling that each room conveys.
Now ask the following questions:

≈ Which colours predominate in the room?
≈ Is there a general colour that is repeated
throughout the house?

≈ Do the main colours reflect your personality
accurately?

If you find that blue predominates, you are probably a quiet, shy person or are seeking peace,
tranquillity and harmony in your life. If you are
often depressed it may be that the blue adds to
the depressive feeling. Dark blue rather than light
blue is more likely to pull you down and leave
you feeling low. You need to contrast a deep blue
room with an uplifting and energizing colour
such as yellow, deep pink, or peach.

Creating your home is something very
personal. To discover your personal colours for
decorating, look at a colour chart or colour wheel
(*see* p 13) and choose the colours to which you
feel immediately attracted. Try not to link these
colours to any person or object, just choose on
instinct. There is no reason why you cannot
include black and white, gold and silver if you
do not have these colours on the chart.

ABOVE AND
RIGHT *Strong
combinations of colour
create a dramatic
effect and suggest a
forceful personality.*

SOUL COLOURS

Choose three colours:

1 The colour you find the most **pleasing.**

2 The colour you find the most **relaxing.**

3 The colour you find the most **inspiring.**

☞ *The most pleasing colour is your "soul" colour and this colour preference usually remains the same over a long period of time. You are drawn to your soul colour intuitively and it will represent your personality and outlook on life.*

☞ *The second colour you choose is your colour of relaxation. It is the colour that has a calming and soothing effect on you, bringing you healing on a physical, emotional, and spiritual level.*

☞ *The third colour is inspirational. It is your mental colour and helps you aspire to your higher self.*

You can use these three colours individually or combined in your room decoration. If your three colours complement each other (*see* p 13) you can use them in one room. If two of them are complementary colours such as yellow and violet, red and turquoise, or orange and blue, these will also work in perfect harmony in the same room. If the colours you have chosen do not complement each other, try using a neutral colour as a backdrop, and add your personal colours in the furnishings and accessories.

Use your soul colour in your living room, your relaxation colour in your bedroom, and your inspirational colour in your work room, rumpus room, studio or sewing room – anywhere you need inspiration. If this colour is very dark or too bright, use it as an accent colour only. Also, adding a white tint can soften the physiological effect of that colour on you. We can also combat the negative effects of a certain colour by adding its complementary colour.

If you do not feel that any particular colour gives you inspiration, remember that light blue is a colour that promotes and releases creative

energy. If you are likely to spend many hours doing close work such as reading, studying, or drawing, too much of a strong or a dark blue can be tiring on the eyes, because reflected or direct blue light makes focusing difficult.

As each rainbow colour vibration has its own powerful energy and quality we can use certain colours to improve our general state of health or alleviate specific problems we may have (*see* p 200). You can manipulate the colours that surround you so that they work together with your body's own healing mechanisms.

BELOW *You can achieve a dramatic effect by using two or three colours that work harmoniously together as accents in a neutral room.*

BLUE AND GOLD ARE A PERFECT COMBINATION FOR FABRICS IN A PLAIN ROOM

THE TWO-COLOUR THEME IS CARRIED THROUGH EVEN IN THIS PICTURE

THE INTENSE BLUE OF THE UPHOLSTERY IS ENHANCED BY GOLDEN CUSHIONS

AN ACCENT OF METALLIC COLOUR IS ADDED

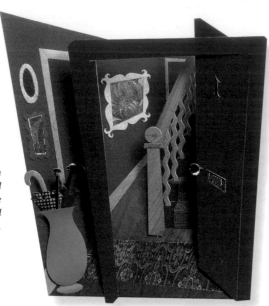

RIGHT *Since it has a stimulating effect, red decor is the perfect choice for rooms that need warmth and movement.*

ailment showing excessive heat in your system (e.g. high blood pressure, fever, rashes, itchy skin).

Pink is made up of red mixed with white. Although usually associated with femininity and love, the therapeutic affects of pink vary according to the tone. A sensitive temperament is most responsive to pale pink and blush-coloured rays, while lovers of home and home life will respond to the pure rose tones. A rose pink is an ideal colour for the bedroom because it helps you develop self-love.

ORANGE

Orange has both the physical stimulation of red and the mental stimulation of yellow. It is a joyful colour and a favorite of people who live close to the Earth. People who like this colour are usually at ease with their own bodies and this is why many dancers are attracted to it. The earthiness of orange also makes it a very creative colour.

Many people do not like orange in their environment, although it may be just the colour they need. Versions of orange that are more acceptable to live with include rust, terra-cotta, amber, peach, and apricot, all of which reflect the positive and lively qualities of this colour.

RED DECOR

*R*ed colours work best in places that require warmth and physical action. A hall, staircase, passage or corridor, kitchen, and playroom are suitable places for red decoration, as is a cold room. A red environment will stimulate physical love, and this is why red sheets and red lights are associated with sexual expression.

RED/PINK

Red is a difficult colour to live with; because of its strength of character most people find it too oppressive and heavy. There are many different variations of red: burgundy, wine, and terra-cotta are often used in homes. Red is physically stimulating and promotes movement and activity.

If you are an impatient person or experiencing frustration you should not surround yourself with red because this will exacerbate the problem. A red environment will also aggravate any

ORANGE DECOR

*O*range has a strong and beneficial effect on the digestive system, so it makes a good colour for a dining room or eating area. Candles glow in a room with orange tones and make you feel warm, secure, and comfortable.

RIGHT *Orange is physically and mentally stimulating, a favorite colour with creative people.*

INSURE THE YELLOW YOU CHOOSE IS GOLDEN, PRIMROSE, OR CREAM. YELLOW-GREEN COLOURS ARE NOT RECOMMENDED

TRY TO EAT IN A ROOM WITH PLENTY OF NATURAL LIGHT

THE BLUE VASE AND BOWLS PROVIDE A COMPLEMENTARY COLOUR AND A FOCUS AT THE TABLE

YELLOW TABLEWARE CAN ENHANCE THE COLOUR OF YOUR FOOD

YELLOW

Yellow is the colour that is the closest to sunshine, and it is an uplifting, happy colour. The positive quality of yellow stimulates the brain, making you alert, clear-headed, and decisive. For this reason, yellow is beneficial when you need to study.

On its own, yellow is a colour that gives us no anchorage, protection, aim or focus although it is a wonderful colour to use in combination with other harmonizing or contrasting tones. Yellow decoration combined with yellow light is not a good environment as the nervous system can be overstimulated. If you have a fractious family relationship, and you have a yellow room in the house, try changing it to a soft cream.

GREEN

As we have discovered, green is the colour of nature. This is why surrounding yourself with green creates a feeling of comfort, laziness and relaxation, which gives you the feeling of calm and space. Green is used therapeutically in interiors to create this feeling of space and connection with nature. It provides an energy balance for all other colours and brings a deep sense of healing at many levels.

Green is soothing only as long as it is a soft and clear tone; when it becomes muddy, dull, or olive, it indicates decay. If you surround yourself with this type of green your environment may reflect a negative aspect of your own personality.

ABOVE *A yellow breakfast or dining room will aid digestion and stimulate conversation.*

BELOW *Soft green tones are therapeutic and relaxing; however, a darker, muddy shade will encourage negative thoughts.*

YELLOW-GREEN COLOURS

At present, lime green is popular as a decorative colour. However, yellow-green colours can make some people feel nauseous. Stick to golden-yellows, clear primrose yellows, and buttery creams and be careful that the yellow does not become tinged with green or turn muddy.

GREEN DECOR MAKES FOR A COMFORTING AND RELAXING ENVIRONMENT

GREEN HELPS CITY DWELLERS TO CONNECT WITH THE FRESHNESS OF NATURE

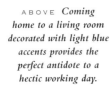

BLUE-TINGED
UPHOLSTERY IS
CALMING AND
RELAXING

BLUE FLOOR TILES
ARE COOLING FOR
THOSE LIVING IN
A HOT CLIMATE

ABOVE *Coming home to a living room decorated with light blue accents provides the perfect antidote to a hectic working day.*

RIGHT *Soothing blue surroundings insure maximum calm!*

TURQUOISE

Mixing green with blue creates turquoise, which transforms green to a cool, refreshing colour with a morning appearance. Turquoise is more successful as a wall colour than green, since the area becomes larger but still holds its static calm appearance. Using turquoise in decoration is an excellent way of making a calming and soothing environment, which is especially helpful if you are suffering from stress. Like green, turquoise is good to use when you are hot or when mental strain has been endured. We associate blue-greens with the homes of people who live in hot climates, and it reminds us of the refreshing and cool colour of the ocean.

BLUE

More people choose blue as their favorite colour than any other (over 50 percent prefer it). Blue rooms and blue-tinged lighting make a calming, expanding, relaxing environment.

Light and soft blue make us feel quiet and protected from all the bustle and activity of the day. Deep blue is relaxing and calm as if we are being soothed by the deep blue of the night sky. The deeper the blue, the more relaxing. A special dark blue, termed "Nila" (a Pali word derived from the Sanskrit), is the most suitable environment for meditation.

Blue-violet is a warm blue, which is comforting and good for those who suffer from claustrophobia or asthma.

VIOLET

Violet is composed of blue and red, providing shelter and protection as well as stimulating and rousing us into activity. The colour has a balancing effect and offers an environment that is similar to green. Yet this colour is not really instrumental in healing, unlike blue or turquoise, although it does provide us with a place to be quiet and compose ourselves. Violet is a colour closely linked to creativity, and many painters and composers prefer to be surrounded by violet when working.

A BLUE-VIOLET
COLOUR IS COMFORTING
AND RELAXING

BLUE WILL HELP YOU
TO SWITCH OFF AND
LOSE YOURSELF IN
A GOOD BOOK

THE COMPLETE BOOK OF COLOUR

Together with violet, a decor scheme in magenta would be as theatrical and futuristic as a birth–death scenario. It is therefore advisable that only trained chromatherapists should use these colours for a healing environment. One can, however, use these colours in small quantities in furnishings. A painting or rug using magenta can be a source of wonderful inspiration, as would a magenta silk lampshade or blind.

LEFT *Violet creates a theatrical mood and hints at the creative nature of the person who lives there.*

Violet used in decorating creates an air of luxury, royalty, and mystery because it has always been associated with kings and spiritual places. It is best to use violet for inspiration in touches in soft furnishings either with harmonizing colours or to complement a yellow scheme.

Shades of purple can be used in areas where dignity and contemplation are required.

COLOUR INFLUENCE

On its own violet can exert strong psychic influences on those who are in the room, so you need to make sure your temperament and inner strength can cope with this.

MAGENTA-VIOLET

From a negative perspective, magenta reinforces the effect of violet, making us desire to be lifted out of the involvement of our present demanding world, avoiding challenges. It can also be too relaxing, which is ultimately dangerous to those who have a tendency to opt out. So if you are chronically depressed or introverted avoid magenta in both your dress and surroundings.

MAGENTA

Magenta is an elusive colour and cannot easily be reproduced. It is best seen through a prism. If you wish to use magenta it is a good idea to find a magenta-coloured flower for inspiration for your scheme. Magenta is a very spiritual colour but with practical overtones. This means that it has a humanizing effect on us. When we are feeling despondent and worried about our condition, and are angry and frustrated, magenta draws us out of this attitude and lets our spirit soar.

ADD ACCENTS OF MAGENTA TO YOUR HOME WITH A RUG OR SCARF

A DASH OF A MAGENTA IN A PICTURE OR PAINTING IS SUFFICIENT

JUST A LITTLE MAGENTA WILL LIFT YOUR SPIRITS

ABOVE *Magenta is a dramatic and spiritual colour; chromatherapists advise that it should only be used in small quantities.*

RIGHT *Gray is associated with control and self-reliance; too much gray can rob you of energy.*

BLACK

Black has the capacity to hold all potential and possibilities so, used in moderation, it can be inspirational and highlight the action of other colours in close proximity. However, it is an extremely hard colour to live with, and a large black wall or ceiling can be extremely draining and promote a negative frame of mind. Often we see dramatic black and white colour schemes in magazines, but that is where they should stay. Black has a negative impact and should only really be used as a backdrop to highlight other colours or in small items to add depth and tone. Although it gives us the impression of space it has the effect of making a room appear smaller so you could end up suffering from claustrophobia.

People who use large amounts of black in their home decoration could find themselves very isolated from other people. Black has the effect of cloaking our real feelings, and others may find it difficult to get close to us.

The Chinese consider black to be a lucky colour in decorating, and you often find black teamed with bright red. The Japanese use black for highlights among soft, warm, natural materials in browns and tan. This softens the effect.

BLACK TONES

Remember there is no true black found in nature, and you should always mix black paint yourself so that you can give it an undertone of blue, violet, or brown.

GRAY

Gray is the colour of evasion and noncommitment since it is neither black nor white. It is the colour of self-sufficiency that sends out a message of "leave me alone." If you have too much gray around it will also drain your energy. Gray has a negative feel to it, depriving us of vital energy.

GRAY

Gray negates our personality and individualism, and people who wear gray find they become very self-critical and end up doing things alone. If you use gray make sure it is a warm dove gray, which will provide a backdrop to other colours.

WARM NEUTRALS — BEIGE, CREAM, AND BUTTERMILK — WILL BALANCE BLACK

BLACK CAN BE VERY HARD AND ISOLATING AND IS BEST USED IN SMALL AMOUNTS

VIBRANT, ENERGIZING RED IS OFTEN COMBINED WITH BLACK, BUT IS BEST USED IN SMALL AMOUNTS

RIGHT *Black is best used sparingly in interiors. Red can be used with black to energize, while pink-toned neutrals provide a softer background.*

WHITE

White is the ultimate purity, but it also holds terrible isolation. An all-white space is as terrifying as an all-black one. Living in a white environment does allow you space to expand and grow, although it is not a colour that promotes action. So if you need time and space to reflect on your life, white can give you a feeling of freedom and uncluttered openness. People who are attracted to white often seek inner cleansing, wishing to purify their emotions, thoughts, and spirit.

For many years white walls were considered to be modern and flexible, allowing the individual to place his or her personal stamp on a place. Unfortunately, this trend often backfired because white can stifle individuality and hinder decision-making. White became popular at a time when we were obsessed with hygiene and cleanliness.

White can still be included in your design colours. White in pigment form can have an infinite variety of tones and need not be a brilliant white. After all, white has many softer shades in the natural world. The Inuit people who live in a white world have several specific words to describe different shades of white. There are the warm whites, having peach and yellow undertones, pinky whites, and bluish whites. Brilliant white is best used to contrast other colours and is effective painted on woodwork and doors, if the walls are painted a colour. Remember that too much white can be stark and lonely, and stay away from bluish whites since they are very cold and unsupportive. So when using white, add several other colours in the decor to make the atmosphere more welcoming.

SHADES OF WHITE

There are many shades of white, and soft whites are not as alienating as brilliant white. White with a hint of colour adds a touch of warmth to your decor, while still retaining freshness.

ADD ACCENTS OF COLOUR TO CREATE INTEREST

BLUE IS CALMING BUT CAN BE COLD

PINK IS WARM AND SUPPORTIVE

CERAMICS

TERRA-COTTA

ABOVE *White creates a spacious and open environment. Try to add other colours to it to create warmth and energy.*

LEFT *It is best to introduce brown through natural materials such as wood or ceramics.*

BROWN

Brown is the colour of Mother Earth and if we surround ourselves with brown furniture, carpets, or clothes we feel protected from the outside world. Brown brings stability to the home, so is a good colour to include when you are suffering from insecurity. Experiment with a wide range of neutrals such as tan, warm pink-beige, earthenware, terra-cotta, and rust that add warmth and provide a nurturing environment.

USING COLOUR FAMILIES

Like musical notes, colours can have differing affects on us depending on which ones we select and how we arrange them. We find some colour rhythms melodious while others jar and grate.

EACH PRIMARY
COLOUR IS CALLED
A HUE

SATURATION
CONCERNS THE
STRENGTH OF
A COLOUR

LIGHTNESS IS THE
PROXIMITY OF COLOUR
TO WHITE

COLOURS HAVE
EITHER A WARM
OR COOL FEEL

It is not only the way the colours (called hues) are arranged in a room but also a number of their qualities that affect the atmosphere in a room. These include how light or dark they are, their hue, their saturation, their temperature, and their degree of "movement."

To help you understand these terms, a simple explanation of them is given.

❧ **Hue** (also called tonality or tone) is the quality of the colour itself; it usually refers to the colours on a colour wheel or mixtures of primary colours. Red, orange, yellow, pink, turquoise, and magenta are all hues. The pure hues are the rainbow colours.

❧ **Saturation** relates to the intensity of the colour from pale to dark. For instance, a yellow surface can appear light, medium, or dark, depending on how much of a yellow pigment has been laid down upon it. A tint is a hue mixed with white, so it is a very pale version of the true colour or hue; pastels are tints. A shade is a darkening of a colour, which is achieved by mixing it with black, so red becomes maroon, yellow becomes brown, orange becomes rust.

❧ **Lightness** (or luminosity) refers to how close a colour is to white or black; yellow is the lightest colour because it is closest to white, and this makes it seem brighter than green or blue, for instance. Violet is the darkest on the colour spectrum because it is closest to black.

❧ **Temperature** refers to whether a colour appears to have a hot or cold feel; for example, blue is generally a cool and soothing colour whereas the colour orange has a hot feel to it, but this can vary a great deal depending on the pureness of the colour.

ABOVE *There are numerous factors involved when deciding how a colour will affect the atmosphere of an interior. These two interiors demonstrate how warm colours advance and cool colours retreat.*

Movement refers to whether a colour appears to be advancing toward you, or retreating. The most luminous colours (e.g. yellow) advance while the least luminous (e.g. blue, violet) retreat.

If you wish to change the mood in a room, you do not have to change the whole decor: there are two ways you can solve the problem. First, you can alter the existing colour, so that a warm bright red becomes a cool bluish red, or a cold gray is given warmth. A brightly coloured room can also be toned down with neutral shades, while a dark room can be improved with light tints. Second, you can introduce your favorite colours into the room in small amounts.

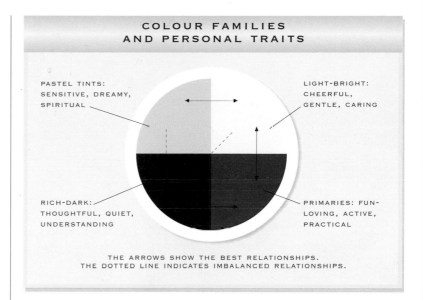

COLOUR FAMILIES AND PERSONAL TRAITS

PASTEL TINTS: SENSITIVE, DREAMY, SPIRITUAL

LIGHT-BRIGHT: CHEERFUL, GENTLE, CARING

RICH-DARK: THOUGHTFUL, QUIET, UNDERSTANDING

PRIMARIES: FUN-LOVING, ACTIVE, PRACTICAL

THE ARROWS SHOW THE BEST RELATIONSHIPS.
THE DOTTED LINE INDICATES IMBALANCED RELATIONSHIPS.

COLOUR TIPS

*W*hen deciding on a colour scheme you need to consider four things:

1 *What are the favorite colours of the person or people using that room? Do they prefer warm or cool colours?*

2 *Is the room itself cold, dark, warm, sunny, large, or small?*

3 *What is the room to be used for? Should it be stimulating, relaxing, or inspirational?*

4 *Does the person, or people, in the room have any special needs; for example, is anyone using the room suffering from stress, physical illness, or any psychological problems?*

FINDING YOUR COLOUR FAMILY

Before deciding on colours for decoration you need to establish which family of colours suits you. First decide on warm or cool colours. If your favorite colour is blue, it is likely that you prefer cool colours, while a preference for red or orange indicates an affinity with warm colours.

You also need to decide if you prefer pastels, light and bright colours, primaries, or rich and darker shades. The brighter and more intense the colour, the stronger your personality.

BELOW *The clothes you wear and the colours and shades that attract you indicate your colour preferences. Ideally, your home should reflect these.*

CHOOSING PALE SHADES AND PASTELS REVEALS A QUIETER, CALMER NATURE

IF YOU WEAR BLUE, WHICH IS A COOL COLOUR, YOU WILL PREFER BLUES, GREENS AND VIOLETS

IF YOU WEAR RED YOU ARE DRAWN TO WARMER COLOURS. VIBRANT SHADES SUGGEST A DOMINANT CHARACTER

THE PALE PINK
FABRIC OF THE
DRAPES AND
CUSHION WARMS
THE ROOM

IT IS BEST TO ADD
SOME COLOUR TO A
WHITE INTERIOR,
PINK IS WELCOMING
AND SUPPORTIVE

THE PALE PINK
PAINTWORK ON
THE CHEST OF
DRAWERS SOFTENS
THE WHITENESS
OF THE WALLS

WHITE WITH WARM
UNDERTONES WILL
PREVENT THE ROOM
FROM FEELING COLD
AND ISOLATING

IT IS IMPORTANT
TO INCORPORATE
TEXTURE WHEN
WHITE DOMINATES
YOUR COLOUR SCHEM

ABOVE Pale decor creates light and space and acts as a tonic for the mind and spirit.

SATURATION:
LIGHT AND DARK COLOURS

Most people want to live in a light and bright environment and our sense of well-being is largely dependent on the amount of light entering our home. Light not only enters our home through doors and windows, it is also reflected off the walls and furnishings.

Light-coloured rooms reflect more light. This has the effect of boosting our energy levels. Light and pastel colours make a room look larger and lighter, and we can stay longer in this type of environment without feeling uncomfortable and use it easily for a variety of different purposes.

Dark colours require more pigment, thus reducing the amount of light reflected. Strong colours also force a specific mood on a room, so are better suited to areas used for a particular purpose. Rooms will appear smaller if painted in any darker shade of a colour, although sometimes it is desirable to have a richly coloured corner. Large rooms, or those with high ceilings, can be made less isolating and more intimate with the use of rich, vibrant colours.

Rooms that receive little light or have been closed for a long period of time contain negative vibrations, which linger in the walls and furnishings, draining our energy, and making us depressed. It is best to decorate these areas in light, warm colours, which have a warming effect on the atmosphere and increase the amount of light reflected into the room.

HOT AND COLD COLOURS

Yin and Yang are present in varying amounts in all things (*see* p 76). In the same way, colours contain both warm and cool energy vibrations in differing proportions.

The hue that gives the greatest sense of warmth is red-orange. Red, orange, gold, and yellow have a stimulating effect on the occupants, so warm colours should be used in rooms that are cold or lack natural light. Pink and lavender also give warmth and affection and help a room look spacious and elegant. At the other end of the scale, blues and mauves are positively cold, and are useful for decoration of small rooms on the sunny side of the house. Green can be either cold or warm depending on its proportions of blue (Yin) and yellow (Yang). A third group is the neutrals, which includes gray, beige, cream, and off-white. These can be used to create a balance between several strong and contrasting colours, or on their own to create a subtle, soft, and relaxing atmosphere. Gray can provide a neutral background, which shows off clear bright colours. However, the recent trend of matching it up with black and white can be dramatic but too severe to live with without using touches of bright or light accent colours.

Although blues are cooler than reds, some blues are warmer than others. For example, when blue is mixed with red it becomes warmer. If mixed with green it becomes colder. Grays too can be warm or cold, depending on whether they have a red or blue undertone. A warm dove gray is very different from a cold steel-blue gray. To judge whether a colour is cold or warm, look for the underlying effect: Is it a grayish slate blue, or a rich or bright blue? Is it a brownish red or a yellowish red?

COOL BLUES AND GREEN

WARMER ACCENTS PROVIDE BALANCE

Generally, the warm colours of red, orange, and yellow are best used in areas where there is physical activity, for example, hallways, stairs, kitchens, playrooms, dining rooms, living rooms, rumpus rooms, and recreation areas. The cool colours, which help us relax and unwind, are best suited to bedrooms, bathrooms, studies, and offices, and also garden rooms and conservatories.

To train your eye to pick out warm and cool colours, get a paint manufacturer's colour chart and note how the colours change from warm to cool or vice versa as they progress through the range.

COLOUR MOVEMENT

In terms of movement, red is a stationary colour, so does not affect the appearance of the size of the room. Yellow is advancing, so a yellow wall will appear nearer, thus making a room appear smaller. Blue is generally a retiring colour, which makes a wall appear to recede, making a room look larger. This is true whether the colours are pure hues, shades or tints.

Bold primary colours generally decrease the size of rooms so it is better to use these colours as accents in smaller items in the room.

PRIMROSE YELLOW HAS A DIMINISHING EFFECT

BELOW LEFT *When blue is mixed with green it becomes cooler. The cool colours are balanced by warmer yellow and terra-cotta accents.*

BELOW *Yellow walls, however pale the shade, will always make a room more intimate.*

COMBINING COLOURS ~ THE NATURAL LAWS OF HARMONY

Just as we need a balanced diet of a variety of food, so too we need the energy from every colour in the spectrum. A colour scheme focused on only one or two colours will cause imbalance within our body system.

We can easily identify an energy imbalance if we like to wear colours from an opposite family to that of our house decoration. If you love to wear red, and live in a house that is predominantly decorated in blue or green colours, your body is unconsciously crying out for warm energy.

A harmonious colour scheme should include both warm and cool tones, although particular areas can be predominantly one or the other. An orange kitchen can provide a warm friendly atmosphere for the cook and family, while a cool

blue bathroom is just the place to destress. You can maintain balance in a room by introducing some warm touches to cool-coloured schemes and cool colours to warm ones. Introduce a variety of colours in blinds, drapes, furnishings, paintings, plants, and lights to balance your dominant colour choice.

The relationship between the colours we choose is as important as the choice of individual colours themselves. There are natural laws of harmony that we can follow as a guide when combining colours.

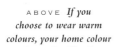

ABOVE *If you choose to wear warm colours, your home colour scheme should reflect this not fight it.*

COLOUR RELATIONSHIPS IN THE COLOUR WHEEL

NEIGHBORING COLOURS

Neighboring colours lie together on the colour wheel and have a natural affinity with one another. Adjoining colours work especially well together in textured paints and paint effects; the partnership of the two colours strengthens the overall effect. Another successful way of using neighboring colours is to use a light tint of one with a deeper shade of the other.

ABOVE *Complementary colours are opposite each other on the colour wheel and naturally balance each other.*

COMPLEMENTARY COLOURS

Complementary colours are opposite each other on the colour wheel. They possess naturally opposing but harmonizing colour energy, so both balance and excite each other. Complementary colours form gray when mixed together as paint, and form white light when the two colour rays are blended. Complementary pairs include yellow-violet, blue-orange, and red-green.

DISSONANT OR DISCORDANT COLOURS

Dissonant colours are one-third of the circle away from each other on the colour wheel. They clash in a similar way as two musical notes can create a discordant sound, but can combine harmoniously if used correctly. You can use dissonant colours together in small amounts (for example, in a patterned fabric or where you wish to make a loud statement!). Remember you will have to live with the results, so think carefully before using such a colour scheme for your home.

THE GREEN IN
THE BLIND AND
PLANT PROVIDE
CONTRAST. GREEN
IS A BALANCING
COLOUR AND CAN
BE ADDED TO ANY
COLOUR SCHEME

TERRA-COTTA
DECORATIONS
COMPLEMENT
AND INJECT
ENERGY INTO
AN OTHERWISE
COOL ROOM

DIFFERENT SHADES
— A MIDNIGHT BLUE
AND A PALER BLUE
— HELP TO BALANCE
THE ROOM

Working with natural colour relationships helps us to create positive energy in the home. We can best do this first by using combinations of colours based on closely related colours, and second by including colours that are complementary. Mixtures of discordant colours tend to be overstimulating and unsettling and therefore less suitable as room colours. A balanced colour scheme should incorporate the following.

☙ *Two or more related colours.* These may be tints or shades of the same hue, or adjacent colours in the same area of the colour wheel. If pink is your main colour, introduce its paler tints and darker shades. This will have a unifying effect while preventing the colour scheme from being flat and uninteresting. The beneficial effect is enhanced with the use of contrasting and balancing colours – for example, blue and green.

☙ *At least one complementary contrasting colour.* The contrasting colour acts as a balancing and

BALANCE

It is a good idea to introduce green into a brown interior, using plants to balance the earthy colours to allow you to grow without making you feeling threatened. Yellow-gold will "lift" a brown room.

harmonizing force and should be lighter or darker than the main colour scheme. If the saturation of the colours used is similar they will compete with one another for attention, and are visually tiring. For example, if your main colour is pale green, your contrasting colour should be a deep shade of apricot or peach (*see* p 124). Red-orange is the complementary colour to turquoise, and when added in small amounts to a room helps focus attention and gives an uplift of energy. Orange is the complementary colour to blue and can be used to lift a rich blue room, which by itself may make you feel too lethargic and depressed.

☙ *Green plants.* Green is the binding force in nature, and plants can be used to harmonize with every colour in any interior. Green can be combined with any natural colour successfully and can also be used to correct any imbalances in a room. Using green is a wonderful way of enlivening a dead or tiring space.

ABOVE *Choosing tints of the same hue – such as blue shown here – will have a unifying effect.*

DESIGNING A COLOUR SCHEME FOR COLOUR-ENERGY BALANCE

Every colour scheme needs a starting point. It is a good idea to build your scheme around one of your "soul" colours or an inspirational item, like a painting or vase; it may also be that you have a favorite piece of furniture or a particular material used in the house that suggests a range of colours to you.

ABOVE *Turning to nature for inspiration – the vibrant golden-yellow of sunflower petals is set off by their green leaves and brown centers.*

Once you have decided on your starting colour, you need to select several different tints and shades of that colour, relating them to your preferred colour family.

If your starting colour is yellow, think of all the different yellows found in nature. There are soft creamy yellow flowers, the golden-yellow of the sun, and deep ochers of the earth. Colour cards from different paint manufacturers can be useful. You may decide to use different yellows in different areas in your home, or use just the one that fits with your preference.

Once you have decided on your main colour you can then select several harmonizing colours to use as highlights. I have found that a good way to do this is to think of a natural object that best represents your colour and tone. Imagine this object in its natural setting. If, for instance, you have chosen a yellow sunflower, create a mental picture of it surrounded by dark green leaves and rich terra-cotta earth. This will give you a harmonizing group of colours with which to work.

If you find it difficult doing this exercise without visual aids, find a natural object like a shell, feather, stone, slate tile, ceramic, or flower that reflects several harmonious colours in line with your soul colours. You can then use this to match up harmonizing colours.

When decorating a home remember that you need to create a balance in the house between warm and cool colours. A colour scheme that limits you to only two or three colours creates imbalance. If your "soul" colour is blue or green, you will need to make sure that you introduce some touches of warm colours, such as terra-cotta or peach, as a contrast. If you are unsure which balancing colour to use, the complementary colour will always work well.

When choosing colour combinations, try to choose three colours of varying saturation and brightness. This means the colours are not competing for your attention. One colour should be light, another medium, and the last can be rich or dark in quality. If you follow this simple rule you will always have an interesting room that is balanced and harmonious. It will be neither sterile and lifeless nor heavy and overpowering.

THE COOLER BLUE
BORDER BALANCES
THE VIVID RED OF
THE WALLS

THE SOFA IS
UPHOLSTERED IN
PINK — A STRONG
RED FABRIC WOULD
HAVE BEEN
OVERPOWERING

THE INTRODUCTION
OF A LIGHTER PINK
RELAXES THE EYE

THE RICH, DARK RED WALLS
PROVIDES A BACKDROP FOR
THE ROOM

BRIGHTLY COLOURED
CUSHIONS IN VIOLET
AND PINK ECHO THE
DOMINANT HUES OF
THE ROOM

LEFT *A sumptuous red is the canvas for a room of paler pinks, varying in intensity and warmth.*

THERAPEUTIC EFFECTS OF COMPLEMENTARY COLOURS

It often happens that you find yourself living in a room that has a colour-energy imbalance. You may find the room is either too hot or too cold, or that the effect of the decor and furnishings is overpowering and has negative effects on your health. When this happens you can easily restore harmony without redecorating by introducing a complementary colour. To help you choose good combinations, look at the table opposite.

TINTS AND SHADES FROM RAINBOW HUES

TINT	HUE	SHADE
rose white	red	wine/maroon
cream	primrose	golden brown
almond blossom	coral	plum or port
lichen	green	dark green
ash rose	deep pink	burgundy
apricot white	peach/apricot	terra-cotta
mercury (gray/blue)	blue	navy
peach	orange	rust
lilac	orchid	magenta

LEFT *If cool, pale green dominates your colour scheme, the contrasting rich apricots and peaches will lift your spirits.*

While it is easy to identify the complementary colours to the rainbow hues, it is not so easy to find those that complement mixed colours. The way to find the exact shade is to stare at an object of that colour without blinking for a minute or two. Then move your gaze quickly to a white piece of paper. You should see the exact complementary colour as an "after-image" on the page. Try to remember this colour and match it as nearly as possible to a paint manufacturer's colour chart. The pure hues will have complementary colours of equal brilliance, but the opposite colour to a light tint will be a darker shade, and vice versa.

The table of complementary colours lists the pure hues, their tints, shades, and complementary colours. Use it to decide on the best contrasts to light and dark shades. Black, white, and gray should not be used on their own since they are not strictly colours. They are best used to highlight a balanced colour scheme. Silver and gold are also useful as accent colours to a colour scheme.

COMPLEMENTARY TINTS AND SHADES	
TINT	COMPLEMENTARY SHADE
red	*green*
pink	*dark green*
maroon	*apple green*
coral	*mint green*
rose	*blue-green*
orange	*blue*
peach	*dark blue*
rust	*light blue*
yellow	*violet*
gold	*mauve*
yellow	*purple*
neutrals	
brown	*mint green*
black	*white*
white	*black*
gray	*none*
silver	*gold*
gold	*silver*

Add to these one contrasting or complementary colour, and you will have a most successful colour scheme.

COMPLEMENTARIES	
COLOUR	COMPLEMENTARY
pure hue	*pure hue (rainbow colour)* *(rainbow colour)*
light tint	*dark shade*
dark shade	*light tint*

LEFT *Maroon, a dark tint of red, has been effectively combined with a light shade, apple, of its complementary colour, green. The pink of the dado rail is a paler tint of red. It is this third colour that helps to complete the colour scheme.*

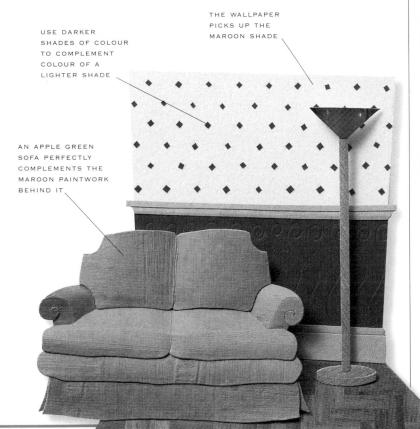

USE DARKER SHADES OF COLOUR TO COMPLEMENT COLOUR OF A LIGHTER SHADE

THE WALLPAPER PICKS UP THE MAROON SHADE

AN APPLE GREEN SOFA PERFECTLY COMPLEMENTS THE MAROON PAINTWORK BEHIND IT

COLOUR COMBINATIONS FOR CREATING STYLES

*The different atmospheres created by colours can be enhanced
by different furnishing styles. Cool schemes lend themselves to uncluttered
but sophisticated interiors; richer colours create a feeling of warmth and
grandeur; and strong, contrasting colours create an interior full of drama.*

COOL, RELAXING ROOMS

A scheme based on soft colours, such as duck-egg blue, warm creamy yellow and deep silvery-green, creates a simple soothing, mentally relaxing feel, reminiscent of colours used in Scandinavia and also by the American Shakers. The harmony of cool blue and warm cream creates an uncluttered and quiet look, which sits well in either a town or a country home. It complements both simple wooden country style and elegant Georgian furniture, and rooms with little pattern or ornamentation, and works well with either period or modern style.

WARM, HOMELY ROOMS

For a homely and nurturing atmosphere, choose a colour scheme based on rich, warm colours. Pink, peach, apricot, and gold have an earthy quality, and feel friendly. Use these colours on walls contrasted with shades of blue and green. Furniture could be old or new and include large overstuffed sofas and softly draped curtains. Small patterns based on natural forms reinforce this emotionally supportive environment.

DRAMATIC ROOMS

Dramatic rooms are difficult to live with for any length of time and are best suited to areas in which you do not wish to linger. Dark green walls may glow by candlelight, but you have to consider whether you would enjoy being surrounded by that colour all day. A sense of drama can be created with the use of strong rich colours or surprising colour combinations. A deep colour can often provide a backdrop for a special piece of artwork or bring life to a little used or uninteresting area in a hall or staircase. Rich purple, gold, black, white, and magenta have always been associated with drama. When used with rich fabrics and heavily ornamented furniture, these hues will create a room with a sense of opulence.

LEFT *A combination of creamy yellow and blue hues creates a clean, timeless look perfectly suited to the simple wooden furniture.*

BELOW *Rich colours in warm tones on the floor and walls and a delicate wallpaper pattern create an interior with a comfortable, traditional feel.*

SMALL PATTERNS AND EARTHY COLOURS HAVE A WELCOMING FEEL

A COMFORTABLE SOFA AND CUSHIONS CREATE A RELAXING ATMOSPHERE

USING BROKEN COLOUR

When we look closely at the natural world, we see that nothing is made up of flat, unbroken colours. An object that might appear to have one overall colour is in fact made up of many different colours whose effects blend together.

ABOVE *Capture the shimmering, luminous surface of the ocean with special paint effects.*

Shiny objects, such as seashells and gemstones, are made up of many colours that combine to create a special luster. Look at an expanse of sky or ocean and you will also notice that the whole atmosphere is created by the strength and direction of the light.

Using broken colours in the home can enhance this feeling of light and movement, and enables you to have a room that is subject to many subtle changes throughout the day and night. Colour washes and paint techniques have been used since ancient times to create atmospheric interiors that reflect this etherial quality.

HOW TO USE BROKEN COLOUR

The simplest way to achieve the distressed effect is to start with the lightest colour you wish to use. Paint on an opaque background or base coat of emulsion or flat oil paint of this colour. Over this you can then build up several layers of thinned-emulsion

RIGHT *The beautiful mix of colours and textures found in gemstones could be an inspiration for a paint effect colour scheme.*

washes or oil glazes, through which the base coat penetrates. The more colours you use, the more subtle and complex are the effects. Broken effects often work better when you use semi-gloss or full gloss finishing coats; this has the effect of giving the combination of colours more depth and richness – an effect that would otherwise be impossible to achieve.

Often we do not like a wall colour or we would like to alter it without having to change our furnishing and completely redecorate a room. An existing wall colour can be improved and given new life by applying a broken effect. For instance, a pink wall in a bedroom could be enlivened with the addition of a peach or apricot glaze or paint effect.

Broken colour can work successfully in many different places. Not only can you apply them to walls, but also to doors, floors, and ceilings. Wooden furniture can also be enhanced by the selective use of

ABOVE *Limitless textures can be achieved using paint effects. On this wall, a marbled texture has been created by applying a tint of the base colour using a scrunched up rag.*

decorative effects. However, in order to avoid creating a room that is too busy it is better to apply broken colour to one area only. The skill is to create a subtle blend of colours that work together to give an overall enriching effect.

It is a good idea to paint some areas with flat colour. This creates the impression of stillness and permanence. Mat wall colours are a perfect foil for decorative effects on furniture, while plain-coloured furniture can be enhanced by a shinier decorative effect on the walls. The inspirational quality of flat and broken effects used together gives a room a multidimensional quality that will change with your moods and provide a more enriching environment.

CHOOSING COLOUR COMBINATIONS

Although in nature all colours work well together, our perception of colours is changed depending on the proximity of other colours. A red colour looks very different when placed next to a violet than it does if placed next to green. Instead of complementing each other, contrasting colours compete when placed side by side. This makes them tiring on the eye, and energetically they may be sending out opposing vibrational messages.

When selecting colours for broken techniques it is best to use colours from the same family, or those adjoining each other on the colour wheel, because each colour increases the intensity of the next, and the overall effect is one of glowing irridescence. If you use contrasting colours you will end up with a muddy effect. Remember also the rules of colour mixing; if you paint blue over yellow you will end up with an impression of green, because even if your final coat is a dark colour, the thinness of the glaze allows the other colours to show through. It is well worthwhile experimenting on a piece of hardboard first.

The glow of sunshine can be achieved by using a light yellow base coat, followed by successive coats of deeper yellows and oranges. This golden surface would shine with warmth and welcoming vibrations and would be uplifting during the dark winter months. A shimmering mother of pearl effect, which is feminine and relaxing, can be achieved by selecting a soft warm white base coat over which is painted light silvery blue, mauve, or green.

LEFT *Enrich plain walls and wooden furniture by applying layers of washes or oil glazes to create a broken surface.*

USING PATTERN, TEXTURE, AND SHAPE

Everything in nature has a rhythm. Colour and sound travel in repeating wave forms, and the movement of the tides and the growth patterns of plants and animals have order and symmetry. Pattern is rhythmic movement created by line, shape, and colour.

ABOVE *Diagonal patterns are good in areas of activity, such as kitchens and bathrooms.*

ABOVE *Patterns based on natural forms and colours are emotionally supportive.*

ABOVE *Horizontal lines can be calming and warm colours will also energize. Vertical patterns are dynamic but cool colours can reduce the effect.*

ABOVE *Geometric patterns create restlessness and are best in muted tones.*

PATTERN

Throughout history, and in every culture, humankind has shown a desire to create pattern. We draw patterns on our skin not just with makeup but in a multitude of ways – from henna designs on a young Indian bride's hands, to the Western art of tattooing. We also weave coloured fabrics for clothes and create patterns for use in the home.

When we base our shapes on those found in nature they are very pleasing to the eye, but if the patterns do not have natural proportions they can be jarring and tiring to live with. Several patterns in one room can confuse the eye, tiring the mind. More than one large pattern in a room often makes us feel uncomfortable and irritable. The best way to combine patterns successfully is to make sure the colours and shapes harmonize with each other.

Patterned fabrics and furnishings send out their own particular messages and feelings. Horizontal lines give a feeling of relaxation and gentleness, while vertical lines have an energy that lifts us and gives a feeling of strength. Rounded shapes and natural forms create a feeling of harmony with nature and give us emotional support. Strong diagonals and geometric shapes encourage movement and change.

The colours found in the pattern will either reinforce or conflict with the energy of the lines. Wavy patterns would be more relaxing if they were coloured in blues and greens than in orange or red. We find florals more appealing if they include tones of green, while geometrics often make use of black and white. Small, repeating wallpapers can be pleasant to live with, provided the patterns are not too complex. Light, fresh prints showing a great deal of background colour do not disturb the eyes or send out confusing messages of which we can easily tire. Large designs send out forceful vibrationary patterns, which can effect our equilibrium especially when we are tired.

So it is better to keep large designs to walls in entrance halls, passageways, and stairways, or any place where you do not spend too much time. If you do want to use a boldly patterned

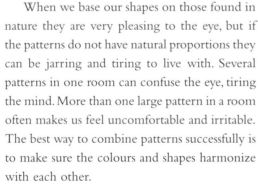

BELOW *Strong designs and colours are best used sparingly. This bold pattern is ideal for drapes or cushions, but would be overpowering used over a large area.*

wallpaper, use it in a large airy room, and only up to the picture rail. Never put patterns on the ceiling unless they are traditional plaster moldings, or a fresco-type painting. Window treatments and furnishings provide a good place to use patterns in a room, because the designs are broken up by the folds of the drapes and lines of the furniture.

PATTERN AND COLOUR

A very simple and inexpensive way to transform a plain or lifeless room is by adding stencils or wallpaper borders at dado (chair) or ceiling height. In this way you can use pattern and colour to lift a dull or dark room.

TEXTURE

If you have a lot of one particular colour in a room, you can add visual interest and enliven the area by using different textures. Many people need a very quiet, unobtrusive environment to relax in, especially if they work in a high- energy and noisy atmosphere. Using a theme of neutral colours interpreted in different textures can provide the peace and solitude you need. It will create a place of peace and space, a sanctuary. This type of simple and neutral decoration is fine if you lead a hectic lifestyle, but if you do not you could find it becomes very isolating and induces lethargy and mental stagnation.

SHADES OF CHANGE

At times in your life when you are going through change, a room decorated in shades of white or neutrals could be a bonus since it is easy to add specific colours to suit your moods and health requirements.

THE PALE COLOUR SCHEME IS A PERFECT BACKDROP FOR THE NATURAL TEXTURES IN THIS ROOM

AN ARRANGEMENT OF SPIKY TWIGS IN UNGLAZED VASES MAKE A STRONG IMPACT

WOVEN CUSHIONS OF COARSE WOOL IN NATURAL PIGMENTS CONTRAST WITH THE BROCADE FABRIC OF THE SOFA

FLOORING FROM NATURAL MATERIALS RETAINS THE EARTHY FEEL

LEFT *A variety of contrasting textures provides a stimulating and tactile quality to an otherwise bland interior.*

ABOVE LEFT The wooden beams across the ceiling have been exposed to give a rustic feel.

ABOVE CENTER This ceiling has become a feature of the room with the use of a darker yellow paint.

ABOVE RIGHT These girders supporting the ceiling are an intrinsic part of this interior. The pale colour of the ceiling is vital to retain the feeling of light and space.

BELOW LEFT Tiles and mosaics add colour pattern with traditional materials.

BELOW CENTER Pale-coloured and synthetic flooring prevents us from feeling grounded.

BELOW RIGHT Earth colours create warmth and make a colourful background for rugs.

Ceilings

Ceilings reflect light downward into the room and therefore should be painted in a light tone. We usually give little thought to the best colour, however, and they are invariably given a cursory coat of white paint. Most interior decorators recommend that the ceiling is painted a paler version of your wall colour. To create a feeling of space, it makes sense to paint ceilings a near-white tint or a lighter version of the wall colour unless the ceiling is particularly high, in which case a darker shade can be used; however, many rooms could be enhanced by using a light contrasting colour instead. Like everything there are always exceptions to the rules.

Waking up to the pinkish or pale yellow light reflected from a ceiling can help kickstart our bodies for the day. Colourful ceilings can also be of benefit to small children who spend many hours looking upward from their cribs.

The Ancient Egyptians preferred to use a pale sky blue on their ceilings, creating the effect of the sky overhead. Pale blue ceilings look wonderful in period rooms, especially where they have been painted with a cloud effect. This idea can also be used in modern rooms, and gives a feeling of air and light. The blue energy can also help cool the hot air that rises to the ceiling in warm weather.

A high ceiling can be made to look less distant with a deeper tone. In period rooms where there are cornices and moldings these can be high-lighted against a darker colour. In a modern home, a wooden tongue-and-groove ceiling and panels can look wonderful sporting bright colours. You do have to make sure all the occupants are happy with the chosen colours, though, or they may weigh heavily upon their shoulders and even be the cause of headaches.

Flooring

It is the floor of our home that has taken the place of the soil on which we used to walk. The floor is important because it has a grounding effect on us and can help build our inner strength. Colours that relate to the earth make the best floor colours for everyday use. Light colours increase our feeling of separation from the earth, and we can literally feel like we are walking on air.

Many people automatically choose synthetic flooring, but there is now a wide choice of natural materials. Wood, stone, and clay have the ability of bringing us down to earth, and if we also take off our shoes we stimulate a very sensitive part of our body – our soles! Some natural floor coverings such as wood and wool are warm to the touch, while others like stone and slate can be used for their cooling properties. They also help keep the internal environment of our home free from toxic pollutants. The inherent colouring of natural materials themselves (*see* p 132) complement any style of room and decoration scheme, and if you need a more colourful floor, try using linoleum or mosaic tiles.

SHAPE AND FORM

Nothing in nature is completely straight or flat, and it is the soft curving lines and undulations that give our world variety and interest. Most people are attracted to shapes found in nature. The shapes and symbols to which you have an affinity can be incorporated into home decorating to create an environment that relaxes and inspires you. The shapes you choose can reinforce the effects of the colour scheme and be appealing and soothing.

The box shapes most of us now live in are very containing spaces. There are many ways to soften the effects of straight lines in your house or apartment. The easiest way to do so is by introducing furniture and furnishings with rounded, flowing lines. The patterns on curtains and soft drapery can make a room more supportive and nurturing. Plants with rounded leaves can be added to a room, as can paintings using flowing lines. Ceramic bowls and vases using rounded forms have a stabilizing effect on a room, and help us connect to more natural forms. If you wish to make some architectural changes to a square room, an archway or arched or round windows can frame a view and provide a feeling of security.

The kitchen is one place where squares and right angles predominate in the modern home. Fill your kitchen with bowls of round fruit and vegetables, rounded plates and cups, and herbs — both fresh and dry. To contrast with the sharp edges of domestic appliances, use hand-crafted furniture, or get a round dining table and dress your chairs with cushions.

RIGHT **Choose furniture and accessories with rounded forms reminiscent of the undulating curves of nature to balance the geometry of our homes.**

A CURVED OR ARCHED WINDOW COUNTERACTS THE HARD EDGES OF THE SPACE WE INHABIT

CERAMICS IN ROUNDED FORMS AND BUSHY PLANTS WILL PROVIDE NATURAL SHAPES AND COLOURS

SINUOUS FURNITURE IN NATURAL MATERIALS BALANCES A ROOM'S STRAIGHT LINES

ABOVE LEFT AND CENTER *Pale wood ceilings can look light and airy in any room, but too much wood can make you feel closed in.*

ABOVE RIGHT *Painting ceiling beams white will make a room feel more spacious.*

BELOW LEFT AND CENTER *The warm, glowing tones of a natural wood and cork flooring give a different feel from manufactured flooring.*

BELOW RIGHT *Natural floor coverings come in neutral colours and can be just as effective as wood, stone, and terra-cotta.*

USING COLOURS OF NATURAL MATERIALS

In recent years the range of synthetic colours has exploded. These colours are never seen in nature and have an unbalancing effect on our system. So from a health point of view it is better to use colours derived from natural pigments, combined with the colours of natural materials themselves, which create a harmonious interchange with our environment.

A WOODEN FLOOR IS HEALTHIER THAN SYNTHETIC CARPET. THESE TWO PALE TONES PROVIDE ALL THE COLOUR IN THE ROOM

ABOVE *Colour a natural wood floor by painting floorboards with natural pigment paints.*

Although you may live in a house where synthetic materials have been used, getting rid of them when they are still serving their function is wasteful of available supplies of energy and materials. It is better to replace them with natural products as they wear out.

PAINTS

Start improving your health by using paint coloured with natural pigments. These are much less noxious than paints that are made using petroleum-based ingredients, which are harmful to the environment. Earth- and mineral-based pigments are ideal for allergy sufferers and for anyone with overstretched or immature immune systems. They come in wonderful natural colours such as ocher, sienna, ultramarine, umber, pinks, creams, and soft and clear greens.

Natural raw materials and paints made from natural pigments provide a healthy, friendly atmosphere free of poisonous emissions. Natural white emulsion, which contains no titanium dioxide, is now available, and its soft white tone can be tinted with natural pigments. Microporous finishes help surfaces to breathe and moisture exchange helps to provide the right atmosphere for our own and our house's long-term well-being. Wallpaper paste free from fungicides can be mixed with pigments and water to make transparent colour washes.

WOOD

Wood comes in a variety of beautiful colours that are rich, nurturing, and earthy. There are a number of traditional treatments for wood that allow the quality of the grain to show through. Colour washing is done with an extremely dilute water-based paint to introduce a very thin translucent layer of colour. Liming introduces a white colour into the grain; it considerably lightens the effect of the wood.

REVIVING WOOD

We can immediately improve the colour quality of wood by using polishes made from natural ingredients. New and old wood can be treated with herb and resin oil, a water repellent antifungal finish, before waxing. A wax made from real beeswax and larch resin brings old beams, stripped wood, or new wood to a natural glow.

STONE, SLATE, AND MARBLE

Slate and stone come in many shades of gray and blue. As their colour tones suggest, the materials themselves are cold to the touch. Slate flooring is most successful in hot climates or in a bright sunny room. In a colder climate, contrast slate or stone with a red, burgundy, or ocher wall colour and add colourful woven rugs to add warmth.

Most of us associate marble with ultimate luxury for a floor, especially in a bathroom. Unfortunately we forget that this is a fast-diminishing resource, and the increased demand internationally is resulting in the devastation of beautiful hillsides and landscape. Use marble in moderation, and only in areas where you can really appreciate the beauty and luster of this material. Remember marble is a very soft and absorbent material that can deteriorate if exposed to prolonged moisture.

TERRA-COTTA TILES

It has only been with the development of modular style building that we have come to expect floors to be flat and even. Handmade terra-cotta tiles come in a variety of rich earthy colours, and when properly treated with turpentine and linseed oil they create a warm, and glowing hard-wearing floor. Each tile is unique with its own subtle colouring and texture. If you

LEFT The soft pinks and creams of unglazed tiles make simple, yet effective, flooring in a garden room.

live in a cold climate and want to use terra-cotta tiles in outdoor areas you need to check whether they are frostproof.

Other handmade tiles are glazed in rich colours and can have a high gloss or mat finish Some are decorated in various traditional and modern designs and can be used individually as wall plaques, or pushed into wet plaster.

Other natural materials that we can introduce into our homes include ceramics, cane, wicker, and fabrics such as cotton, wool, and silk.

ABOVE Tiles can be bought to achieve any effect, from hand-painted, traditional patterns and bold designs to plain tiles in rich, vivid hues.

NATURAL MATERIALS HAVE A WARMTH AND VIBRANCY THAT LIGHT UP A ROOM

THIS FITTED KITCHEN WOULD LOOK HARD AND STARK WITHOUT THE EARTHY TONES OF THE FLOORING

LEFT The rich colours and elaborate patterns of these tiles are a dominant feature of this sleek, modern kitchen.

LIGHTING

Light has different qualities depending on the weather, season, time of day, and location. It can be direct, reflected, or diffused. The brightness and quality of both natural and artificial lighting can be used to create different moods and atmospheres.

THE SIMPLE, JAPANESE-INSPIRED ARRANGEMENT IS IN HARMONY WITH THE WINDOW, WHICH DOMINATES THE ROOM

THE SIZE OF THIS WINDOW ALLOWS IN A LOT OF LIGHT, WHILE THE TEXTURED GLASS BLOCKS FILTER LIGHT GENTLY SO DRAPES AND BLINDS ARE NOT NEEDED

THE WHITE WALLS WILL REFLECT AND CREATE LIGHT IN A ROOM

RIGHT *This large window insures the maximum amount of natural light, essential to our mental and emotional well-being.*

SEASONAL AFFECTIVE DISORDER

SAD (seasonal affective disorder) is a major cause of many sleep and emotional problems. Depressive symptoms can be significantly improved within two to four days when a person is exposed to full-spectrum lighting. Bright artificial light has also been successfully used in the treatment of premenstrual syndrome, bulimia, and other eating disorders.

NATURAL LIGHT

Natural light encourages the action of the pituitary and pineal glands, both of which are the "master glands" of our endocrine system, controlling the release of hormones into the body that are closely linked to our moods and emotions. The pineal gland, which produces the hormone serotonin, is also sensitive to light and has been found experimentally to control seasonal rhythms.

We all need a daily minimum of 30 minutes exposure to natural daylight without screens or sunglasses. Certain individuals suffer from SAD (seasonal affective disorder) during the winter, a form of depression that is brought on by lack of exposure to sunlight (*see* box opposite). No form of artificial lighting can match the wonders of natural sunlight, so allow light and air to come into your home by opening a window. If this is not possible you can install full-spectrum lighting. Fluorescent or striplights have a blue bias, while common incandescent bulbs have a yellowish tint. This causes energy imbalances in our system.

In his book *The Natural House*, David Pearson recommended the best locations for rooms to maximize sunlight. Bedrooms should be oriented toward the sunrise to put us in touch with the natural cycle of day and night, so that we wake up with the rising sun. Breakfast rooms should also face the early morning sun, so that you can enjoy your first meal in natural daylight. This ensures that your activities are synchronized with your biorhythms. Kitchens, living rooms, and play areas should be located where they can make the most of late morning and afternoon sunshine. Offices and working areas benefit from daylight during the middle of the day, while studies that are used in the evening can be located on the darker side of the house. Storage areas, larders, and garages are best located away from the sunlight. If these have been added to the main house, they will provide extra insulation if they are located on the cold side of the house.

Filtered natural daylight creates a gentle, quiet feeling. We can create filtered light through blinds and shutters, fine fabrics, screens, shutters, frosted or coloured glass. It is especially useful in bedrooms, treatment rooms for therapists, relaxation areas, and bathrooms.

ABOVE *However small your patio or garden, it is an invaluable space to benefit from sunlight all year round.*

FRENCH WINDOWS THAT OPEN TO THE OUTSIDE WILL HELP BRING LIGHT INTO THE HOUSE

WHITE WALLS WILL HELP TO CREATE MORE LIGHT

INCREASING NATURAL LIGHT

- *Keep windows clean and check that they all open.*
- *Design window treatments to allow the maximum amount of natural light into the room.*
- *Draw curtains back as far as possible and keep blinds up during the day.*
- *Move away any plants or objects that obstruct light coming into your home.*
- *Place mirrors opposite windows in rooms with low light levels.*
- *Create skylights, courtyards and sunrooms to enjoy the benefits of sunlight.*

A GLASS ROOF OR WINDOW WITH LARGE PANES OF GLASS WILL FLOOD A ROOM WITH LIGHT

ABOVE *Garden rooms, conservatories, and attic conversions are all areas where glass roofs can be installed. This fills a room with a maximum amount of light where plants and humans thrive.*

ARTIFICIAL LIGHTING

We can reproduce each of the different types of light (direct, reflected, and diffused) artificially in the home; the type of lighting we choose has a strong effect on our interaction with each room – both the tasks we can perform there, and the atmosphere it acquires.

Direct light is needed when we have to perform a task requiring precision and concentration. Reading, writing, drawing, and sewing are all activities that require bright, concentrated light. The colours on the walls will affect the amount of light in a room; some colours will absorb light while others will reflect it, thus altering the brightness. The size, colour, and height of pieces of furniture will also affect the amount of light in a room.

Reflected light is suitable in a room where you need an even distribution of light. Light can be bounced off walls and ceilings to give a softer effect; in a dark or small room strategically placed mirrors increase the general light levels in the room.

The following table shows the percentage reflection of different colours when they are illuminated by white light (natural or artificial). Lighter tints would reflect more light, while darker shades would reflect less light.

BELOW
Water reflects light beautifully and lends an air of tranquillity to any room. Position a spotlight so that the water will catch its light.

LIGHT REFLECTION

COLOUR	PERCENTAGE
white	85
intense yellow	60
light gray	35
intense green	25
dark gray	15
intense red	15
black	2
intense blue	10

FOCUSED LIGHTS

The pinpoint focus of a beam of light can be used to highlight certain objects in a room. A picture, sculpture, flower arrangement, plant, or special piece of furniture can benefit from accent lighting. You have to remember that spotlights give off heat, so always place a light away from any objects or surfaces that could be damaged or are potentially flammable.

When we require good general lighting but also need areas of bright light, we can use reflected and direct lighting together to give a harmonious and functional light to a room.

Until recently, all artificial lights were biased to a particular colour range in the spectrum. This can produce headaches, eyestrain, loss of energy, nausea, and even fits. Incandescent bulbs, which are ordinary household bulbs, are biased toward the red end of the spectrum. They therefore make the colours in the room more yellow than they are; this has a warming effect, but will also alter blues to look green, and reds to look orange.

Fluorescent bulbs on the other hand give off light in the ultraviolet and blue part of the spectrum; you may have noticed this when you have tried to colour match something in a department store or shop. The blue colouring can make you feel cold and all the colours in the room will take on a bluish tinge. A new generation of compact

fluorescent lamps are now available that are much more efficient and longer lasting than the older type. They cut down on heat production and do not attract as much dust and pollution as other types of bulbs.

Tungsten-halogen lamps give a bright, white light close to daylight in quality. They are powerful lights and good for general illumination. Low-voltage lights are more energy efficient and ideal for spot lighting and accent.

Full-spectrum lamps more closely resemble the balance of spectral light found in daylight. These lights improve mood and performance and have no long-term side effects like other artificial lights, but they can increase the levels of ultraviolet radiation in a room.

THE EFFECTS OF COLOURED LIGHTS

ABOVE *Enjoy the romance of candlelight, not just in the dining room, but in the bathroom!*

Candlelight is very therapeutic; it creates a gentle and peaceful atmosphere that is in harmony with nature. Try putting a candelabra in the bathroom and experiencing the relaxation of a bath by candlelight. A meal by candlelight helps you to relax and digest the meal, while filling your living room with candles can create an intimate and mystical atmosphere.

- *A deep pink blind on a bedroom window gives a loving pink glow.*

- *Red light increases heartbeat, circulation, and breathing, and stimulates self-awareness.*

- *Orange-toned blinds warm a cold room and bring it alive. Use terra-cotta, peach, or apricot to give warmth without being harsh.*

- *Yellow light can be beneficial, but should not be used together with a yellow decor scheme. Ordinary electric lights give an uplifting effect, provided the room has enough everyday objects of varying colours. A gold curtain or blind will lift up a dull room.*

- *Green light is never pleasant. Plants that are exposed to green light for any length of time fail to thrive. Green lighting with green decoration is too strong an environment to use in interior design, although it has been used successfully in therapy rooms.*

- *Blue light has a very calming effect. It lowers the pulse and makes us exhale deeply, promoting a feeling of release and safe retreat. A blue lightbulb in a bedside light is particularly useful to aid sleep, and for hyperactive children. Blue light is also soothing and healing for anyone with a fever, suffering from headaches, sunburn, or itchy skin. Blue blinds filter light successfully, especially in a bathroom, where the cool light will combat the heat from your bath or shower. A hot bedroom or living room will also benefit from the filtering effects of pale blue curtains.*

- *Violet light creates peace and tranquillity. When violet light shines on brown and honey-coloured shades, it appears almost gold. Used as a light source, it has a gentle contracting effect and is good for inflammation.*

BELOW *Simple coloured lampshades provide a glowing focal point in a room.*

COLOUR THROUGHOUT THE HOUSE

The colour scheme should create unity and flow not only between different areas in your home but also between the individuals who live there.

ABOVE *Choose colours that work in harmony with each other, such as earthy browns and greens.*

RIGHT *Make sure that connecting rooms in your home are decorated in harmonious colours, with no shocking changes as you walk from one room into the next.*

The home is usually a shared place, so we must think carefully about the needs and colour preferences of everyone in it before deciding on a colour scheme. This is because when people live together one may have stronger colour vibrations than the others, with the result that the people with the softer colour vibrations become overwhelmed by others' preferences.

To create a feeling of harmony in your home you should be able to move between the main living areas without shocking colour changes. Adjacent rooms can be viewed through open doors so rooms that adjoin should form a harmony of colour. It is a good idea to choose one family of colours – warm, cool, or neutral – for the main rooms. Or use different shades and tints of one or two colours.

Choose warm colours in rooms where activity is to take place. The magnetic colours of red, orange, and yellow have a physically stimulating and energizing effect on our bodies. The living room, dining room, study, television room, playroom, workroom, studio, reception room, halls, and stairways are all areas in which the strengthening qualities of warm colours are appropriate. For rooms in which you wish to create a restful and peaceful atmosphere, choose cool or pastel colours to give out relaxed harmonious vibrations.

Living and dining areas are generally used by everyone in the house, so these rooms should not be decorated in a colour that one person hates. There are compromises within the same colour families that will work for everyone. For instance, if one of your family hates yellow, try a light butter-cream instead.

In rooms that are used exclusively by one person, select a colour that is in tune with his or her inner colours and particular needs. In a bedroom or study, the therapeutic aspects of a colour will contribute to making the right atmosphere in the room. Teenagers may use their bedrooms for entertainment and home study, so their rooms would need a more warming and uplifting colour scheme than those rooms were used solely for relaxation and sleep.

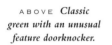

ABOVE *Classic green with an unusual feature doorknocker.*

ABOVE *Yellow walls highlighted with strong-coloured flowers.*

ABOVE *Bright-coloured renderings harmonize with neighboring properties.*

ABOVE *A rainbow of colour cheers up a narrow street.*

EXTERIORS AND FRONT DOORS

The outside of your home sends welcoming messages to everyone who sees it. A house is not only an extension of ourselves but also part of the surrounding environment. We must, therefore, bear in mind that the exterior of our house influences and reflects the environment around it. Every house should be in harmony with the elements of style, materials, and colours that are found nearby. The colour of a house should blend in with the natural colours found in the buildings and landscape in the locality.

If you are looking for an appropriate colour for the exterior of your home, the best possible colours are those found in the textures and colouring of the materials used – especially if they are brick, stone, or wood. Rocks and earth pigments found in your locality can yield a beautiful yellow-cream, rust, or pinky-tan, which can enhance a house, making it look as though it has grown naturally out of the earth.

Many houses have rendered walls, which need to be painted; there are many colours more appropriate than white. Brilliant white is rarely found in nature, so consider as an alternative a soft creamy white or pinky white.

The doorway is the protector of the house, keeping out the wind and rain and strangers. It should also give out a welcoming message to you and your visitors. It is a good idea to assess the impact of the colour presently on your front door. When deciding what colour to paint it, ask yourself what impression you get from your existing door when returning home. Do you get a welcoming feeling from the colour, an oppressive feeling, or no feeling at all? If your door provides you with only a feeling of relief at being home, you need to change the colour.

INDIVIDUAL EXPRESSION

The colour of the front door affords you the opportunity to express your individuality so that the colour energy welcomes you to your private haven. Paint the front door your favorite colour or a colour that best expresses the personality both of the occupants and of the house itself.

COLOUR OPPOSITES,
BLUE GREEN AND
YELLOW ORANGE
ENHANCE EACH OTHER

A COLLECTION OF
PEBBLES BRINGS THE
OUTDOORS INDOORS

A VIEW INTO THE
BACKYARD IS FRAMED AND
ECHOED BY VIBRANT GREEN

THE ORGANIC SHAPE OF THE
CHAIR AND ITS RED COLOUR
CONTRAST WITH THE SURROUNDINGS

ABOVE *Modern urban industrial elements have been softened by bright colours and the warm tones of wood.*

ENHANCING THE ENTRANCE AND DOORWAY

- *Place a welcome mat made from natural fiber outside the front door. It may be coloured or have a welcoming design woven into it.*

- *Make a path leading up to the door, planted on either side with aromatic shrubs, trees, or flowers.*

- *Find a door knocker in the shape of a favorite animal or symbol.*

- *Get a brass bell or bell pull so that the sound of the door bell is pleasing and musical.*

- *Stained-glass panels with a design incorporating the sun's rays or other symbol can be a welcoming sight when you come home.*

- *Paint the door in a welcoming colour of your choice or a protective colour.*

ENTRANCES, HALLWAYS, AND STAIRS

Once you are through the front door, an entrance hall provides you with a further opportunity to adjust from the outside world and to slow down. The hall is the place where you first come into contact with the personality and atmosphere in the home. The colours here can be dramatic or relaxing, depending on the mood you wish to create. We usually spend little time in the hall, passing through it to other rooms or up a staircase, so it is essentially a place of movement. For this reason you can use more intense and vibrant colours than you might use in areas for relaxing in the house. It is possible to use a deeper version of your main colour or a contrasting colour so that you can look through to other rooms. Warm rich colours create a cozy and welcoming feeling especially when you come inside from bad weather, but people who lead a hectic or stressful lifestyle may prefer to enter a softer, lighter, and more calming space. Halls, passageways, and stairs often look large, long, and vacant if painted white or cream. Instead, try painting these areas with a rich or vibrant colour. Remember, you are always on the move, passing through a hall or passage, and a more striking inspirational colour may be just what you need.

It is not only the colours of the walls but also that of the floors that will have a strong impact when entering a house. Some older homes have terra-cotta tiles in hallways and entrances. These are easy to clean and hard wearing. The natural colouring of the tiles enhances our Earth connection, slowing down our mental energy and stabilizing our energy system.

Wood is also a lovely material for hallways and indeed any area inside the house. Outdoors we have to protect ourselves against the elements and harsh environmental conditions but inside we can connect to our true selves by shedding our outer defenses. Walking barefoot on your floor or changing into soft slippers also helps to alter your state of mind.

Connecting yourself to the floor also provides a very soothing and earthing feeling – especially after work. The Earth connection helps to relax the mind, which is often overstimulated during the day. It puts you in touch with the simple things in life, including your family and home, and you can draw up Earth energy to support and give you strength.

In many cultures the front door or surrounds are painted in a protective colour. Turquoise was used by both Middle Eastern people and Native North Americans around their entrances. Black is another colour that absorbs bad vibrations, while white deflects detrimental influences. Purple, midnight blue, and blue-violet are also protective colours that look stunning on a front door, making a strong backdrop for foliage and plants grown around the doorway.

Windows and doors are strongly linked since these are the sources of light vibrations entering your home. Try painting these in the same colour or in colours that harmonize with the front door.

EASTERN TRADITIONS

In the East it is traditional for the front door to face the rising sun and it will be decorated with good-luck charms and painted in colours that are thought to ward off evil.

BOLD CURTAINS
FRAMING AN ENTRANCE
CREATE A DRAMATIC EFFECT

LAMPS SHED A WELCOMING
GLOW AND GIVE AN INVITING
FIRST IMPRESSION TO VISITORS

RUGS ADD A SOFT
TOUCH TO THE POLISHED
WOOD BLOCK FLOOR

ABOVE
Traditional style enriched by warm colours that burnish the tones of the antique furniture.

RICH RUSSET WALLS
ARE REMINISCENT
OF MEDIEVAL ITALY
SUGGESTED IN THE MURAL

THE DIAMOND
THEME IS REPEATED
ON THE TABLE AND
THE UPHOLSTERY

ABOVE *A trompe-l'oeil mural enlarges the room. The patterned living room floor leads the eye naturally into the mural and out onto its balcony.*

LIVING ROOMS

The living rooms in your house are your "image" rooms, which best reflect the personalities of the people in the home. The living area should reflect your identity back to you, telling you what kind of person you are, and expressing your lifestyle and interests. It is a place where you should be able to relax and be yourself, where you can enjoy being surrounded by objects and colours with which you feel in tune. The living room is also a place where you can welcome and entertain friends and family, so you need to decide whether you wish the place to be cozy, peaceful, dramatic, or welcoming. Living rooms are best decorated in tones relating to the atmosphere you wish to create there and to your individual lifestyle. To create a warm and friendly room, use strong colours in the warm range such as deep rusts, apricot, gold, or sandy yellows. Balance these colours with smaller amounts of cool colours. You can lighten or darken these colours to suit your identity and soul-colour preferences (*see* p 30). A quiet room can be successfully decorated in several calming subtle or light tones of one relaxing colour.

If you want a dramatic look, try contrasting two colours only, with less furniture, ornaments, and general clutter. Use textiles and textures to add variety and interest. Rooms decorated in two colours can become tiring and mentally restrictive, however, so only do this if you are feel confident and secure with all aspects of your life. We do need variety and stimulation for our minds and bodies: living in a home lacking in colours will make us introspective and introverted.

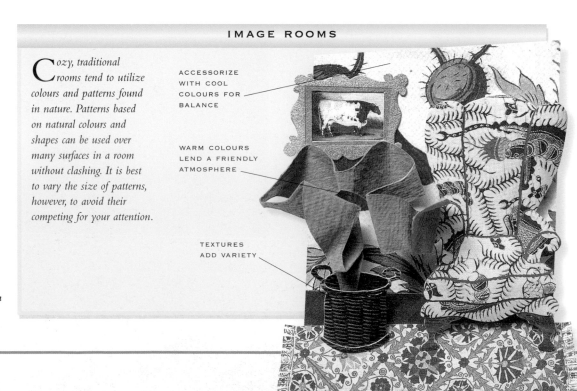

IMAGE ROOMS

Cozy, traditional rooms tend to utilize colours and patterns found in nature. Patterns based on natural colours and shapes can be used over many surfaces in a room without clashing. It is best to vary the size of patterns, however, to avoid their competing for your attention.

ACCESSORIZE
WITH COOL
COLOURS FOR
BALANCE

WARM COLOURS
LEND A FRIENDLY
ATMOSPHERE

TEXTURES
ADD VARIETY

RIGHT *Living rooms reflect our personalities and are best decorated in warm, strong colours.*

Turquoise, lilac, orchid, and lavender contain blue energy and are all excellent colours for a study area. The warm pink undertone gives you active support and determination while the blue tone promotes a calm atmosphere that helps you to concentrate on tasks at hand.

If you live in a modern house or enjoy modern styles, a strong, dramatic room can be made using some modern furniture and bold flat areas of colours and texture rather than pattern. An entirely modern room can lack soul, however, if there are no links to natural shapes, materials, and colours. In fact, large planters with palms, cacti, or both look wonderful in a modern setting.

If your living area is shared by several family members, a neutral background may be the best way to unite all their soul colours, but often you can find a colour with which everybody is happy.

Whatever your colour scheme, try to include one or two main colours, plus a contrasting balancing colour. Remember to link these colours to your soul colours. The effect of your soul colour will be enhanced by placing its complementary colour in the room. You may also wish to introduce a colour you have been attracted to recently in the form of a movable decorative object such as a vase of flowers, rug, or ornament.

Black can be used successfully in many places as an accent colour, for instance, in furniture, picture frames, and rugs, or where there is sufficient contrast for it not to dominate. Gray is restful but should never be used alone. Silver is luxurious and gold elegant, but I recommend using these colours as highlights only – to add sparkle and richness to a room.

HARMONY

If you are going through major changes in your life, it is perhaps best to paint your living room in a neutral colour, so that you can introduce different colours in the furnishings, lighting, and accessories to suit your ongoing needs. A wide variety of beautiful furnishings – fabrics, rugs, ceramics, and pictures – can provide an array of colours. If you are skilled at mixing several patterns and colours together, you can create a room with interesting textures, colours, and patterns. Take care not to make it too busy because too many colours can often send out confusing and conflicting energy. A busy room is not beneficial to those who are nervous, confused, or have bad memories, for mixing several patterns together does not soothe the nerves or promote concentration.

BELOW A strong colour theme has been used for walls and paintwork, based on striking opposites: yellow and purple.

ALTHOUGH THIS ROOM IS BUSY WITH PATTERNS AND TEXTURES, A RESTRICTED COLOUR PALETTE PREVENTS IT FROM BEING OVERWHELMING

THE EFFECT IS ENRICHED BY THE MULTITUDE OF PATTERNS IN THE ETHNIC EMBROIDERY

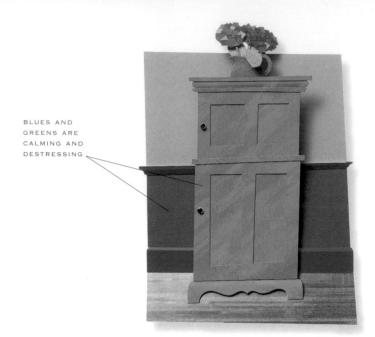

BLUES AND GREENS ARE CALMING AND DESTRESSING

ABOVE *Harmonizing tones of blue and green, together with natural wood, provide a relaxing environment.*

KITCHENS

A kitchen should be a warm and nurturing place, a place for a social gathering, and somewhere where you can express creativity while nourishing your body. If you are a working family, it is even more important that your time in the kitchen is enjoyable and that you look upon it as a place to unwind and relax. The colours in your kitchen can stimulate your senses and help release the stress you have accumulated in the day. Even if you live in a sophisticated apartment or condominium, colour can be used to enhance a kitchen and dining area so that you can feel energized and inspired. A single bright blue glass bowl full of lemons or tomatoes on a table can make a colourful and enriching feature.

The chief task performed in a kitchen is the preparation, serving, and eating of food. The quality and enjoyment of the meal will greatly depend on the mood and creativity of the cook as well as the quality and freshness of the ingredients used. Colour in the kitchen can be mood-enhancing and used to create a cozy atmosphere, aid creativity, stimulate the digestion, help you to unwind or relax, and set you up for the day ahead.

RIGHT *A cool slate floor is complemented by a splash of yellow, which in turn is accented by turquoise walls.*

UPLIFTING COLOUR

*Y*ou could put a vase of bright yellow flowers such as daffodils in the kitchen or breakfast bar. These will be uplifting to whoever is cooking.

Country kitchens have become popular because the smells and colours stimulate the senses, Kitchens naturally lend themselves to all the rich, warm, earthy colours – nut brown, golden-yellows, terra-cotta, peach, and red. These can be set off with lots of green, which provides the complementary colour needed to set off warm tones. Green is a colour that is often associated with the kitchen since it reminds us of the natural delicious food that nature provides for us.

GREEN ACCENTS

*R*ather than painting the kitchen walls green, which could be cold or dreary, use green in furnishing accessories, kitchen implements, tableware, and kitchen furniture.

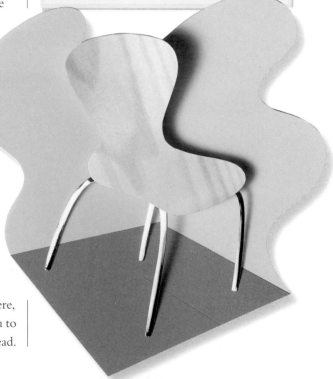

A SPLASH OF COLOUR ENLIVENS A NEUTRAL DECOR

WHITE OR NEUTRAL COLOURS GIVE THE KITCHEN A LIGHT AND AIRY FEEL

airy feeling, as long as it is used together with lots of colour. If you do have a white or neutral-coloured kitchen, use bowls of natural foods to bring colour into the room. If you lust after a particular colour, the kitchen is a wonderful place to introduce this colour energy. A bowl of fruit or vegetables is inexpensive and your body will benefit by drawing off energizing and healing colour vibrations from the fruit and vegetables.

Colour can be introduced into a neutral-coloured kitchen in the form of tiles, worktops, and flooring. If you use natural materials, you will end up with a healthy kitchen and one where the colours naturally blend and enhance one another. For instance, if you have a terracotta tile or rich wooden floor, you could introduce turquoise or green tiles to provide the perfect harmony.

LEFT *Use hotspots of colour to relieve an otherwise restrained colour palette of neutrals.*

On a therapeutic level, warm shades of brown, orange, red, and yellow instill us with vitality. Orange stimulates appetite and aids digestion.

An all-white kitchen may feel very clean and tidy, but white is not a relaxing colour and will not encourage you to spend time there. However, white can still be used in the kitchen to give a bright and

BRINGING COLOUR TO YOUR KITCHEN

Try some of the following accessories to bring colour and energy to your kitchen.

- Coloured glass bottles
- Bunches of dried flowers and herbs hanging from the ceiling
- Brightly painted flower pots with herbs on the window sills
- Ceramic or coloured glass bowls of fruit or vegetables
- Glass bottles containing spices, lentils, and other legumes
- Tiles hand painted with ceramic or glass paints
- Colourful cook books
- Plates, cups, copper, old jelly molds, and straw baskets

- Colour-washed kitchen cupboards
- Colourful cotton rag rugs
- Bright printed blinds and curtains

LEFT *Dried herbs not only look attractive but are also readily available for cooking and impart a delicious fragrance to the kitchen.*

ABOVE *Rustic furnishings and chunky tableware combine well with a tiled tabletop.*

BELOW *An alcove is the obvious site to place a table, particularly when there is light from a window and a view to enhance the area.*

DINING ROOMS

Dining rooms should be places of social gathering where you can relax and enjoy your meal. If you live alone, a small table set near a window or in an alcove can provide a special place where you can take time to replenish your depleted energy resources.

All shades of orange are appetite stimulants and aid digestion. So peaches, apricots, and peachy yellows make the best colours for a dining area. If you do not like these warm colours, or if you eat in the kitchen, having a tablecloth and napkins in these colours will have a similar effect and would look perfect set off

against a blue, green, or turquoise wall. The main colours of your kitchen and dining area can be set off with vibrantly coloured tablecloths, mats, table decorations, napkins, and tableware.

If your dining room is used mostly in the evening, dark, rich green can make a relaxing environment for eating as long as there are warm colours elsewhere in the room. Candles would make darker walls glow and create an intimate and cozy atmosphere. Dining rooms are often located on the cold side of the house, and this really does not matter if you have a lighter place to eat your breakfast and daytime meals. A darker dining room could quite easily have the walls painted a rich colour, like a deep red, burnt orange, or golden-yellow. A glaze or slightly reflective eggshell paint would create a wonderful glow by candlelight in the evening and the room would feel warm and inspiring by day.

Sometimes your lifestyle or even the building itself requires a more restrained colour palette for the kitchen and dining area. This works exceptionally well if you are using a Japanese or American Shaker style for the house. There is a difference, however, between subtle shades of natural colours found in the materials themselves and cold neutrals often found in synthetic materials. So make sure your soft colour tones reflect these natural vibrations.

Gray, brown, or beige with a warm undertone can provide a warm and supportive environment in which to eat, and can also have a calming and relaxing effect on our whole system. Even if you have decided to use restrained colours in the kitchen and dining area, you can make use of spot colour with a flower arrangement or display of fruit or vegetables.

Conservatories are becoming very popular eating areas, where you can enjoy the uplifting rays of natural light throughout the year. Eating breakfast in a conservatory will give you the best start to the day. Sunlight helps you absorb the maximum energy from our food and you will

NATURAL BLOND WOOD FURNITURE HARMONIZES WITH THE PINE CEILING

NEUTRAL COLOURS BRING OUT THE BEAUTY OF THE WOOD, RATHER THAN COMPETE WITH IT draw nourishment from contact with a more natural surrounding. Eating breakfast in dreary dark surroundings is likely to make you feel as dreary and lethargic as the environment in which you have eaten it.

Light clear yellow and cream are particularly useful as colours for the dining areas in a home, as long as the yellows do not have a green under-tone. Be aware, however, that yellow has the annoying property of changing tone when viewed under different types of light. The type of light bulb you have in the home will affect the yellow, making it either more green or more blue at night, so that your beautiful yellow wall can be transformed into a horrible lime green. When using yellow for a wall colour it is wise to prepare a sample board so that you can view the colour under both natural and artificial light. Yellow is a very sociable and lively colour and will encourage conversational flow and exchange at the dinner table.

If your kitchen or dining area is on the cold side of the house, it is a good idea to use the warming and stimulating colours of red and orange, or choose a softer version like a deep salmon or peach. All magnetic colours stimulate our metabolism, aid digestion, and are wonder-fully warming in the winter. A tired cook can draw red energy into his or her system after a long day, although too much red energy in the kitchen can make you hot and irritable when cooking, so only choose it if you enjoy cooking and do not suffer from medical problems such as high blood pressure or a heart condition.

LEFT *The glass roof of a conservatory will make you feel as though you're eating outside, at any time of the year!*

A MIDNIGHT BLUE CEILING HINTS AT A NIGHT SKY AND IS REFLECTED IN THE TEXTILES

THE FOLDS OF THIS MYSTERIOUS SHOT-SATIN DRAPERY ARE EMPHASIZED BY CAREFUL LIGHTING

SPONGED WALLS CREATE TEXTURAL INTEREST

A CLEAR GLASS DINING TABLE AND A WOODEN FLOOR INJECT ELEMENTS OF LIGHT AND REFLECTIVENESS

LEFT *High drama can be created with rich royal blue and opulent drapery, but too much could tend to be claustrophobic.*

GLASS BLOCKS GIVE A DEGREE OF
PRIVACY, YET LET IN MAXIMUM LIGHT

ABOVE *A pure white backdrop gives scope for instant transformation by coloured lights, to create different effects.*

BEDROOMS

Bedrooms are very special rooms, because they are generally the rooms where we start and finish the day. The colours we wake up to will affect us throughout the day, and the cumulative effect will stay with us much longer. Often we devote all our attention to the activity centers in our home, and neglect these more private areas. We need to redress the balance in our lifestyle, which means paying more attention to creating healing rooms where we can relax, unwind, and find time to energize ourselves.

Try to locate the main bedroom and other quiet rooms away from a road or place where there is a lot of noise. Ideally, a bedroom should be located on the east or south easterly side of the house, which allows you to wake up with the natural dawn. We need the rhythm of the natural light cycles to keep our metabolism in balance, allowing our brain and our glands to produce hormones related to rest and activity.

Even though we use a bedroom primarily as a place to sleep there are many other activities we can enjoy if it is well designed. Since the bedroom is also the first choice for a room in which to make love, it would be an ideal place to create a space for a massage or a place where you can give or receive a therapeutic healing treatment. If the colours for the bedroom have been chosen to be conducive to love-making they may not provide the right atmosphere for sleeping. So decorate the bedroom in restful colours, and introduce some red love vibrations through the bedcovers, sheets, coloured light bulbs and sensual aromas. In this way you can move and change the atmosphere of the room to suit your mood.

WOODEN SHUTTERS
EFFECTIVELY EXCLUDE
THE LIGHT AND
BREAK UP WHAT
WOULD OTHERWISE
BE A LARGE EXPANSE
OF DRAPERY

LEFT *Masculine, subdued colours and simple furnishings are given a boost by voluminous drapes and swags.*

EXCLUDING DAYLIGHT

If you have a problem waking up in the morning, replace heavy curtains with those with light-filtering qualities. When light rays penetrate a bedroom you will also feel much brighter and alert when you get up. If, on the other hand, you have difficulty sleeping, you need to make sure light is blocked out from the room during the night – thicker curtains will do the trick.

COORDINATING
CURTAINS AND
CUSHIONS IN
STRIKING REGAL
CRIMSON AND RICH
GOLDEN YELLOW
ADD TO THE WARMTH
CREATED BY THE
WOOD PANELING

A BOLD FRINGE
ON THE BEDCOVER
VISUALLY LINKS
THE SCROLLED
HEADBOARD AND
FOOTBOARD

LEFT *An aristocratic,
French-style bedroom
where rich reds and soft
fabrics stimulate our
senses.*

DRESSING-ROOM RETREAT

The bedroom is a personal room – a place where
we can retreat not only from the world but also
from our family and sometimes even our partners. We
may use a bedroom for many other activities such as
reading, writing, eating, all types of toilette, bathing,
and dressing, and the colours we choose can help make
the bedroom a special and nurturing place.

If you have any extra space in the bedroom, try to
create a dressing-room retreat. It would be better to have
a separate room, but an area of bedroom that is draped
to muffle noise and intrusion is sufficient. Screen off
this part of the room to make your private retreat where
you can dress, read, have tea, relax, and generally
dedicate time to yourself. Restful pastels will underline
the quiet mood. Soft pink, lilac, mauve, green, and blue
(as pictured here) are all colours that will create a mood
of tranquillity and support. If you are lavish with both
floral patterns and flowers you will not be in danger of
making the small dressing area appear visually smaller.
The effect will then be romantic and relaxing, homey
and reassuring, rather than claustrophobic.

ABOVE *A small seating area bathed in natural
light makes the perfect retreat in which to enjoy an
engrossing book.*

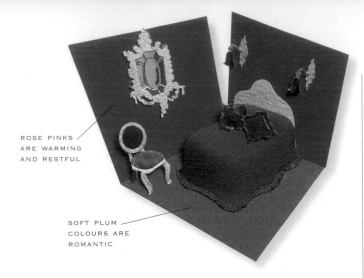

ROSE PINKS
ARE WARMING
AND RESTFUL

SOFT PLUM
COLOURS ARE
ROMANTIC

ABOVE *Plum tones are also warming, but less strident and more relaxing than reds.*

COLOUR THERAPY FOR THE BEDROOM

The colour we need in the morning may not be the colour we want at night. Burgundy, scarlet, or Chinese red are very energetic and physical colours, and red is also the colour of sex. This energizing colour is wonderful when we want to be stimulated in this way, but not so good if we are tired and want a peaceful night's sleep. Pink and plums are softer and more romantic. Peach and apricot are emotionally supportive, providing feelings of love from their pink tone and energy from their yellow tone.

Lemon yellow and honey yellows are cheerful, but they are also mentally stimulating and they should not be used in a bedroom if you suffer from insomnia. If you have yellow in the bedroom, make sure it is a pale tint – buttercup, primrose, or cream.

Blue makes a bright bedroom serene, but if you have a quiet disposition or are prone to depression it would be better to use lilac, orchid, lavender, or almond blossom, which are both soothing and supportive. Mulberry, salmon, or rose pink are stronger pink tones for people who do not like pastels. These provide warmth and affection while still being restful.

Blues and greens are soothing and refreshing in a bedroom, but are best used in the soft furnishings and plants. The relaxing and restful energy of cool colours is restful to the mind so

RIGHT *Hot, vibrant reds are challenging, but in the winter they can provide a comforting cocoon.*

they make good main bedroom colours for someone who suffers from stress. Blue-green and turquoise are both peaceful and fresh, especially if you live in a hot climate or if a room is particularly bright and sunny.

FEMININE BEDROOMS

Women often like to have a feminine bedroom with white walls and plenty of crisp white lace bedlinen. White creates an atmosphere that is old-fashioned, clean, and cool. Plenty of wood in the room and rugs in warm tones, would set off the white, as would natural textures of wicker or prettily decorated ceramics. Plants in ceramic planters soften the effect of an all-white room, contributing to its simple and fresh atmosphere.

If you live alone, or have suffered a bereavement, don't surround yourself with too much white. While soft white or shades of white have a supporting and uplifting effect on the psyche, a stark white can promote feelings of loneliness and isolation. If you want to create an all-white room, mix and match many tones of white, off-white, and cream together to give a rich tapestry of textures and subtle colour changes.

You can achieve a feminine bedroom without using white by introducing soft curves and flowing lines in your window treatments. Aim

BRIGHT REDS ARE WARM,
BUT STIMULATING AND
ENERGIZING COLOURS

YELLOW MAKES A ROOM BRIGHT AND CHEERFUL

APRICOT IS EMOTIONALLY SUPPORTIVE

BLUE ADDS A RELAXING TOUCH

to achieve a personal bedroom, with framed photographs and personal items to make your room much more feminine.

Pink is popular colour for feminine bedrooms, and since it is often the female partner who decorates the bedroom, many men complain that they have to suffer pink sleeping areas. Fortunately, they will unconsciously benefit from the muscle-relaxing, affectionate, and loving qualities of pink. A pink bedroom does not necessary have to be prissy. Deep rose pinks, orchid, or peachy pink can create a sophisticated but feminine room that exudes an aura of warmth, luxury, and love.

MASCULINE BEDROOMS

Black bedrooms and bathrooms have been trendy from time to time, especially in bachelor pads. There may be no problem going to sleep in a black room, but waking up in a room that reflects no light is certain to affect your energy levels during the day. Black signifies rejection and fear, and creates a feeling that the world is not right. People who are drawn to black are often the very people who need to be stimulated with air, light, and colour. They desperately need love, support, and understanding, but are hiding under the

cloak of black. Introducing colour into the room will be their first major step to paving the way on their path of self-development.

Many people who use black in decorating are reluctant to change the scheme. The best way to deal with this is to introduce touches of other colours into the room. After a while the colour energy received from these areas or items will change the person's energy balance, and he will gradually become drawn more and more to other colours. Eventually he may decide to substitute the black room for different colours that allow personal growth and help the person to communicate with the world.

Men can unwittingly choose so-called masculine colours such as navy blue and burgundy for a bedroom scheme because of past associations with these colours. However, dark blue, maroon, and gray have a stultifying effect with the result that men are prevented from expressing their own individuality and creativity. Wide expanses of dark blue can also be depressing, and burgundy in large doses can reflect the negative aspects of red, so it is important that men break away from this colour mold. Use light and bright complementary colours in order to balance the effects of dark blue and red.

LEFT *Yellow is uplifting, but choose the strength of colour carefully: bright yellows stimulate rather than calm.*

BELOW *White is classic and has a fresh appeal, but take care you don't achieve a stark, clinical effect.*

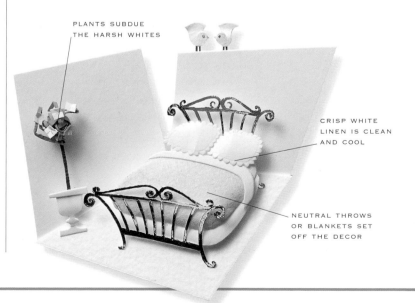

PLANTS SUBDUE THE HARSH WHITES

CRISP WHITE LINEN IS CLEAN AND COOL

NEUTRAL THROWS OR BLANKETS SET OFF THE DECOR

NATURAL MATERIALS

*U*se natural materials such as wood and plants in your bathroom to create a restful and relaxing space. Choose tiles made of clay or decorated in warm soothing colours of your choice since these create a feeling of warmth. If you decide to use ceramic or decorated tiles that incorporate cool blues and greens, make sure you contrast these with warm wall colours, drapes, or blinds, and bathroom accessories such as towels, robes, and even toiletries.

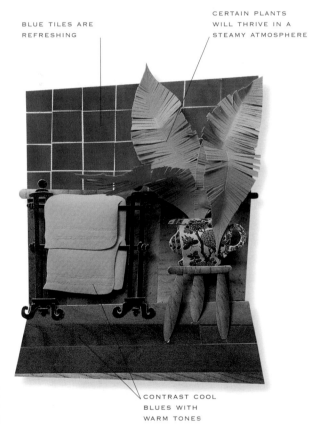

BLUE TILES ARE
REFRESHING

CERTAIN PLANTS
WILL THRIVE IN A
STEAMY ATMOSPHERE

CONTRAST COOL
BLUES WITH
WARM TONES

BATHROOMS

For centuries bathing was an essential part of social life, an activity central to the fabric of society. The baths were an important meeting place, a social center for relaxation and debate, and at the same time a place to be massaged and pampered. It is only during the past century that bathing has become a private affair, in what is often the smallest and darkest room in the house.

Bathtubs do not have to be housed in bathrooms; we can alternatively incorporate bathing spaces into the heart of the home. They can be part of a bedroom, a loft, or a cellar. A place of bathing can also be enhanced and linked to nature by opening it to a courtyard or garden, or providing a skylight.

En-suite bathrooms have gained popularity but, while it is convenient to have a shower and sink next to the bedroom, too often the bathtub is squeezed into a small, airless space. This means that bathing for the most part takes place in cramped conditions. The bathroom itself does not need to be entirely separate from the bedroom. Creating a bathroom adjoining a bedroom could mean changing the level of the floor, or using a screen of plants as an informal low divider.

Warm peach or pink tones work well in a bathroom because they give skin a healthy glow; in countries with cool climates these pinky tones are particularly warming and affectionate. You can also introduce warming and supportive colours into a bathroom by allowing diffused light to shine through a fabric blind. Natural light will bring the therapeutic and healing affects of colour into the room. Peach, pink, terra-cotta, and gold have the effect of uplifting our spirits and fortifying our energy resources. This is particularly useful when we are confronted by our bodies in the bathroom. Soft warm colours help us feel comfortable with our physical form and thus boost our self-confidence and self-esteem.

If you are after a more Mediterranean feel to your home, turquoise teamed up with deep blue is a wonderful colour for a bathroom. It is a refreshing, soothing colour for a hot, tired, or aching body, and it encourages your mind to relax as you think of the cool clear colours of the sea and sky. Blue on bathroom walls can prove cold in the winter, but is particularly welcoming if you take a shower after exercise. Blue curtains or blinds, however, will provide cooling, soothing filtered light after a hot bath or shower.

An all-white bathroom can be cold and draining, and will not encourage you to linger. Bathing in a white room becomes a clinical chore. So if you have an all-white bathroom, try introducing other colours to encourage you to enjoy the special time you spend there.

Do not use bright strip or spot lights in a bathroom, since the light from these fittings has a blue bias, which will make you feel uncomfortable and skin look dull and lifeless. Try incorporating soft overall lighting, using light bulbs of a yellow or peachy tint. You will also need a good light over the mirror. Try to design a bathroom so that there is a permanent wall or hanging candelabra. Candles in the bathroom add wonderful living light that is perfect for relaxation in a bath. If this is not possible, a selection of candlesticks with candles on a bathroom shelf is both attractive and colourful when unlit or lit.

FAMILY BATHROOMS

If space permits, create a relaxation area in the bathroom. A chair and colourful rag rug can encourage your family to enjoy bathing together. Keep a selection of colourful bottles of aromatic bath salts and oils, as well as some humidity-loving plants on a shelf or table.

LEFT *White walls make the most of the sunlight shining in through a muslin-draped window.*

CHILDREN'S ROOMS

There is a cycle of changing colours in our aura through the different stages in our lives. These inner colours are reflected in our changing colour preferences. Children have colour likes and dislikes according to their individual character and stage of development. Having a knowledge of the therapeutic qualities of colours can help you make a child's home environment a place that nurtures learning skills and personality, while providing a safe haven to play and grow.

Rudolph Steiner (*see* p 165) was one of the first modern thinkers who brought attention to the fact that colour and shape can have a beneficial effect on our mental and physical development. As a result of his work there is an international network of Steiner communities, which are designed using the therapeutic qualities of colour and form.

Infants and small children

Parents are usually the designers of the nursery and most new parents design the nursery from scratch by converting a study or spare room. They usually redecorate the walls with paints and wallpapers, buying furniture and accessories in anticipation of the happy event. This is an ideal opportunity to use colours that will give your child the best start in life.

A small child needs to sleep, but also to be alert and interested in his or her new surroundings. An infant needs to be surrounded with soft light colours, since these are in keeping with the pastel shades found in the aura during the first years of life. The custom of dressing babies in pastel blue or pink probably derives from an intuitive awareness of the subtle inner vibrations of a new baby. We also unconsciously link blue to the masculine Yin force of the sky, while pink is

STRONG COLOURS

Strong, bright colours have the affect of shocking the baby's inner vibrations, which could make the infant unsettled and restless. Bright, intense colours such as primary red, yellow, and orange can stop a child, sleeping well, as well as causing him or her to cry. Strong contrasting colours and bold patterns are also likely to be overstimulating, so for a small infant choose soft tones of yellow or cream, peach or pink, which radiate peace and are emotionally soothing and comforting.

BELOW LEFT
Conventional colour choices help strangers to identify a baby's sex!

BELOW RIGHT
Soft, pastel tones suit the light shades of a young child's aura.

derived from red of Mother Earth. Although we often associate pink with girls and blue with boys, creamy yellow and apricot and peach are excellent colours for both sexes. Add a few bright accessories after birth to give the room a personal touch.

Green is calming but can be cold when used as a wall colour, especially in a cold or dark room. If you do use green make sure it is a soft, light tone. Blue on its own can also be cold and may make the child susceptible to colic and colds. Blue is a good colour for your child if he or she is overactive, but will not offer much emotional or physical support. Therefore, it is a good idea to use blue on the walls, making sure there is a contrasting warm colour in the drapes and other furnishings. Pink, peach, apricot, pale almond white, and lavender all provide love and security for the child.

Babies spend most of their time lying on their backs looking upward. Most people are aware of

this and try to provide stimulation for the child by hanging toys and mobiles above the baby carriage or crib. Once the baby is able to focus on more distant objects, it is a good idea to provide a wealth of colour and shape on the ceiling, too. Most ceilings in the home are painted pure white, a light but visually uninteresting colour. You can do so much more to improve the well-being of a small child if you pay attention to the colours and shapes on the ceiling.

Paint the ceiling a single light colour so it does not have to be repainted for some time and from it hang lots of mobiles. Stores sell a wealth of fun designs, or you can make your own. Let your imagination run riot to create an original mobile using natural objects suspended from brightly coloured ribbon. Think about providing a variety of different shapes and textures, and don't forget the benefits of soft musical sounds. Shells, bamboo, wood, or metal windchimes can bring gentle reassuring vibrations to the nursery.

LEFT *Choose an assortment of bright, primary colours to attract a baby's attention and offer visual stimulation.*

NEGATIVE PATTERNS

The colours of the child's bedclothes and bedding have a direct effect on his or her physical and psychological well-being because the subtle colour vibrations permeate the aura while the child is asleep. Unless the child is well balanced and outgoing, be careful not to have strong, large, or geometric patterns on drapes, blinds, or walls. These shapes can send off jarring vibrations. Distraught parents have often come to me for advice regarding restless children who suffer from recurring dreams and nightmares. Often the child has a quilt or pillow decorated with black, red, purple, and other bright colours, covered with large cars, trains, or comic figures. Removing these negative vibrational patterns from the room is the best thing to help your child get a good night's sleep.

LEFT *Peach is appropriate for babies of either sex and provides a warming glow.*

A baby is extremely sensitive to light so make sure the nursery is filled with reflected or filtered light through sunlight-filtering drapes, blinds, and an opaque glass lampshade. It is helpful to put a soft nightlight with a pink or peach tint near the cradle so that the warm and nurturing glow gives out vibrations of love and security. A soft yellow-tinted light bulb also gives a friendly light. You can change the light bulb from time to time, especially when a child cannot sleep or is suffering from a childhood disease such as chickenpox or measles. Blue works best for any hot condition where the child is running a temperature or has itchy skin. Blue light is calming and soothing for an overactive young child.

Older children

Once a child has outgrown the nursery environment, you may decide to update the decor to reflect your child's changing needs. Parents remain the chief room designers of children's rooms, although a growing child can have very strong and individual taste.

Children grow and develop fast, and as they explore their world they become attracted to brighter and more striking colours. A child will be attracted to his or her own colours intuitively, which will meet the energetic needs of the child at that point in time. Try to introduce these colours into the room, even if they alarm you! The best policy is to keep the walls in a soft peach or cream, but to add more brightly coloured drapes, bedcovers, a wall mural or frieze, all of which stimulate the child's enquiring mind and encourage emotional development.

As your child's colour preferences and emotional and mental needs change, you will be able to alter the room without the need for any major redecoration.

Older children will probably have to use their bedrooms for study purposes at some time or another. A room full of bright colours can be very distracting when concentration is needed. Try to introduce wall colours that are less visually exciting, and stay away from busy patterns and wallpapers, especially strong geometric shapes,

BELOW LEFT
Keep a pastel base colour for the walls, which can be spiced up with areas of bright colour.

BELOW RIGHT
A room crammed with bright colours is not conducive to study: bear this in mind if the bedroom doubles as a homework area.

A PEACH BASE CAN BE ENLIVENED WITH BRIGHT ACCESSORIES. ADD BRIGHT DRAPES TO STIMULATE AN ENQUIRING MIND

TOO MANY BRIGHT COLOURS ARE NOT CONDUCIVE TO STUDY. INTRODUCE SHADES OF YELLOW TO HELP THE MENTAL PROCESS, AND KEEP PATTERNS SIMPLE.

which emit disharmonious vibrations. Various shades of blue-green work well in a study/bedroom, and contrasting warming colours would be better if confined to bedcovers, drapes and blinds, cushions, and rugs. If your child has a brightly coloured room it may be possible to create a quiet corner in a room, where the colours are more muted and quiet. Pale yellow-cream contains yellow energy, which gently aids the mental processes, helping logical processes and clear thinking, while at the same time not being too disturbing for your child.

PERSONALITY COLOURS

*L*ike *adults, children have distinct personalities and soul colours. This means that some children want a sophisticated bedroom, while others are happy in a brightly coloured "rumpus room." A more sensitive child will naturally be attracted to softer, lighter colours, while an active, outgoing child will be attracted to bright primaries. You need to be sensitive to these individual tastes when choosing colours for the growing child so that you can provide colours that are in tune with his or her personality and psychological requirements.*

VIBRATIONS EMANATING FROM STRONG GEOMETRIC SHAPES CAN BE DISRUPTIVE

LEFT *Striking patterns can also be distracting and do not combine well with the multifarious clutter children accumulate.*

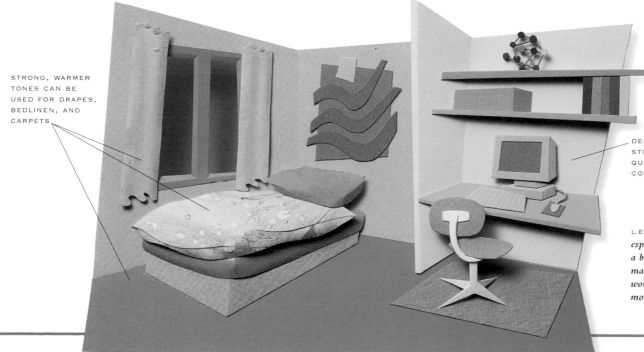

STRONG, WARMER TONES CAN BE USED FOR DRAPES, BEDLINEN, AND CARPETS

DECORATE THE STUDY AREA WITH QUIETENING, COOL SHADES.

LEFT *If your child is especially eager to have a brightly coloured room, make sure that there is a work area decorated in more muted tones.*

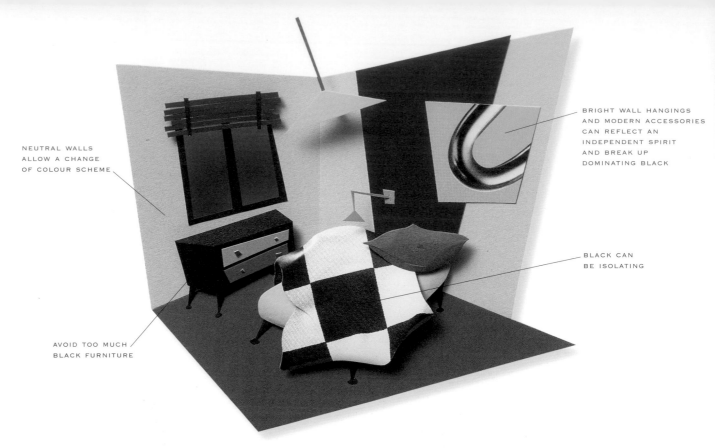

NEUTRAL WALLS
ALLOW A CHANGE
OF COLOUR SCHEME

BRIGHT WALL HANGINGS
AND MODERN ACCESSORIES
CAN REFLECT AN
INDEPENDENT SPIRIT
AND BREAK UP
DOMINATING BLACK

BLACK CAN
BE ISOLATING

AVOID TOO MUCH
BLACK FURNITURE

ABOVE *Bright colours and cheerful accents enhance a neutral colour scheme.*

TEENAGERS' ROOMS

By the time children become teenagers, they will want to assert their individuality, and one of the best ways of letting them do so is to encourage them to decorate their rooms. As it is part of the home, the teenager still has the natural support of the family, familiar surroundings, and colours provided by the rest of the house.

It is not surprising that red is often a teenager's favorite colour. Red expresses sexual development and intense energy. Pink shows a great need for love and affection. Blue suits a quieter nature and a search for a calm, soothing atmosphere, especially if there is tension in the home or at school. Green shows a need for individual space and time to reflect and develop ideas and ideals.

Most teenagers go through an emotional crisis as they search for their adult identity. A love of black often reflects a difficulty in taking on adult responsibility and a rejection of the new adult role. Parents should be encouraged to view this colour preference as a natural phase that their son or daughter is going through. It is similar to

creating a cocoon around themselves, where they feel safe and hidden from the world. This allows them to spend time finding their own real identity and giving them space for introspection. If you know someone who is going through a "black phase," you can help him or her mature by encouraging the combining of black with other colours. A bright cushion or wall hanging or a piece of jewelry can be set off well by black, making the impact of that colour stronger. This will help lift the young person away from the feeling of isolation or withdrawal from the world.

COLOUR INDICATORS

The colours your son or daughter chooses during the teenage years will tell you a great deal about what he or she is experiencing, thinking, and feeling at that particular moment. So pay heed to these colours, read your child, and try to provide all the love and support that he or she will need during this often difficult period.

ROOMS FOR OLDER PEOPLE

Decorating a room for an elderly relative can play an important part in the harmony of the home and the quality of life that person will enjoy for the rest of his or her days. Becoming old can bring with it a great sense of loneliness and fear, and loving and supportive colours can be a great comfort. Variety in the colours of the immediate environment can boost interest in the world and stimulate the mind. Living in a dark, dreary environment encourages us to withdraw, but this attitude to life can be dramatically reversed with lively and varied stimulation from colours.

As our physical body declines we often find that our colour preferences become softer and lighter. While we are drawn to these paler shades, we also need to replace the vitality of the colours we are drawing away from. As a result our sensitivity to the colour vibrations around us will become greater, and strong bright colours may have an unsettling effect.

If we are to keep up our stamina and ensure that our immune systems remain strong, it is during our latter years that we can make use of the therapeutic action of colour. Red and orange are the warming and stimulating colours of the spectrum, so softer shades of these colours can stimulate the circulation and contribute to maintaining stamina. Since few senior citizens are attracted to strong reds and oranges, we should make use of softer versions of these colours, for example, peach, apricot, warm tans, terra-cotta, and pink for decorating their rooms.

In our latter years it is natural for our thoughts to turn toward spiritual matters, and this can be reflected in colour choices. Soft blue, lavender, mauve, and violet are colours that connect us to our spiritual side – and it is interesting to note that elderly ladies often use lavender water, and may choose to have a blue hair rinse.

In studies carried out in nursing homes, it was discovered that residents and staff responded well to soft pinky beige colours contrasted with soft blue-greens. These tones are emotionally supporting, physically nourishing, and mentally soothing and peaceful. In addition, the judicious use of floral patterns can evoke the peace and tranquillity of rural life.

BELOW *Soft colours and pretty floral motifs have a light, airy appeal.*

THE FLOWERS HARMONIZE WITH THE DECOR

THE PLUM COLOURED VELVET CHAIR IS A HARMONIZING SHADE FOR THE REST OF THE ROOM

WALLS ARE DELICATELY STRIPED IN A SHADE OF THE BASE COLOUR

THE CRISP WHITENESS OF THE BEDSPREAD PROVIDES RELIEF FROM THE SURROUNDING COLOUR AND TEXTURE

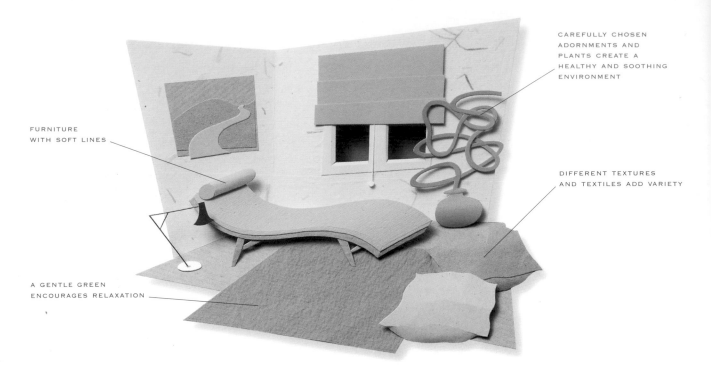

CAREFULLY CHOSEN
ADORNMENTS AND
PLANTS CREATE A
HEALTHY AND SOOTHING
ENVIRONMENT

FURNITURE
WITH SOFT LINES

DIFFERENT TEXTURES
AND TEXTILES ADD VARIETY

A GENTLE GREEN
ENCOURAGES RELAXATION

ABOVE Therapy rooms can achieve a peaceful aura through shades of green associated with nature.

HEALING AND THERAPY ROOMS

The therapeutic qualities of colour lend themselves to healing interiors whether therapy rooms or relaxation areas. Here, colours should encourage relaxation and peace while stimulating and supporting the body's self-healing ability. Warming but gentle colours connect you with the earth's healing energies and give a feeling of safety and protection.

Green has particular beneficial effects. Soft green induces a gentle relaxation because this colour works in harmony with the body's own healing mechanisms. Green and blue have a constrictive therapeutic action, reducing bleeding. However, attention must be paid to the exact tone of green used. Using green on its own can be cold and uninteresting, and it is important to introduce an element of variety and support from soft nurturing colours such as pinks, peaches, warm tans, or creamy yellows.

Although many hospitals are still painted white, presumably because there is a belief that white does not distract the attention of the occupants or disturb patients, recent research has proved that a predominantly white environment does nothing to promote learning or healing. Soothing combinations of soft green, blue, peach, and sunny yellow can make people more alert and physically and mentally healthier, avoiding monotony by stimulating the mental processes while soothing the emotions.

Pastel tints of light blue and green are particularly useful if you need to provide a waiting room, as long as the room is not too dark and cold (in which case use primrose or creamy yellow, apricot or a stronger peach tone). A waiting room is a place where anxieties are amplified; blue can minimize this anxiety.

People with psychological problems require an environment that is mentally uplifting and emotionally nurturing and one that encourages interaction with others and the world around them. The environment should offer interest, variety, and the opportunity to interact with living things, natural materials, textures, colours, and aromas.

The following general guidelines can be used as a basis for colour schemes that are appropriate for people with specific problems.

People who suffer mental debility or depression or who are autistic, have been found to respond particularly well to bright orange and yellow. These colours are mentally stimulating and aid communication and alertness.

People who suffer from insomnia or hyper-activity, or who display aggressive behavior or anger, require the mentally pacifying and balancing effects of green together with the emotionally and physically pacifying and loving vibrations of pink.

People who suffer from delusions, fears, or anxieties need the balancing and soothing qualities of shades of violet such as lavender, mauve, or orchid. These colour energies cleanse the mind of negative thoughts and balance the system through the pineal and pituitary glands.

WORK AREAS

People working in places where little thought has been given to colour schemes, ventilation, and lighting are likely to become ill. Mentally stimulating colours can improve motivation and enhance health, improving productivity, while properly designed rest areas can ensure that we work at optimum levels during working hours. Unfortunately too many workplaces are still painted in dull brown and beige or cold gray and white. These colours are harsh, unfriendly, and often depressing, offering little brightness and relief to a monochrome work environment.

Colour can transform the working conditions of the self-employed from a tiring and oppressive environment to one where they feel motivated and inspired. Work areas can easily be made more pleasing and spacious. Many self-employed people find that they put in longer hours and are under more stress than they were at their employer's place of work. They also tend to duplicate the work environment they have been eager to leave.

ABOVE
Utilitarian "rabbit-hutch" work areas can be demoralizing and depressing.

ABOVE *The Mondrian-inspired storage table is the key to colour accents in this predominantly white room.*

WORKPLACE COLOURS

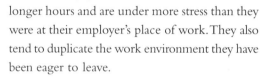

When assessing colours that will benefit a place of work ask yourself the following questions:

- ·Do you have the space and amount of light you need?

- Is your workplace comfortable for you?

- Do you have plants that lend a healing energy to your space?

- Does your environment have the colours you like and feel you need?

- Is the air you breathe fresh?

- Is your work place hot, cold, damp or dry?

- Do you feel you are working to your full capacity?

- Do you feel tired, lethargic, unmotivated, depressed, ill, frustrated, or trapped?

A QUICK GUIDE TO COLOURS FOR ROOM INTERIORS

The following table will provide you with a guide to which colours are appropriate for the various rooms of your house.

COLOUR	EFFECT	USE IN	AVOID IN
Red, *burgundy, brick, wine, Pompeiian red*	*warms, enriches, makes rooms smaller*	*small areas, finishing touches, kitchen, hall, stairs exercise room, playroom*	*bedroom, workshop, healing room, study*
Pink, *rose, blush, salmon, shell*	*nurturing, gently relaxing, sedating, restful*	*nursery (pale), bedroom, kitchen (salmon), therapy room, room for the elderly, young child's room*	*living room, bathroom hall, stairs, study*
Orange, *peach, rust, terra-cotta*	*warming, aids digestion relaxing, gives feeling of support and friendliness*	*kitchen, playroom, living room, dining room, recreation room, bathroom hall, study, bedroom (peach)*	*study, bedroom, office relaxation/therapy room*
Yellow, *primrose, cream, ocher, gold*	*brightens, enlivens, warming sunny, mentally stimulating*	*living room, dining room, family room, kitchen, bedroom (cream only), study (cream)*	*bathroom, bedroom*
Green, *mint, sea green apple green, leaf, fern*	*cools and enlarges space, can be cold and neutral on its own; creates a quiet and tranquil room; darker green gives a rich but natural look*	*kitchen, bedroom, breakfast/dining room, patio conservatory, sitting/living room, relaxation area*	*activity room, cold or dark room*
Turquoise	*creates a cool, larger room fresh, uplifting; does not distract if you need to work but clears the head and aids communication*	*Small room, bathroom, bedroom, study, teenagers room, home gym*	*dining room, playroom*
Blue, *duck egg, Wedgwood, periwinkle, sky, royal*	*creates large cool airy space can be cold and sterile unless balanced with warm colours; relaxing and peaceful*	*treatment room, relaxation area, bedroom, bathroom, sauna, nursery (light blues), study if combined with warm colours*	*dining area, cold or dark room, entertainment area, hallway, stairs*

A QUICK GUIDE TO COLOURS FOR ROOM INTERIORS

COLOUR	EFFECT	USE IN	AVOID IN
Violet, lilac, lavender, orchid	*ensure occupants have personalities that can cope with violet*	*treatment room, bedroom study, meditation room, sanctuary*	*where anyone suffers from mental problems*
Purple	*as above; creates a rich enclosed space, warm but powerful*	*hall (use sparingly), living room, dining room (only with contrasting colour), meditation space*	*kitchen, dining room, office*
Magenta, mulberry, rose salmon, almond, blossom	*as above*	*entrance hall, bedroom, study, room for the elderly (light tints only)*	*office, kitchen, bathroom*
White	*creates a cool and airy feeling*	*use pure white as accent to highlight colours; off-whites come in many shades; all rooms with contrasting colours*	*pure white can be as frightening as pure black, and can also be cold and clinical; use with other colours or soft whites*
Black	*black makes space smaller; like gray it can also be cold and tiring*	*use sparingly to highlight other colours*	*kitchen, dining room, hall, stairway*
Brown	*warm, nurturing, earthy, safe*	*use warm neutrals all areas in floors to set off other colours, furniture.*	*bedroom, living room kitchen, dining room, relaxation room*
Gray, dove gray (warm), steel gray (cold)	*the most neutral of all colours; undistracting, but bland and uninspiring alone*	*use sparingly to highlight other colours*	*where there is anyone suffering from chronic tiredness, fatigue, or depression*
Gold	*sparkle, richness, inspiration*	*use to accent other colours*	*avoid large expanses*
Silver	*coolness, change, feminine*	*use to accent other colours*	*avoid large expanses*

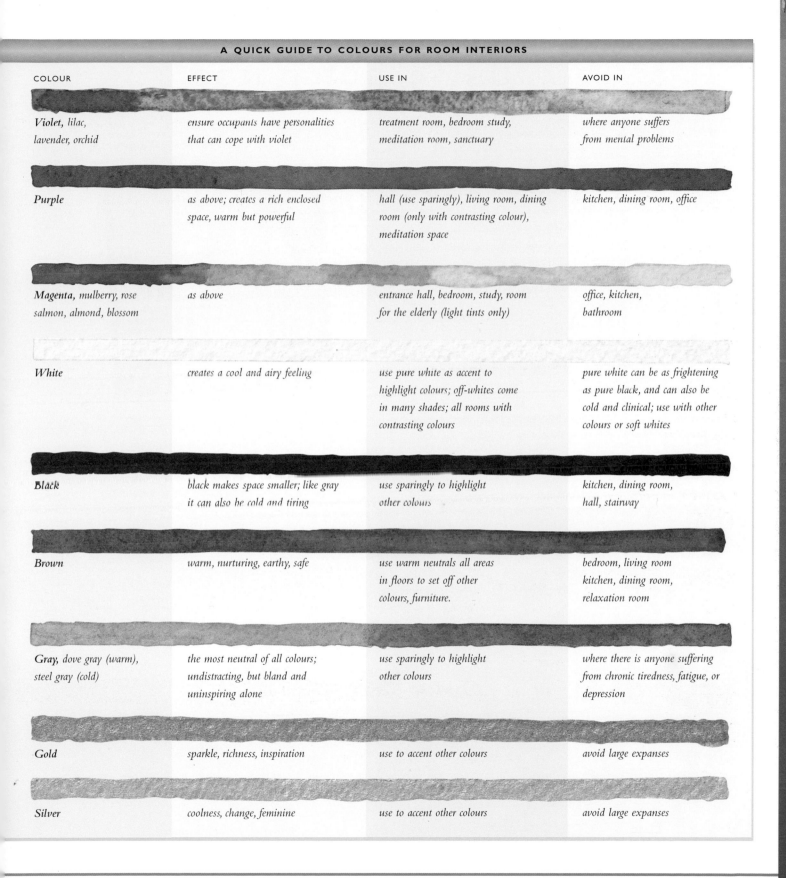

COLOUR IN PUBLIC BUILDINGS

IN LOVE OF HOME, THE LOVE OF COUNTRY HAS ITS RISE.
CHARLES DICKENS, *The Old Curiosity Shop*

RIGHT *Bold geometric designs make these apartment blocks in Salvador, Brazil, unmissable.*

Our local environment is an extension of our home, and being aware of and caring for our immediate surroundings can be a positive step to solving so many problems facing our society today, including our ability to live more harmoniously with each other and conservation of our natural environment.

EFFECTS OF COLOUR

Look at the colours that surround you, in the stores, supermarkets, public library, and school. On your next visit to the dentist, or to see your doctor, look at the colours in the room. Are they helping you relax and feel better, or do they make you feel anxious or ill?

BELOW *A wealth of colourful imagery provides a stimulating educational environment for young children.*

Buildings can be life-suppressing or life-enhancing. The increasingly common condition "sick building syndrome" has resulted in thousands of lost working hours a year. We need to understand how to create environmentally friendly buildings, using colours both inside and out that reflect the atmosphere of the environment in which they are built. The introduction of colour therapeutics into offices and factories can help to humanize the work area.

Colourless public buildings, including doctors' waiting rooms, hospitals, schools, and offices, may appear clean and bright when newly painted, but they soon look shoddy and uninviting. The commonly chosen white or dark, muddy colours are oppressive. Colour can play a major part in providing a relaxing and supporting environment; for instance, it could help provide calming surroundings when visiting a health practitioner. Tests in the U.K. have revealed that people are likely to have a higher blood pressure than normal when visiting a doctor, resulting from the stress felt when waiting for a consultation.

HOUSING DEVELOPMENTS

In many high-rise apartment buildings and public places, muggings, filth, and graffiti have become a scourge. Buildings are often poorly maintained, with no one person taking responsibility for the environment. Interestingly, the trend toward handing the power and the responsibility back to the tenants has proved revelatory. Front doors are now painted a wealth of inspiring colours, lighting is installed in corridors and stairways, and gardens with coloured fences are created. When buildings are brought alive with colour, this acts to foster community spirit. Many dark, dreary places that had been vandalized and defaced on a regular basis are less often the focus of vandals after a clean, brightly coloured coat of paint has been applied. Community gardens have also proved a success in many inner city areas. The garden provides a green space where residents can enjoy, and find inspiration among aromatic and colourful plants.

SCHOOLS

In New York City, colour was used to curb disruptive behavior. Half of a school was painted in therapeutic colours – shades of pink in the corridors and warm beige, creams, blues, and greens in classrooms. Not only was there a marked decrease in violent behavior, but the pupils using this half of the school were reported to be more cooperative, had a greater attention span and obtained higher marks. Some of these ideas on using colours have now been applied in prisons and reform schools in both the United States and the U.K.

PUBLIC RECEPTION AREAS

Many leading hotels use colour therapists to create a friendly atmosphere. Rich bright colours are being used to aid relaxation and give an aura of luxury and comfort, so that hotel lobbies look less impersonal. Green and deep blue are used to aid relaxation, while deep red, peach, and yellow are welcoming.

STEINER SCHOOLS

A hundred years ago, the pioneering educationalist Rudolph Steiner believed that when people were surrounded by living architectural forms and particular colours it had a spiritual influence and an objectively moral effect on their emotional life, in addition to benefiting physical health and mental well-being. Steiner's followers introduced his philosophy of colour into their network of communities, including their schools, using different colours to aid, influence and encourage children through their physical, emotional, and mental development. Young children entering the school were first housed in rounded rooms painted in soft pastel colours. Older children moved into a central shared learning area where stronger and more vibrant colours were used. They then progressed to larger shared work areas in which soft blues and greens were used; these colours were believed to be less distracting to the mental concentration needed at this age.

RIGHT *Younger children at a Steiner school work in soft, pastel-toned classrooms that provide a nurturing environment.*

PART FIVE

COLOUR IN THE GARDEN

The garden is a special place that is just as important as the inside of our home. Through the garden we can directly interact with nature, and the love and attention we give to our gardens will return to us in many ways. Plants give us nourishing food, and more and more people are coming to learn the joys of growing their own fresh produce. Herbs too not only make wonderful additions to meals but also have medicinal qualities.

In this age of technological development the garden is even more important to our emotional and mental well-being. The more we live indoors and away from natural sunlight, the more we will succumb to illness. The plant and animal kingdom can provide us with a form of relaxation and unconditional love we will not be able to find anywhere else. Gardens are good for the soul. The colours found there give us immediate enjoyment and penetrate our subconscious, their influence staying with us for a long time afterward.

Our gardens, like our homes, reflect specific colour preferences and needs. Every garden in some way reflects the personality and attitude of the designer or owner. Therefore we should learn to show sensitivity to the environment while at the same time envelop the art of gardening to enhance our lives with colourful living forms.

If we have a particular imbalance in our lives, whether it be physical, mental, or emotional, a garden can play an important part in the healing process. We can make much more of the healing powers of flowers by creating a garden full of therapeutic colours and scents.

USING SINGLE COLOURS IN THE GARDEN

Different colour vibrations have different healing qualities and single colours in the garden are an opportunity to use the colour group that will set our own natural healing system in motion.

RED TULIPS   BLUE MUSCARI   YELLOW TULIPS   YELLOW FRITILLARIES

ABOVE *A bright spring bulb display: red and yellow tulips mixed with blue muscari and yellow crown imperial fritillaries.*

Some people do not like bright yellow or orange, yet it is often exactly the colour energy these people need. Red, orange, and yellow flowers raise the spirits, and a bed of poppies, marigolds, or zinnias brings a feeling of joy and happiness. At the other end of the spectrum, lavender and blue flowers calm and soothe our nerves.

RED AND PINK

Red is the colour of blood and is full of life-force energy. It is stimulating and eye-catching. Use red in the garden to create a feeling of warmth, movement, and drama. The Japanese use red and white flowers together to signify happiness. Red is especially welcome in colder months, reflecting an air of cheerfulness and warm-heartedness.

If you need to bring more love into your life, plant and think pink. A rose garden of different shades of white, pink, deep rose, and red will send out a message of deep unconditional love through its perfume and

RIGHT *Bulbs can be combined for exciting effects and a welcome splash of colour after a dreary winter.*

colour. By surrounding ourselves with these loving colours, we pick up the pink vibrations and start to exude loving thoughts and vibrations ourselves. A rose garden is particularly healing for those who are suffering from grief, anxiety or emotional trauma, although everyone can enjoy the uplifting qualities.

ORANGE AND GOLD

Gold and orange are the colours of sunshine. If your environment is dark, wet, and cold, then gold and orange flowers can redress the balance, bringing sunny bright vibrations into your life. They will give out a feeling of warmth, like the flames of a fire, and recharge you with energy and vitality. A window box with bright orange-red tulips and orange-yellow daffodils has an uplifting and warming effect in the spring.

Orange flowers particularly have an iridescent quality about their petals and have been known since ancient times as cures for depression.

Orange and golden nasturtium flowers can be eaten in salads or with ice cream, and they are a wonderful cure for nervous anxiety, depression, and tiredness.

YELLOW

Soft yellows are the colours of many spring flowers. Daffodils, narcissi, and primroses herald the new cycle and their energy clears and purifies the ground and air after the decay of winter. Yellow petals reflect ultraviolet light well, especially in the early spring. Primroses, cowslips, daffodils, gorse, and yellow star of Bethlehem attract insects for this reason. If you have a study or desk that is situated near a window, plant yellow flowers outside because the sunny yellow rays will help stimulate the brain.

GREEN

Green is the primary healing colour of any garden, and we all know the benefits of walking in a park, garden, or forest. Green works on the parasympathetic nervous system, which helps the heart relax. When we are surrounded by green we quite naturally start to breathe more slowly and deeply. A tapestry of green foliage on its own will create a tranquil impression, especially if a few coloured flowers are dotted around.

If you need emotional healing, or need to get away from a restrictive situation, think green.

Green creates a feeling of space, which lets you grow in your own time, bringing equilibrium back into a busy or stressful life. It is easy to enjoy the soothing space-giving qualities of green indoors by surrounding your favorite sitting place with green plants.

You can never tire of the unlimited shades of green in a garden, and using foliage colour and architectural leaves gives structure and form to any garden space. Green is naturally the best background colour for a single colour garden, for most colours are complemented and create vivid contrasts or subtle blends with green.

BLUE

Blue combines well with all the other colours in the garden. Planted with white, blue flowers appear fresh and cool and convey the peacefulness of the sky and ocean. Blue flowers add depth and strong healing vibrations to a border filled with pink, lilac and white flowers. As well as herbaceous plants, many shrubs bear beautiful blue flowers. Many types of conifer have blue green or blue-gray needles. These trees cleanse the air. Some grasses have a bluish tinge and bring healing through sound and movement.

LEFT *Golden tulips and buttery wallflowers kick-start the gardening year in the spring.*

BELOW *A blue border is restful and sets off contrasting colours such as yellow.*

NARCISSUS "NICOLE"

HYACINTHUS "BLUE STAR"

ANEMONE BLANDA

RIGHT *The delicate petals of* **Aster amellus** *"King George" decorate the fall garden with misty violet stars.*

INDIGO-VIOLET

If you are tense, fraught, hyped up or suffering from any nervous or mental disorder, a lilac-coloured garden will help soothe the mind. Plant soft mauves and lavenders for when there is tension in the family or anger and violence. These soft, gentle colours help dissolve and purify strong emotions and provide an atmosphere of love and protection. Lavender flowers are particularly useful for the protective and cleansing vibrations that they give out. It is known that during times of plague in the Middle Ages, many lavender sellers survived the disease because of the antiseptic qualities of this beautiful herb, which was constantly with them.

In order to feed your spirituality and to encourage your quest for inner guidance, meditate in a violet and indigo garden. Planting violet flowers will also encourage an array of beautiful butterflies to visit your garden. Some species of butterflies prefer purple flowers, and these delightful visitors can lighten your spirit. Use a cut violet flower, such as a pansy or viola, to act as a reminder of your highest aspirations.

WHITE GARDEN

*A*n all-white garden has a very special healing quality. White is a symbol of purity and reverence and is linked to the feminine energy of the moon. Many night-flowering plants have white flowers whose scent is pervasive and sweet. This scent is of a very high vibration and has a purifying effect on the psyche. People who live in cities and work in a polluted or unhealthy atmosphere may find white flowers particularly cleansing and refreshing.

A green enclosure with white flowers is a special place to sit on a summer's evening or on a hot day. In the late summer evenings, white flowers take on a special iridescent quality, making them stand out dramatically from the dark foliage. An elegant, peaceful setting can be created by adding a white bench and white pergola in a secluded white garden.

White looks good in any garden, so fill yours with white lilies, jasmine, iceberg roses, white valerian, white agapanthus, white foxgloves (digitalis), alyssum, perennial candytuft, hyacinths, iris, dianthus, and campanula. Shrubs and climbers to include are clematis, gardenia, hydrangea, jasmine, magnolia, and azalea. Trees with contrasting foliage include Halesia caroliniana, or for a small garden, Styrax japonica.

White light contains all the other colours within it, and contemplating flowers of this colour instill us with the feeling of the possibility of all things. White roses, carnations, primulas, and daisies make a fresh garden of purity and spirituality. Spending time meditating in a white garden can be a wonderful experience; the fragile beauty will center your mind and uplift you.

ABOVE *The lush petals of* **Rosa** *"Iceberg," backed by fragrant* **Philadelphus**, *light up a summer evening.*

THE COLOURS OF FLOWERS

There are far too many flowers to group effectively by colour, but the following rough
guide lists widely available flower types to help you choose colours that suit you.

POPPIES

RED-ORANGE TO CORAL

- rose, ⟡ poppy ⟡ carnation ⟡ Lychnis
- chalcedonica ⟡ peony ⟡ nasturtium
- dahlia ⟡ kniphofia (red-hot poker) ⟡ zinnia
- pelargonium ⟡ tulip ⟡ begonia ⟡ gladiolus

PANSY

LAVENDER TO PURPLE

- lilac ⟡ violet ⟡ Michaelmas daisy
- sweet pea ⟡ iris ⟡ orchid ⟡ pansy
- freesia ⟡ clematis ⟡ foxglove ⟡ iris
- lavender ⟡ crocus ⟡ anemone ⟡ allium

MARIGOLD

YELLOW TO CREAM

- rose ⟡ honeysuckle ⟡ gladiolus ⟡ tulip
- mimosa ⟡ sunflower ⟡ cowslip ⟡ primrose
- orchid ⟡ Welsh poppy ⟡ dahlia ⟡ crocus
- chrysanthemum ⟡ freesia ⟡ winter jasmine

HOLLYHOCK

MAUVE TO PINK

- rose ⟡ carnation ⟡ sweet william
- sweet pea ⟡ hyacinth ⟡ aster ⟡ peony
- pinks ⟡ delphinium ⟡ hydrangea
- geranium ⟡ pelargonium ⟡ hollyhock

ZINNIA

GREEN

- alchemilla ⟡ moluccella (bells of Ireland)
- bupleurum ⟡ euphorbia ⟡ hellebore
- nicotiniana (tobacco plant – "Lime")
- zinnia ("Envy") ⟡ amaranthus ("Viridis")

JASMINE

IVORY TO WHITE

- rose ⟡ carnation ⟡ gypsophila ⟡ camellia
- magnolia ⟡ peony ⟡ gladiolus ⟡ tulip
- ox-eye daisy ⟡ hyacinth ⟡ syringa
- lily-of-the-valley ⟡ gardenia ⟡ jasmine

DELPHINIUM

BLUE TO INDIGO

- delphinium ⟡ larkspur ⟡ iris ⟡ pansy
- anemone ⟡ bluebell ⟡ hyacinth ⟡ lobelia
- veronica ⟡ ageratum ⟡ anagallis ⟡ aconite
(monkshood) ⟡ centaurea ⟡ meconopsis

BLACK TULIP

BLACK

- black narcissus ⟡ hollyhock ("Nigra")
- Iris ("Black Night") ⟡ black tulip ⟡ pansy
("Bowles Black") ⟡ tacca ("bat plant")

COLOUR COMBINATIONS

*Every colour is modified by the colour next to it. Colours planted
in harmonies are just like the gently rising and falling notes on a musical
scale. So these combinations are restful and gentle on the eye.*

RIGHT *The
harmonizing shades of*
Achillea *"Forncett
Candy,"* **Salvia viridis,
Papaver somniferum,**
and **Dianthus** *make a
delightful blend.*

We can never completely control the colours in the garden because of colour associations. There are times when we wish to create gardens reflecting certain colours, but however carefully we control the flower colour scheme, the colours from the sky, buildings, earth, and those created by people and animals will intrude and contrast with our chosen colours. Remember, however, that in nature no colours clash; the colours of many indigenous plants are very subtle, and mingle to create beautiful and surprising effects. You can use the laws of colour to create colour combinations that give different effects in the garden, using the colours of flowers, berries, and foliage to weave a flower tapestry.

COLOUR HARMONIES

To achieve a harmonious effect, choose colours that lie next to each other on the colour wheel; or use different tints and shades of the same colour. For instance, you can plant a corner of the garden with flowers of white, pink and rosy hues; fill another area with blues and lilacs.

The healing effects of colour harmonies in the garden work together more gently than those that rely on strong contrasts. Related colours are more relaxing and subtle in their effects and a garden of this type is good for spending time sitting quietly. This allows you to slow down and relax so that you become more sensitive to the softer colour vibrations.

BELOW *Use the
colour wheel to select
complementary colours,
placed opposite
each other.*

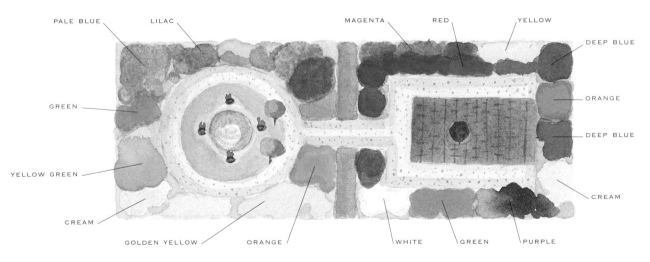

PALE BLUE   LILAC   MAGENTA   RED   YELLOW

DEEP BLUE

GREEN

ORANGE

YELLOW GREEN

DEEP BLUE

CREAM

CREAM   GOLDEN YELLOW   ORANGE   WHITE   GREEN   PURPLE

COLOUR CONTRASTS

If you wish to achieve a more dramatic look, you can strengthen the effect of the colours by planting complementary colours next to each other. Here, each colour enhances its partner and makes it appear more intense. Gardens made with striking contrasting colours send out powerful vibrations. They create an impact when viewed from a distance and their individual healing qualities become more pronounced as you move in closer.

You can use this approach with any shape of bed. For instance, try an all blue and pink border with a splash of orange, the complementary colour to blue. Violet flowers are best planted with yellow, their complementary and harmonizing colour energy. Yellow is also the colour of the mind, so using these colours together will help you to communicate with your inner wisdom. Violet and yellow are also linked to creativity, so while walking in this dual colour garden you will find creative inspiration. For extra impact, try a purple and yellow border, with a splash of red as an accent colour. Green and red are also complementary contrasts. Green is a perfect foil for both red and pink.

UNUSUAL COLOUR COMBINATIONS

In one part of the garden, you may wish to create a particularly vivid and dramatic effect. You can easily do this by using a broad variety of non-complementary combinations.

As a strong background for yellow flowers, blue makes them look more intense. Similarly, deep pink looks vivid against a pale blue.

Dissonant colours (see p 120) are useful in gardens in which you wish to emphasize the healing qualities of a particular colour. Bright red or magenta planted with deep violet would help you heal through physical regeneration and transformation. If you planted orange with pink and lilac, the orange energy would fortify and stimulate emotional and spiritual healing.

Late summer produces some of the best and most violent colour combinations. Dahlias, gladioli, chrysanthemums, red-hot pokers, heliotropes – the list is endless.

A RAINBOW EFFECT

One way of making sure your garden reflects all the colours of the rainbow is to plant a colour wheel. This concept was popularized by the 19th-century British artist and gardener Gertrude Jekyll. Mark out a wheel and divide it into 12 segments. For a restful scheme, plant each of the colours in the same order as adjacent colours on the wheel, so that blue moves gently into lilac and purple, red into orange, and orange into yellow.

LEFT *A park bedding scheme makes effective use of colour contrasts.*

BELOW *Create a striking impact at one end of the garden with a flower bed of vibrant rainbow colours.*

HOT AND COLD COMBINATIONS

Colour themes can be used to create effects such as warmth or coolness, and visually increasing depth (*see* p 116). Yellows and apricots combined with green achieve warmth, while red is the warmest colour of all. The degree of warmth depends on the shade; deep shocking pink is much warmer than a soft pale pink.

Warm gardens are energizing and work well in city gardens where the endless gray environment drains us of energy. In dull, rainy weather the bright colours of a warm garden lift our spirits and help keep us optimistic and bright. Plants that have red orange or gold colours are particularly welcome in a dark area of a garden or planted in tubs close to the house.

Green is nature's harmonizing force and in itself is cool and relaxing. It is a perfect foil to almost every colour. Other cool colours include shades of blue, lilac, lavender, and white. Many herbs have flowers reflecting paler and cooler colours and often have very refined aromas. If you plant medicinal and culinary herbs you will appreciate the healing effects of the subtle colouring and scents while you are working in the garden (*see* p 181).

FOLIAGE COLOURS

RED CHOKEBERRY

HEUCHERA

RED

❧ cornus (dogwood) ❧ Parrotia persica ❧ cotinus (smoke tree) ❧ fothergilla ❧ vitis (Japanese glory vine) ❧ Virginia creeper ❧ Rosa virginiana ❧ acer (ornamental maple) ❧ liquidambar ❧ katsura tree ❧ red oak ❧ scarlet oak ❧ stag's horn sumach ❧ red chokeberry ❧ Euonymus alatus

PURPLE-BRONZE

❧ castor oil plant ❧ heuchera ("Purple Palace") ❧ euphorbia ("Fireglow") ❧ ajuga ("Atropurpurea") ❧ sedum ("Atropurpureum") ❧ phormium ("Purpureum") ❧ rodgersia, berberis ("Atropurpurea") ❧ Rosa glauca ❧ prunus ("Pissardii") ❧ Acer palmatum ("Atropurpureum")

GOLDEN CYPRESS

SEA HOLLY

GOLD

❧ golden heather ❧ berberis ("Aurea") ❧ golden elder ❧ golden hop ❧ ivy ("Buttercup") ❧ philadelphus ("Aureus") ❧ hosta ("Golden Prayers") ❧ lonicera ("Baggessen's Gold") ❧ holly ("Flavescens") ❧ corylus ("Aurea") ❧ gleditsia ("sunburst") ❧ robinia ("Frisia")

SILVER-GRAY

❧ sea holly ❧ Stachys lanata (lamb's ears) ❧ artemisia ("Lambrook Silver") ❧ cineraria ❧ santolina ❧ pinks ❧ buddleia ("Argentia") ❧ Helichrysum splendidum ❧ blue-gray cypress (Cupressus glauba)

If you plant light or bright colours in front of darker hues they will appear to advance, giving greater depth. Planting hot colours such as red or orange in front of cool blues and violets, or green, will also give a greater impression of depth.

FOLIAGE COLOURS AND SHAPES

Often a garden can provide the most enriching experience when we have to look closely at the subtle changes of colours in the leaves and foliage. When considering what foliage to plant in a garden, introduce gold and silver colours for extra sparkle. Golden leaves are often shiny and reflect more light on dull or wet days. Many silvery gray leaves are soft or covered with fine hairs. This foliage stands out against darker greens and adds an air of mystery and luxury. Gray foliage is an excellent colour background for pink and creates a feeling of freshness when combined with white. Many gray-leaved plants are drought resistant, so they are good for a hot, dry spot.

The form and structure of the plant create areas of light and dark; this can also play an important part in the colour scheme. Large leaves can add height and provide a cool shelter for smaller shade-loving plants. Leaf shapes can also provide contrast of colour and texture especially against garden ornaments and buildings.

Bamboo and grasses

Grasses come in a range of eye-catching colours. Their leaves vary between green, green-gray, bronze, silver, and yellow. Other grasses can be used to create movement and whispering sounds in the garden. Each has its own characteristic sound; giant bamboo (*Bambusa multiplex*, which grows up to 50 feet) creaks and moans, while the tiny squirrel-tail grass (*Hordeum jubatum*, which grows to 2 feet), whispers softly in the wind.

Grasses need not be planted individually and can be integrated into the mixed planting of a border, but there are some grasses, such as *Glyceria maxima variegata* which can spread voraciously. You can create an area of grasses in the garden especially if you have a dry sunny spot. A pampas looks especially good when grown on its own. Put one in the lawn or graveled area, in an atrium or courtyard garden.

Grasses give shape and form to a Japanese-style garden and blend in particularly well with a modern style house or building. Grow potted grasses and bamboos in a conservatory or roof terrace, surrounding the pots with stones, or place them in a pebble or graveled area.

COLOURS OF GRASSES

SEDGE GRASS

RED

- *sedge* (Carex buchananii)
- Inperata cylindrica (*"Rubra"*)
- *feather grass* (Stipa arundinacea *"Autumn Tints"*) *prairie cord grass* (Panicum virgatum *"Rubrum"*)

SUGAR CANE GRASS

YELLOW

- Hakonechloa macra (*"Aureola"*) *hardy sugar cane* (Miscanthus sinensis *"Zebrinus"*)
- Spartina pectinata (*"Aureomarginata"*)

SHEEP'S FESCUE

BLUE

- *sheep's fescue* (Festuca glauca)
- Helictotrichon sempervirens
- Kowleria glauca Sasleria caerulea

MANNA GRASS

WHITE

- *manna grass* (Glyceria maxima *"Variegata"*) *hardy sugar cane* (Miscanthus sinensis *"Variegatus"*)
- *gardeners' garters* (Phalaris arundinacea *"Picta"*)

CHANGING COLOURS
IN THE GARDEN

A garden is more than a careful placing of plants. Its atmosphere is created by life in its many forms. This is subject to constant change in the weather, movement of the materials in the paths and structures, and the presence of visiting birds, insects, and mammals.

Colours will vary according to the growth of the plant. Colour changes occur not only with different-coloured flowers and foliage but also with changes in weather and the time of day. Throughout the year also, each season has its distinctive colours, feelings, sensations, and energy flow. Nature is full of changing colours that create different harmonies and beauty.

COLOUR CHANGES
THROUGH THE DAY

Certain colours tend to be more prevalent at particular times of the day and this ever-changing quality of light helps regulate our body clock and psychological rhythms. The sun's rays have been found to have a bias to a particular colour as the

rays lengthen and shorten, and as the Earth moves around the sun. Each day therefore gives us a cycle of colours from the pale morning light through the brightness of the day to the splendid colours of sunset.

Just before sunrise the early morning light is tinged with a pale green and as the sun comes up the light takes on a stronger yellow tone. The colours in the garden in the early morning will be more reflective and softer especially if there has been an early morning dew. As the morning progresses, the rays get hotter and the light changes to a strong golden-yellow, which we associate with the midday sun. During the middle of the day, colours become more brilliant, standing out in contrast against dark shadows.

BELOW LEFT
A garden year: in the spring, this garden has a palette of pinks, blues, and mauves.

BELOW RIGHT
The same garden in the summer. An expanded colour scheme brings in highlights of yellow and white.

During the afternoon the golden–orange ray becomes stronger, casting a peachy glow on everything. sunset is the time we see the sky streaked with bright pinks and crimson. In the late afternoon, colours take on a sharp and iridescent quality. In the summer months the sun may tinge everything with a golden hue. Photographers often choose the late afternoon as the best time to take pictures because of this clarity of colour.

As the sun sinks low on the horizon, the colour of the sky intensifies, first revealing a violet hue and then a deep indigo. Later in the evening the sky changes to a deep midnight blue. Even on the darkest night there is always some light, but we can only see the deep-coloured rays of the night sky when they are reflected to the Earth by the moon. Deep blue changes to green in the early hours and the daily colour cycle starts again.

COLOUR CHANGES THROUGH THE SEASONS

The cycle of colour energy found in nature throughout the year has a profound effect on our lives. Without it our own internal rhythms become confused and we start to loose a feeling of connection with ourselves and others. If our life is in harmony with the seasonal colours we feel in tune with nature resulting in a feeling of wholeness and contentment.

In the spring, as the sap rises, our spirits feel light and airy after the short dark days of winter. By the time summer arrives we are highly active and busy, so we respond and appreciate the bright rich colours of action and vitality. In the fall, the colours of fallen leaves and earth become all-important, drawing our energy downward and inward. At no other time is the quality of the light such a major contributing factor to the achievement of the overall effect. During the winter we conserve our physical energy and turn our thoughts to study and inner development.

Spring colours start off pale and deepen to beautiful yellows, blues, and mauves. In the summer, fill your garden with flowering trees, shrubs, and plants in red, orange, and yellow. Follow this by late summer and fall flowers in golden oranges. Plant deciduous trees for fall colours. Wintertime should include red-stemmed trees and plants bearing deep indigo and crimson berries.

BELOW LEFT
By the fall, the colours are toasted orange, cinnamon, and russet: ripe, warm, earthy tones.

BELOW RIGHT
In the winter, skeletal plant forms have their own beauty, especially when iced with snow.

PRIMULA VULGARIS
(PRIMROSE)

Summer

Red, orange and yellow flowers provide the stimulating vibrations we need during the active season of summer. These bright, warm hues reflect the colours of the sun and sky and provide a joyful summer energy. A country garden in full bloom is a rainbow of beautiful colours. The colours are bright and wondrous and are set off against a carpet of rich green.

PLANTS FOR SEASONAL COLOUR

Spring

At first the soft pastel colours of the blossoms help us stir slowly and happily. Little white snowdrops start the process of cleansing as they help purify the earth after months of decay. We are then uplifted by the bright, clear colours of the spring bulbs; these are mostly yellow, which lifts the spirits, stimulates the mind, and has a warming effect, and purple, which helps purify and cleanse the body and soul.

PLANTS FOR SPRING COLOUR

- *Plant white and pink early-flowering bulbs to wake you gently after the dark winter. Use snowdrops, anemone, aconites, and pink and white crocuses followed by early-flowering tulips and irises.*

- *Create a feature of* Magnolia stellata. *This tree has delicate star-shaped white flowers, which send out sparkling healing rays of white light. Plant pink primula underneath it.*

- *Plant blue grape hyacinths with daffodils, tulips, and narcissus in a sunny position to focus and stimulate the mind.*

- *Create a glowing carpet with yellow primroses interspersed with bluebells in the shade.*

- *Use shrubs to create a woodland effect: magnolia, forsythia, rhododendron, and azalea.*

PLANTS FOR SUMMER COLOUR

- *You can enrich orange and yellow flowers by planting them close to shrubs with copper and bronze foliage. Grow* Prunus x cistena *as a backing hedge.* Calendula officinalis *can be planted with lilies and euphorbia.*

- *Grow complementary colours such as a catmint (blue-violet) border in front of yellow roses, and lavender bushes between pink and red roses.*

- *Deep pinks, white, and crimson hollyhocks create an uplifting border.*

- *Create an arbor or archway planted with intermingling creamy yellow and violet-coloured climbers. Use clematis, honeysuckle, jasmine, and passionflowers. Their sweet perfume and colours provide a perfect place to read or just to sit and contemplate.*

ALCEA ROSEA (HOLLYHOCK)

Fall

In the fall there is a deepening and richness to the colour tones – oranges and russet browns of the fall flowers and leaves, ripened ears of wheat and barley, poppy buds, vine leaves, fruits, and berries. Yellow turns to gold, orange turns to russet, and red turns to rust. Blue and violet berries appear, reminding us that it is time to store our energy for the cold and short days ahead.

PLANTS FOR FALL COLOUR

- *Create perfect harmonies of colour with ornamental vines, Japanese maples, sedums, and polygonums.*
- *Plant shrubs that bear vivid-coloured fruits: pyracanthas, holly, cotoneaster, or berberis.*
- *Create a gold garden with sunflowers, Michaelmas daisies, dahlias, goldenseal, helianthus, and ornamental cabbages.*

HELIANTHUS (SUNFLOWER)

PLANTS FOR WINTER COLOUR

- *Red and yellow-stemmed dogwood glows in the winter light.*
- *Plant a window box with the complementary colours of gold and violet for winter inspiration. Use variegated herbs and ivy with winter heathers.*
- *For a splash of fire in a winter garden, plant a trio of firethorns (pyrancanthas) bearing gold, orange, and red berries. Your garden will come alive with colourful birds.*
- *Christmas and Lenten roses (hellebores) have blooms of exquisite colours – green edged with purple, white tinged with purple or deep maroon.*
- *Plant clusters of early-flowering snowdrops. Plant these lovingly even in a small garden and take delight in discovering them each year.*

HELEBORUS ORIENTALIS (LENTEN ROSE)

Winter

Winter is a time of strong contrasts. Bright red berries are set against dark greens of evergreen trees and shrubs, and small white flowers stand out against the dark silhouettes of the landscape. White flowers show up against the dark shapes of the trees. Magestic reds and purples contrasted with gold provide us with inspiration and a feeling of celebration. Winter gardens come into their own if they are planted with evergreens and fruit-bearing shrubs and trees. A red-fruited crab apple makes a spectacular display against a frosty winter border. Red-stemmed boxwoods shine in the winter sunlight, and silvery blue cypress reminds us that there is still life in the dormant winter months.

WILD GARDENS

If we are to preserve our indigenous plant and wildlife, every garden should have a wild area. Few people have a garden large enough to create a full-scale woodland garden, but the joys of a shady dell can be made by scaling down the features found in nature.

ABOVE *Wild flowers in the countryside–a beautiful palette that can be a source of inspiration when planting flower borders in the garden.*

In a corner of a garden you could plant small trees to provide dappled shade. Paths should meander and look as natural as possible. The shade cast by the trees provides a home for many lovely woodland plants. For the spring you can plant a carpet of bluebells and yellow–green spurge (euphorbia), and if you plant carefully you will also enjoy dainty woodland anemones, violets, snowdrops and primroses. A woodland garden can also be full of wildlife; include some nesting boxes for birds and animals.

A wild part of the garden does not have to be located in the shade. In sunny conditions it should include unpruned native wild roses and herbs such as marjoram, chicory, and thyme, and the flowers of salvia, wild bellflower, creamy meadowsweet, and pale harebells.

We may contrive the colours in our garden, but although we think we can see clearly the colour of plants, they have many colours that are seen by animals but not by us (*see* p 22). So do keep a natural part in your garden, where nature can arrange the colours and change them for you.

WILDFLOWER COLOURS

RED-PINK

- poppy
- scarlet pimpernel (Anagallis)
- corn cockle (Agrostemma)
- mallow
- foxglove
- hellebore (Silene)
- germander
- pink campion
- dog rose (Rosa canina)
- briar rose (Rosa eglanteria)
- coneflower (Echinacea)
- soapwort

YELLOW-ORANGE

- marsh marigold
- primrose
- cowslip
- St. John's wort
- tansy
- yellow flag
- broom
- mullein (Verbascum)
- elecampane
- arnica
- wallflower
- poppy
- yellow foxglove

BLUE

- bellflower (Campanula)
- forget-me-not (Myosotis)
- scabious
- gentian
- bluebell
- harebell
- cornflower (Centaurea)

INDIGO-VIOLET

- fritillary
- milk thistle (Silybum)
- violet
- periwinkle
- pasque flower (Pulsatilla)
- heartsease (wild pansy)

WHITE

- hellebore
- daisy
- meadowsweet
- wild clematis
- bellflower (Campanula)
- white campion (Silene)
- lily of the valley
- sweet woodruff
- sweet cicely
- white foxglove

If you don't have space for a "wild" garden, bring yourself closer to nature by introducing less formal features – a stream, pond, trees or stones can all contribute to the feeling of natural beauty and imbue the garden with healing vibrations.

HERB GARDENS

Herbs are wonderful plants for small spaces. Planted outside a window they bring calm and balance into the day. Place them near a kitchen, bathroom, or any area where you wish to relax.

≪ Grow edible flowers. A basket or tub of brightly coloured heartsease, nasturtiums, and marigolds reflects the joy and energy of summer.

≪ The flowers of many herbs are edible. Try borage, camomile, chervil, chives, wild garlic, lavender, wild marjoram, mint, sage, thyme, and lemon verbena.

≪ Outline a formal herb garden in golden box; fill in with cotton lavender, purple sage, golden thyme or marjoram, salvia, iris, and rosemary.

≪ Grow a container filled with different aromatic mints. Combine applemint, ginger mint, spearmint, catmint, and peppermint.

HERB COLOURS

RED-PINK

≪ *bergamot (oswego tea)*
≪ *thyme* ≪ *coriander*
≪ *caraway* ≪ *hyssop*
≪ *pink lavender*
≪ *lungwort*
≪ *apothecaries' rose*
≪ *pink rosemary*

ORANGE

≪ *marigold* ≪ *nasturtium*

YELLOW-GOLD

≪ *rue* ≪ *fennel* ≪ *dill*
≪ *camomile* ≪ *marjoram*
≪ *golden feverfew* ≪ *lemon balm*
≪ *thyme* ≪ *golden sage*

GREEN

≪ *lovage* ≪ *ginger* ≪ *hops*

BLUE

≪ *borage* ≪ *hyssop*
≪ *rosemary* ≪ *lungwort*
≪ *chicory* ≪ *rue*
≪ *linseed (foliage)*

INDIGO-VIOLET

≪ *chives* ≪ *lavender*
≪ *mint* ≪ *sage* ≪ *savory*
≪ *thyme* ≪ *basil*
≪ *oregano* ≪ *marjoram*
≪ *verbena* ≪ *comfrey*

PURPLE-BRONZE

≪ *purple sage (foliage)*
≪ *purple basil* ≪ *castor oil plant*
≪ *bronze fennel*

WHITE

≪ *white lavender* ≪ *white rosemary* ≪ *anise* ≪ *angelica*
≪ *caraway* ≪ *thyme*
≪ *sweet marjoram* ≪ *verbena*
≪ *lemon balm (Melissa)*

SILVER-GRAY

≪ *lavender*
≪ *curry plant* ≪ *southernwood*
≪ *cotton lavender (Santolina)*

VARIEGATED

≪ *silver thyme (foliage)* ≪ *sage "Tricolour"* ≪ *gilded rosemary*
≪ *lungwort* ≪ *ginger mint*

CALENDULA
(MARIGOLD)

ALLIUM
SHOENOPRASUM
(CHIVES)

MELISSA OFFICINALIS
(LEMON BALM)

THYMUS
(THYME)

LEFT *Grow an aromatic herb garden, filling it with both medicinal and culinary herbs, creating fragrance and colour.*

BRINGING FLOWERS INDOORS

If we are unable to get out into the wilderness, we can tune into natural colour cycles by bringing the outside in.

The use of cut flowers, floral arrangements, and pot plants in the home, office, schools, and hospitals can bring a burst of colour into our lives and have an uplifting effect on the body, mind, and soul. A container with a bright red poinsettia or red and yellow tulips will bring sparkle to illuminate any dark room.

Using cut flowers in our homes is one of the best ways we can harmonize with nature's changing colour patterns. This is especially important in towns and cities where we are cut off from nature's parade of colours. Not only can we help our mood with a bunch of flowers in a certain colour, but we can enrich our homes and offices with arrangements of fresh or dry flowers for a longer-lasting effect. Even the most humble home can be transformed by a bowl of flowers. A small arrangement on a simple table by the front door can give out a colourful and aromatic welcome on your return home.

When flowers are expensive or scarce, try using greenery only. Herbs can make an informal, fragrant centerpiece on a dining table, which will not go unnoticed.

You can also create wonderful arrangements full of texture and colour using berries, dried branches with moss or lichen, or by placing just one or two flowers in a vase.

COLOUR ENERGY

If you have access to a garden or flower market, a bowl of blue hydrangeas sends out calming energy and has the effect of drawing the eye, providing a focus for the mind. The heady perfume is a feast for the senses. A vase of vibrant tulips virtually explodes with starlike energy rays in all directions.

CHOOSE VIBRANT COLOURS

COMPLEMENT YOUR ROOM'S COLOUR SCHEME WITH THE RIGHT COLOUR FLOWER

RIGHT *Create a welcoming burst of colour in your hallway with a brightly coloured arrangement.*

LARGE LEAVES ADD CONTRAST

FLOWERS AT THE DINING TABLE

It is not only the dining table that benefits from an arrangement of flowers. A couple of flowers on a breakfast tray or picnic blanket will be appreciated and can make any occasion into a special one. Use flowers in cooking, and in the bath for an exquisite sensation and healing effect.

Most of us no longer eat or sit together at the dining table on a regular basis, so we are losing out on the wonderful benefits of eating together. However, mealtimes can provide an opportunity each day to spend time with our families; if you live alone, having a meal with a friend allows natural and essential social interaction.

The benefits to our digestion from feeling relaxed while we eat are obvious since we are better able to absorb nutrition from our food.

Low, wide vases are best for a table arrangement; they are stable and don't obscure people at the other side of the table. To create a sumptuous centerpiece, fill a large round bowl with damp foam or crumpled wire. Add flowers all over combined with touches of variegated foliage. Work around the bowl to achieve a domed effect.

If you have a small garden or live in an apartment, collect some petals and interesting shaped leaves. Float these in a wide bowl. Add floating candles of harmonious colours to this simple but spectacular feature.

A romantic dinner can be enhanced if you crown the table with an intoxicating glass of roses. Pack blooms densely in varying shades of the same colours. Add deep crimson touches in the form of rosebuds.

When eating alone it is important to spoil yourself by setting a table properly, including placing a vase of flowers in front of you. While enjoying your dinner you can soak up their positive radiations.

ABOVE *Use your imagination to create an original table centerpiece when you are expecting guests.*

FOLIAGE CREATES BALANCE

A MIXTURE OF BOLD COLOURS

FLOWER COLOUR COMBINATIONS FOR INDOOR ARRANGEMENTS

❧ *A posy of vibrant violets, pansies, or violas harmonizes with a country-style bedroom and complements a small room decorated in yellow.*

❧ *Use large leaves, vines, dried twigs, and branches to add height and contrast to an arrangement in a large room. These will set off a few big flowerheads. Choose hydrangeas, lilies, gladioli, or euphorbia with hosta leaves.*

❧ *For pure simplicity, and to add an air of serenity to a room, place a few pure white arum lilies or white irises in a clear glass vase.*

❧ *Bring a sunburst of colour to a dark room or when you feel depressed with a blue or green vase full of poppies. Watch the flowers as they move and dance with each new day.*

LEFT AND CENTER *Tables can be enhanced with floral arrangements of either fresh or dried flowers.*

POTPOURRI

*Potpourri is a wonderful source of year-round enjoyment of colour
and scent. If you have a garden it is very satisfying to make your own, but
if you buy potpourri from a store think about the colours, aromas, and
textures that create the feelings you need at that time of year.*

Many commercial potpourris have been treated with artificial sprays and dyes, but you can spot these easily for the colours look unnaturally bright.

Potpourri can be displayed in all sorts of containers and in almost every room in the house. The combination of the colour energy and the aroma will pervade the room with subtle and healing vibrations. It is best to choose a container whose colour is either in the same range as the flowers or of a contrasting or complementary colour, which will accentuate the colour vibrations.

The following recipes will help you to create your own potpourri using specific colours and scents (*see* p 17 for specific flower colours). The colours will magnify the effect of the fragrance and will give your home a permanent aura of freshness and harmony.

☙ To make the following potpourris by the dry method, place the spices, fixatives, and oils in a plastic airtight container. Mix thoroughly.

☙ In a mixing bowl place all the floral material and then pour over the fixative mixture, making sure it is thoroughly stirred.

☙ Place the potpourri in an airtight container and leave in a dark place for six weeks. Shake the container every day for the first week.

☙ After six weeks the potpourri will be ready to display in an open container. Remember to stir it every so often and add oils when necessary.

BELOW *Enjoy the scent and colour of your favorite flowers all year round by making an aromatic potpourri.*

Pink and white mix

This sweet and floral potpourri has delicate colour and aromatic vibrations that give out loving and emotional healing. They help balance the feminine aspect within us so that we become more caring and nurturing of ourselves and each other.

INGREDIENTS

- *4 cups mixed fresh flower petals in shades of pink and white*
- *2oz/50g mixed fresh mint, marjoram, rosemary*
- *2oz/50g lavender flowers*
- *4 bay leaves*
- *1 tbsp/15g cinnamon powder*
- *2.5ml cloves*
- *½ oz/12g finely ground gum benzoin*
- *¼tsp nutmeg*

METHOD

Divide the mixture in half, using white petals for one half and pink for the other. Layer the two colours in a tall glass jar or vase.

LEFT *The delicate colours and fragrance of the pink and white mix potpourri send out loving vibrations.*

Yellow and orange mix

This lemony potpourri has sweet-smelling yellow and orange flowers. A lively coloured mixture, it is suitable for a study, family room or dining room. Put this pot-pourri in a green bowl.

INGREDIENTS

- *4 cups flowers and petals in shades of yellow and orange*
- *2tbsp/30g mixed sweet herbs*
- *1tbsp/15g orris root powder*
- *1tbsp/15g lavender*
- *2tsp/10g cinnamon powder*
- *½tsp grated nutmeg*
- *½tsp of whole cloves*
- *a few pieces of lemon and orange peel*
- *3 drops lemon oil*
- *3 drops geranium oil*

RIGHT *This yellow and orange mix will enhance any study, living room or dining room.*

Blue and violet mix

Blue and violet potpourri has a lovely calming, soothing effect for any room. It will suit a traditional living room, placed in a blue and white china dish or basket, or suit a modern interior if displayed in a blue glass bowl.

INGREDIENTS

- *4 cups petals and flowers in shades of blue, lavender and violet*
- *2tbsp/30g mixed green-leafed sweet herbs*
- *1tbsp/15g lavender*
- *1tbsp/15g orris root powder*
- *½tsp/2.5g whole cloves*
- *½tsp/2.5g allspice*
- *3 blades ground mace*
- *3 drops lavender oil*
- *2 drops of bergamot oil*

Woody mix

This traditional masculine mix has a sharp and pervasive aroma and rich warm colours. Make a scented sachet and place it in a drawer, or an attractive wicker basket on a table or desk.

INGREDIENTS

- *4 cups sandalwood shavings*
- *12 small fir cones*
- *1tbsp/15g bergamot leaves*
- *1tbsp/15g orris root powder*
- *4 drops sandalwood oil*
- *4 drops bergamot oil*
- *½tbsp whole cloves*

RIGHT *This pungent woody mix is a warming, earthy addition to any room.*

GIVING FLOWERS

*We give flowers to show emotion on many occasions, but it is a
pity that so few of us are aware of the personal messages we could send
with flowers. We all send bunches of flowers on occasions of births, weddings,
deaths, and illnesses, and to display thanks and love, but we could say so
much more by more careful choice of the flowers.*

ABOVE *In Hawaii,
flower garlands, or leis,
originally had religious
significance. Today they
are presented as a
greeting or worn on
special occasions.*

Both flowers and herbs carry a wealth of meanings and messages that have been used since
antiquity and are rapidly being lost.

It is not only the symbolism we have given
to the flowers but also their colour and scent that
makes our choice for special occasions appropriate or not. When sending flowers to someone
who is ill, try to choose the flowers of a colour
beneficial to that illness. (*See the list of ailments*
p 200.) Also, remember that if the patient is very
ill then bright rich colours will be too heavy on
the eye. So stick to lovely soft pastels until the
person is well on the road to recovery.

THE COLOURS OF FLOWERS

- *Red flowers have traditionally meant love (of a
  sexual and passionate nature).*

- *Pink flowers are associated with a higher love
  and affection, and white with pure spiritual love.
  Someone who is grieving will appreciate a gift of
  a bouquet of deep pink flowers, which sends out
  a deep and powerful message of universal love
  and tenderness.*

- *New homeowners will be pleased to receive a
  pot plant or bunch of brightly coloured orange,
  pink, and red flowers. (Include peppermint for
  warmth and marigolds for happiness.)*

- *Yellow flowers would be a good choice for a
  student about to write an exam since yellow
  stimulates and aids clarity of thought.*

- *If you wish to send flowers to a mother with a
  newborn child, send a posy of blue/lilac flowers.*

- *Violet and magenta send out strong rays of
  aspiration and inspiration and are best used in
  ceremonial settings or spiritual places. A tiny
  bowl of violets can brighten up any corner with
  intense colour and hidden aroma.*

ABOVE *Soft blue and
lilac make a suitable
bouquet for a new mother
and her baby.*

ANCIENT BELIEFS

- *Hyacinth was a favorite flower for bridal
  wreaths in Ancient Greece and Rome and
  is still a favorite today.*

- *Myrtle, with its white, sweet-smelling flowers and
  lustrous dark leaves, preceded orange blossom in the
  bridal bouquet.*

- *Laurel leaves were much used as victory wreaths in*

*Ancient Rome and Greece. These were a lovely
deep green, showing a harmony between body
and mind.*

- *Many island cultures offer strangers a garland of
  flowers to welcome them.*

- *White flowers with a sweet scent such as jasmine,
  or frangipani, show respect and friendship.*

People love to be given flowers; they uplift the spirit and pervade the house with their colour and perfume, so don't wait for a special occasion to spoil yourself or a friend. Choose your bouquet according to the language of flowers. Attach a card telling your friend the meaning of the flowers you have chosen, so he or she can focus on (and enjoy!) the message contained in them.

THE LOST LANGUAGE OF FLOWERS

- *Red rosebuds and roses are for love.*
- *Red tulips are for a declaration of love.*
- *Red nasturtiums are for patriotism.*
- *Scarlet poppies are for consolation.*
- *Pink carnations are for deep love.*

ABOVE *A bouquet of red roses sends a message of love and is traditionally given on Valentine's Day. Pink carnations or red tulips also communicate love.*

- *Orange blossom is for fertility and happiness.*
- *Yellow buttercups are for memories of childhood, or riches.*
- *Yellow camomile is for wisdom or serenity.*
- *Blue cornflowers are for hope and unity.*
- *Blue forget-me-nots are for fidelity.*
- *Blue violets are for loyalty.*
- *Lilac is for first love.*
- *White lilies are for purity.*

- *White violets are for innocence.*
- *White chrysanthemums are for truth.*
- *White honeysuckle is for fidelity.*
- *Honeysuckle is for secret affection.*
- *Pansies are for love.*
- *Hyacinths are for constancy, or for sport or play.*
- *Daisies are for faithfulness.*
- *Fern is for fascination.*
- *Jasmine is for joy.*
- *Lavender is for silence.*
- *Rosemary is for remembrance.*
- *Basil is for love.*
- *Parsley is for festivity.*
- *Mint is for virtue.*
- *Coriander is for worthiness.*
- *Marjoram is for joy and fertility.*
- *Mint is for wisdom.*
- *Peppermint is for warmth.*
- *Sage is for esteem.*
- *Purple sage is for riches or health.*

RIGHT *A gift of white lilies represents purity.*

PART SIX

HEALING WITH COLOUR

A BODILY DISEASE, WHICH WE LOOK
UPON AS WHOLE AND ENTIRE IN ITSELF,
MAY AFTER ALL, BE BUT A SYMPTOM OF SOME AILMENT
IN THE SPIRITUAL PART.
NATHANIEL HAWTHORNE, *The Scarlet Letter*, 1850

T*he idea of using colour to heal is not a new one; there have been many systems of colour healing throughout history. Modern colour therapy makes use of the wisdom upon which these ancient medical practices were based, combining it with a contemporary understanding of light technology, to create a modern, vibrant holistic form of health care that is suitable for our present needs.*

Research has now begun to validate the importance of colour in the treatment of disease. Colour therapy is being used increasingly as part of the treatment of a wide range of chronic health complaints, such as asthma, arthritis, nervous and mental disorders, depression, eating disorders, skin diseases, digestive ailments, blood and circulation problems, fevers and shock, including serious illnesses, such as paralysis, multiple sclerosis, and ME (myalgic encephalomyelitis). Great strides are now being made with colour acupuncture and laser light to relieve pain and encourage recovery.

Colour therapy can make a wonderful contribution by helping to build up vitality and rebuild health after an operation or illness. Colour treatments can be given safely and effectively alongside other remedies, helping to boost the immune system and promote healing from within.

COLOUR AND HEALING

The healing effects of colour were recognized in the 1930s in both Italy and the United States, when colour therapy was first used successfully in many hospitals and institutions to help the mentally and emotionally disturbed.

While colour can be used to fight problems in the physical body, its most important and long-lasting contribution is in the area of emotional and mental disorders. So much of how we feel physically can be related to our response to the people we associate with, and our home and work environment. Using colour to alter emotional energy results in changed perceptions of the world, and our experience of it. By introducing positive vibrations into the mind, we can drive out negative patterns, which will be detrimental to our overall health. Colour therapy therefore treats the cause of the disease, rather than its symptoms, working towards creating a balance within the body that allows it to fight off disease. Since colour directly links to the subconscious, we can use it to diagnose the root cause of a problem, treating it at a deep level. This is why colour therapy has such an impact on chronic illnesses that have no apparent cause.

Throughout our lives we are blocking certain emotional feelings, fears, and anxieties, and these get locked into our body tissues. They reveal themselves as physical ailments but are, in fact, psychosomatic in origin. Release of these feelings restores the channels through which energy flows, relieving pressures and pain. It is only by clearing deep blockages that may be inside our cells and muscle tissue that we can hope to cure ourselves.

We probably all have a disposition to illness, but whether we develop a particular disease depends on a progression of situations developing in our being over a length of time. There are many triggers to ill-health, and serious illness has many layers and blocks originating from deep within us. External factors, such as our lifestyle, diet, and our emotional and mental state, can all contribute to deep-rooted imbalances. Illness occurs when we have too much or too little of a particular colour in our energy systems. For instance, if we have too much red energy, we are hyperactive, suffer from hot flushes and heat exhaustion, and often have a bad temper; people with an excess of red energy can be recognized by their ruddy complexion and inability to relax. On the other

ABOVE *Those suffering from stress, especially work-related, may find colour therapy beneficial to relieve the pressure and symptoms.*

RIGHT *Colour therapy uses the chakra system: energy centers in the body that absorb colour vibrations.*

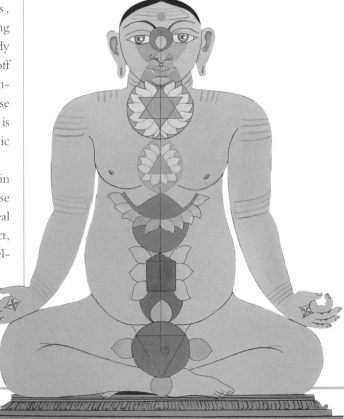

hand, with an excess of blue energy the body systems will tend to be sluggish, the person may suffer from cold hands and feet and, if the imbalance is left unchecked, may develop anemia, low blood pressure, and depression. By consciously rebalancing the colour energy in our body systems we can return it to a state of harmonious functioning, regain balance in our lives and create a feeling of well-being. When this happens many physical ailments disappear of their own accord. By using colour to heal at a very deep level, we are giving support to other medical practices in a holistic way.

There are many ways in which we can use colour to heal ourselves. According to colour therapists, we take in colour energy not only through our eyes but through our skin. We also ingest colour energy in our food and drink and through the air we breathe, and direct it using our minds or hands to particular parts of our bodies. We can solarize water, imbuing it with the quality of a certain colour wavelength, or use solar ray therapy, which involves bathing in a bath using herbs, flowers, and oils that correspond to particular healing colours. Most important, we take in colour vibrations through the subtle energetic system – known as the aura.

As a form of vibration, colour, like sound, has a very special capacity to alter energy patterns. If we can change the energy patterns in our body, we can alter disharmonious vibrations in particular parts of our system, restoring order and balance. Physicists have suggested that matter itself is formed from "crystalized light" – that is, from high-energy light photons. Since the cells

in our bodies are formed from light, it is only a small step to argue that they will also respond to coloured light; colour therapists state also that colour vibrations can not only affect our physical cells and organs and our emotional, mental, and nervous activity, but in addition have a powerful effect on our spiritual well-being.

ABOVE *These aura bottles provide a complete colour system that works on our spiritual, physical, mental, and emotional well-being.*

ALTERNATIVE MEDICINE

While conventional medicine is searching for a complete cure to serious illnesses, there are many alternative methods we can use to alleviate the problem, bringing comfort, understanding, and peace. In cases where serious illness cannot be cured, colour breathing and visualizations can help a person come to terms with his or her illness and sometimes sufferers go into spontaneous remission.

COLOURS AND
THE ORGAN SYSTEMS

*Wearing certain colours and surrounding oneself with certain colours
will also reinforce the action of the colour internally. If we have a problem
with any particular area of our body, we can combine all our self-help
colour treatments to combat the problem.*

Each body system, organ, and gland is made up of a number of cells that are clustered together. Each cluster forms a unit that operates at a particular frequency. This frequency corresponds to the frequency of vibration of a particular colour and sound. For instance, the liver has a sympathetic vibration to the colour yellow, while the heart is in tune with the colour green.

When an organ or gland is malfunctioning, it will loose its correct vibration, in much the same way as a radio station may lose its signal. By strengthening the vibration of the sympathetic colour, the organ will be retuned and clear reception will be restored. The organ will be re-energized and balance in the body regained. For instance, if we had a bad stomach we could wear yellow, visualize yellow, drink a soothing herbal drink with a yellow colouring, and eat soft yellow and orange foods such as squash and bananas, use the correct exercise for the stomach, and lie in a bath of yellow essential oil such as camomile and lavender.

The principal colours used in colour therapy are red, blue/violet, and green. The secondary colours of magenta, turquoise, and yellow are also used for healing. These colours are made up of two of the primary colours (*see* p 13). Paler shades (tints) of these seven colours are also useful in cases where someone is very weak or ill.

● ADRENALS

● REPRODUCTIVE ORGANS

● PANCREAS

● THYMUS

● THYROID, PARATHYROIDS

● PITUITARY

● PINEAL

● GLANDS

ABOVE *The various parts of the body, our organs and glands, operate at different rates that correspond to the vibrations of certain colours.*

BELIEFS ABOUT COLOUR

The correspondence of the colours to certain organs of the body has given rise to many sayings:

❦ *"Seeing red" corresponds to anger; this anger surges up from the base of the spine, raises our temperature and pulse, and makes us literally turn red.*

❦ *"Yellow bellied" means nervous or fearful; the solar-plexus is linked to yellow, the colour that rules the nervous system.*

❦ *Green corresponds to the heart area, so when we are "green with envy" we are acknowledging that envy arises from the heart, the center of our emotions.*

LEFT *Poor digestion can signal a lack of yellow energy. Eating yellow foods, wearing yellow, and bathing in yellow oils will reintroduce this colour back into your life.*

HEALTH WEAKNESSES

Our preferred colours not only complement our personal colouring but also lend support to certain physical and emotional problems we may be inclined to suffer from.

TRADITIONAL MEDICINE

ABOVE *Some alternative medical practitioners can ascertain your health by the colour of your tongue.*

Both ancient and modern medicine make use of colour for diagnosis of many ailments, because colouration of certain parts of the body can indicate mental and emotional ill-health. The colour of the skin, hair, nails, and eyes can all give a good indication of the general health of an individual, and can also help a skilled person diagnose many physical ailments.

A white tongue, for instance, reveals a system in need of alkalis, while a person with a red tongue is likely to need acids. A dark red tongue is often a sign of infection, while a brownish tongue may be a sign of typhoid.

Pigmentation of skin is probably more important. Yellow skin and eyes reveals malfunction of the liver or gall bladder. Dark rings under the eyes will indicate depleted energy in the kidneys. A red skin can indicate high blood pressure or blood disorder and a grayish complexion can show problems with the immune system and general tiredness or depression.

Our physical type and colouring, as well as our ruling planet and soul colour (*see* pp 199 and 30), will predispose us to health problems of a certain kind. People with an abundance of blue energy (cool people) may find they suffer from poor circulation, asthma, or low blood pressure. Cool people often have a sallow or dark complexion, or blue or green eyes, and they will feel the need for stimulation and heating from the red ray. Red is often a favorite colour of people with black hair and cool complexions because this is the colour energy they need.

People with ruddy complexions or with red hair have an abundance of red in their system and are likely to be predisposed to high blood pressure and heart problems. They will be attracted to cooling and soothing blues and greens.

Fair people with light blue or green eyes often may suffer from indecision and pessimism and need the beneficial radiation of yellow, which gives confidence and aids clear-thinking.

ABOVE *People with dark colouring find that the colour red has an energizing effect.*

ABOVE *Those with fair hair and skin will benefit from the optimistic effect of yellow.*

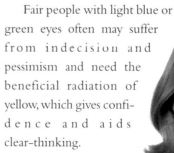

RIGHT *Cool, calming colours such as blue and green are ideal for balancing with red hair.*

USING COLOUR
TO DIAGNOSE YOUR
ENERGY IMBALANCES

*Psychologists over the last hundred years have been using
colour tests to aid with understanding personality traits, deep feelings,
and desires of their patients.*

ABOVE *The colours
you select indicate an
intuitive recognition of
your inner colour
vibrations.*

A well respected colour test was devised by Dr. Max Luscher in 1969, to gain accurate psychological information about a person through his or her choices and rejections of colours. Some more recent colour tests also employ shapes as a cue for choice. Flower colour cards include the shape and associations of each flower in addition to its colour. If you self-administer one of these colour tests, or have a colour test or reading done for you, you will be surprised how accurately they reveal your state of mind at the time.

Part Two of this book introduced the idea of identity colours. These are the colours that you have liked over a long period of time and reflect your personality. Your colour preferences and any changes in likes and dislikes also form an early warning system for your health, since stresses show up in the colour tests long before any physiological symptoms can be found. Our colour preferences are often dictated by the past or learned associations we have with these colours. We subconsciously link colours to people and places, and often these have negative associations for us, as certain colours may conjure up bad memories from the past. These subtle connections can lead us to choose colours that are not good for us or reject colours we need.

Colours are neither good nor bad, for like everything in the universe they are made up of both good and bad qualities. However, if we have an abundance of one colour energy it is likely we will have too little of another. This will encourage the negative side of the colour to become dominant. Clear, bright colours reflect the positive qualities of a colour, while dark or muddy colours indicate a negative aspect. If you choose a tint or light colour, this will reflect its rainbow colour, only the effect will be softer. A shade or darker

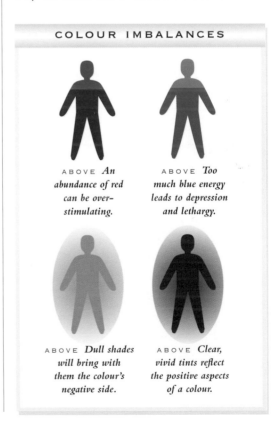

COLOUR IMBALANCES

ABOVE *An abundance of red can be over-stimulating.*

ABOVE *Too much blue energy leads to depression and lethargy.*

ABOVE *Dull shades will bring with them the colour's negative side.*

ABOVE *Clear, vivid tints reflect the positive aspects of a colour.*

version of a rainbow colour will have the same qualities but a stronger effect. (Black and white are not really colours, but people sometimes have strong attractions to or dislike of these.)

ABOVE *Red is the colour of energy, physical action, and adrenaline.*

RED

Red is the colour of blood and life-force energy. It is the colour of physical love and love is the great healer. It gives strength and the release of epinephrine (adrenaline), activating the nerves and blood. A love or preponderance of red shows you are motivated to do well and succeed, and are brave. It also shows movement and a desire for travel and change. Red helps you overcome negative thoughts through perseverance and determination, but shows a tendency to act without thinking things through. It may show a need to take action. It can connect you to your purpose in life and help you on your journey. Too much red can make you angry and impatient.

PINK

Rose pink is uplifting and gently stimulating. It is a muscle relaxant, and supports and soothes. Pink is the colour of unconditional love and a compassionate, caring person. Baby pink indicates emotional immaturity and a need to be loved for yourself. It connects the heart to the soul.

ORANGE

Orange is an antidepressant. It is uplifting and warming and generally stimulates the mind and so renews interest in life. It strengthens the immune system and aids digestion, with a releasing action on the body fluids. It strengthens the spleen, lungs, and pancreas. A love of orange shows a person in touch with his or her body. Orange is a cheerful joyous colour, showing a need to communicate about a relationship at home or work that is important to you. It shows a desire to let go of the past and a need to look at your energy levels.

YELLOW-GOLD

Yellow strengthens the nervous system and the brain. It creates energy in the muscles by activating motor nerves. It activates the lymph system and cleanses the digestive tract. Yellow is a bright and stimulating colour. It links to your inner wisdom when making your decisions. It can also be the colour of fear, which may show itself in emotions such as jealousy, resentment or envy. Mentally stimulating, yellow aids memory and clarity of thought. It encourages expansion so we can go ahead with new ideas. Gold is the colour of higher ideals.

RIGHT *A colour of vitality and joy, orange is physically stimulating and is often worn by those who are at ease with their bodies.*

RIGHT *Green surroundings relax, calm, and soothe the mind, body, and spirit. Green is a colour of nature and connects us to the Earth.*

TURQUOISE

Turquoise strengthens the immune system by stimulating the thymus gland, thyroid, and lungs. It adds sparkle and vitality when you are tired or feeling washed-out and shows a need to be refreshed and cleansed. Turquoise also shows the need for protection and to communicate with your inner being, and for new ideas.

BLUE

Cooling and calming, blue aids the healing process and can relieve pain. It promotes the healing of wounds and burns. Blue calms the mind and shows a need to use your intuition. Too much dark blue can be depressing, however. Blue shows a desire for peace and harmony in your life. It encourages you to put your trust in others and have hope. Blue indicates a need to express your real thoughts and feelings in a non-threatening environment.

GREEN

Green brings physical equilibrium and is physically relaxing. It stimulates the pituitary gland, helping to balance our emotions. Green shows a strong affinity with nature. It can also reveal a desire for harmony and balance in your life and a need for space for yourself. Green is mentally relaxing and good for stress. It promotes harmony between body, mind, and soul. It helps us connect with empathy to others and the natural world. It reminds us "What you sow, so shall you reap."

VIOLET

Violet balances the body's metabolism, and helps maintain the potassium balance in the body. It suppresses hunger and has a cleansing and purifying effect. It balances the mind and helps deal with obsessions and fears. Violet has a transformative quality, helping us make changes in our lives. It brings peace, and helps us connect with our creativity and spiritual side so that we can change and grow. An attraction to violet indicates a time to let go of the past and look forward to the future.

LEFT *Shades of blue suggest the need for self-expression in a tranquil environment.*

ABOVE *To dowse for your colour preferences, you will first need to make a circle made up of eight colours.*

If you wish to find your colour preferences, imbalances and needs in a more intuitive way, you might prefer to dowse for them using a pendulum. This will help you to bypass your conscious mind, which is constantly censoring impulses that are coming in from a deeper, subconscious level.

≪ You can make a pendulum out of a button or some sort of small weighted object, such as a natural quartz crystal. Suspend this object on a short length of chain or thin string about 6 inches (15cm) in length.

≪ Draw a circle on a piece of paper. Divide it into eight equal segments. Colour each of the segments as follows, starting at the top of the circle and working clockwise; red, orange, yellow, green, turquoise, blue, indigo, violet.

≪ Hold the pendulum out in front of you and try to calm and clear your mind of any particular thoughts.

≪ Hold the pendulum directly above the center of your colour circle.

≪ First, you need to determine which way your pendulum will swing for you. To do this, "ask" the pendulum (aloud or silently) which way it will swing for a "yes" answer. Note the direction. Next find out the direction for a "no" response, and then for "unsure, try again." (If it does not swing on its own, start it moving and the pendulum will correct itself if this is the wrong direction.) These directions will remain constant for you, no matter what questions you then ask.

≪ Hold the pendulum over a particular colour. Decide which colour you wish to find first (for example, the colour for relaxation).

≪ Ask the question. You need to be specific and clear about what you are asking, and frame your question so that you get a "yes" or "no" answer. For instance, you may say "Is this the best colour for relaxation?" Note the direction of the swing. Keep repeating this process around the circle until you find that the pendulum swings in the "yes" direction. If in doubt about an answer, repeat the question until the response is clear.

≪ You can further ask the pendulum whether you need a light or dark version of the colour, or the pure rainbow hue itself.

CIRCLE OF
EIGHT
COLOURS

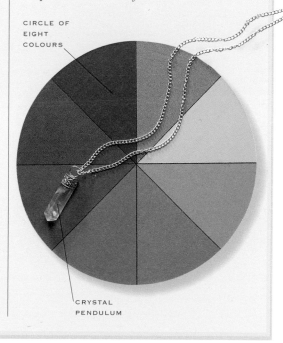

CRYSTAL
PENDULUM

LEFT *Holding your pendulum above the colour wheel, it responds to your questions and reveals your true colours.*

BODY AND PERSONALITY TYPES AND THE ELEMENTS

Human types and their characteristic colour traits were classified by Plato (428–347 B.C.E.) into four distinct groups corresponding to the elements of earth, air, fire, and water.

ABOVE LEFT *The element of air dominates sanguine types, who need violet for balance.*

ABOVE CENTER LEFT *Water rules phlegmatics; green will calm the emotions.*

ABOVE CENTER RIGHT *Cool colours benefit hot-tempered fire signs.*

ABOVE *Earthy melancholics need red or orange to instill energy.*

THE FOUR ELEMENTS

This elemental classification was used throughout Europe and the Near East until relatively recent times, dominating medical thinking for many centuries (note that it is different from the Chinese elemental system – *see* p 37). We are all made up of different combinations of these elements, with one of the elements tending to predominate over the others.

By looking at your physical characteristics and colouring you will be able to identify your predominant element. If you have soft, supple skin and doelike eyes you will probably be ruled by the element Water, or by Fire if you have a hot, fiery temperament and colouring. If you have dry skin and dry, dull hair you are likely to be ruled by Air, and by earth if you have a large, strong build and are slow.

The body types came to be known as phlegmatic, choleric, sanguine, and melancholic, based on the common health problems of each. The element of Fire was considered dominant in choleric people, whose heads, throats, and chests were most prone to health problems; they tended to be overactive, bad-tempered, and nervous. Sanguine people were ruled by Air and often had problems with their hips, upper arms, and lower legs. Phlegmatic types were Water ruled, and prone to problems in the chest and sexual organs; since Water is the element of the emotions, these people were very emotional. Earthy melancholics were prone to health problems relating to their shoulders, thighs, and knees; they were likely to have an earthy colouring with a golden skin, golden blond, or nut brown hair, and brown or hazel eyes.

Each of these types have an imbalance of one of the colours. Cholerics tend to be ruddy in appearance due to an abundance of red and orange rays and need more green and blue in their lives. Sanguine people need more violet, helping to balance the dryness of their skin and hair. Phlegmatics should focus on mood-balancing green. Melancholic people, prone to depression and lethargy, need red, orange, or yellow.

Each element therefore bestows specific qualities, which are a guide when using therapeutic treatment for psychological and physical problems. By looking at our own body type and colouring, we can pinpoint the areas where emotional and physical problems may occur. (Do note, however, that just because you have a predisposition to certain ailments does not mean you will contract them. Knowing our weak points allows us to strengthen our problem areas, and they can act as an early warning system.)

HEALTH AND THE ZODIAC

As well as the basic elements, each person has a governing planet and sign of the Zodiac, which relates to a particular element, providing a further clue to our natures. The governing Zodiac sign and planet are each related to a particular colour, and also indicate health weakness in one part of the body and dominant emotional states.

ELEMENTAL QUALITIES

ELEMENT	SIGNS	QUALITIES
Air	Aquarius, Gemini, Libra	mentally oriented, good communicators
Fire	Aries, Leo, Sagittarius	action-oriented with leadership qualities
Water	Cancer, Pisces, Scorpio	emotional and sensitive
Earth	Taurus, Virgo, Capricorn	practical and calm

HEALTH INDICATIONS FOR ZODIAC SIGNS

COLOUR	ZODIAC	PLANET	BODY PART/PROBLEMS	RELATED EMOTIONS
red	Aries	Mars	headaches	impatience, irritability
green	Taurus	Venus	neck, throat troubles, thyroid	laziness, indulgence
orange	Gemini	Mercury	lungs, respiration, chest, upper arms	noncommital, indecisive
orange	Cancer	Moon	breast area	emotional problems, insecurity
yellow/gold	Leo	Sun	back/spine, rheumatism, arthritis	withdrawn, resentful
yellow-green	Virgo	Mercury	stomach, digestion, uterus	inflexible, critical
green	Libra	Venus	kidneys, lumbar area, lower back, urinary tract	indecision, noncommital
green-blue	Scorpio	Mars/Pluto	sex organs, constipation, intoxication	resentment, suppressed emotions
blue	Sagittarius	Jupiter	hips, thighs, liver, bone problems	exhaustion, stress, envy
indigo	Capricorn	Saturn	skeleton, nerves, teeth, skin, tendons in knees	duty bound, insecurity
violet	Aquarius	Saturn/Uranus	skin, hay fever, eczema, ankles, circulation	oversensitive, dreamy
red-violet	Pisces	Jupiter/Neptune	kidneys, feet, chills, rheumatism, bladder	worry, low self-esteem

SOLAR RAY THERAPY

Solar ray therapy is an old practice originating in India, where the person sits outdoors in a tub of water covered with a sheet of coloured glass, silk, or cotton. The glass or cloth acts as a large colour filter in the same way that clothing does and has wonderfully revitalizing effects.

Natural fiber allows light and air to pass through to our skin. When light passes through the cloth this reflects a certain colour; we feed that colour energy into our system. We can therefore give ourselves solar ray therapy by choosing to wear certain colours of clothing (*see* p 44), and also by choosing light-filtering cloth for drapes and blinds, and through our choice of bedlinen. It is also possible to increase its effect by practicing a visualization method such as colour breathing (*see* p 226) as well.

COLOUR TREATMENTS USING SILK SCARVES

Silk has the highest vibration of any cloth, its reflective finely woven threads absorb natural dyes giving a clear and iridescent quality to the colours. This luminous quality increases the purity of the colour vibration passing through the cloth. If you cannot get silk cloth, a fine cotton is also good.

Here are some silk scarf treatments you can easily do at home on yourself, your family, and friends to treat common problems.

COLOUR TREATMENT FOR EXHAUSTION, LOW ENERGY, COLD

In Traditional Chinese Medicine, the kidneys are the organs where we hold vital energy and it is often the kidneys together with the adrenal glands, which straddle them, that become overworked and malfunction in times of prolonged stress. Red is the colour that activates the liver to make new red corpuscles, thus building up our entire system. It has a warming and releasing action and is excellent when we are tired, run down, and suffering from cold.

RIGHT *The warm vibrations emanating from a red blanket or scarf draped over the pelvic area will energize the kidneys and adrenals.*

- *Place a red blanket or scarf over the pelvis or back. The energy of the red ray will penetrate and boost the energy within the kidneys and adrenals so that you can build up your reserves and replenish your immune system.*

- *Red socks are useful if you are suffering from cold feet or chilblains and will help move the blood around the body.*

BELOW *Red socks will help boost circulation and benefit those suffering from chilblains.*

FOR GRIEF, HEARTACHE, HEALING THE HEART

Put a pink scarf over your chest area and close your eyes. Visualize sending out love rays to someone you care about, who may be distressed, and imagine that person bathed in pink light.

❧ You can also wear a pink shirt or place a pink gemstone, for example rose quartz, on a chain around your neck so it rests against your heart. Have faith that you will soon be able to give and receive love unconditionally.

ABOVE **A pink gemstone worn close to your heart will generate feelings of love.**

FOR LOW SELF-ESTEEM AND RELATIONSHIP PROBLEMS

Orange energy is a vital tonic that tones and releases fluids within the body, and is strongly linked to the release of our emotions.

❧ Tie or place an orange-, peach-, or apricot-colored scarf around the hips and pelvis.

❧ Color breathe using orange to bring joy and release to your system. Feel it filling up your pelvic area with warmth and energy. If you wish to release deep feelings of hurt from the past, this is the best time to do this. You may feel like expressing your feelings through tears.

RIGHT **Tie an orange scarf around your hips to lift your spirits and revitalize the system.**

FOR FEAR AND PROTECTION

Lay a yellow scarf over your middle while lying down on a bed or on the floor. Our solar plexus is the area in the body where we hold fear.

❧ If you are anticipating going into a frightening or emotionally disturbing situation it is best to wear something yellow around your waist. Try a yellow top or belt. This will protect your solar plexus from hurtful vibrations.

❧ In addition, practice some deep color breathing, concentrating on releasing the fear through your breath. As you take in the yellow energy you will be aware of regaining your own power once more until you feel your own yellow energy radiating once again.

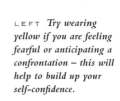

LEFT **Try wearing yellow if you are feeling fearful or anticipating a confrontation – this will help to build up your self-confidence.**

FOR SLUGGISHNESS, INDIGESTION AND BAD SKIN

Yellow is nature's purgative and blood cleanser. Think of citrus and cider vinegar, both excellent antacids that neutralize acid imbalances in the blood. Yellow has a stimulating action without raising the heartbeat; this means that your metabolism is stimulated without placing pressure on your heart. Yellow links to the pancreas and spleen, stimulating the pancreas to produce insulin.

❧ Place a yellow scarf over the abdomen area for half an hour. The action of the yellow energy can be enhanced by drinking a tumbler of yellow solarized water (see p 209) in the morning.

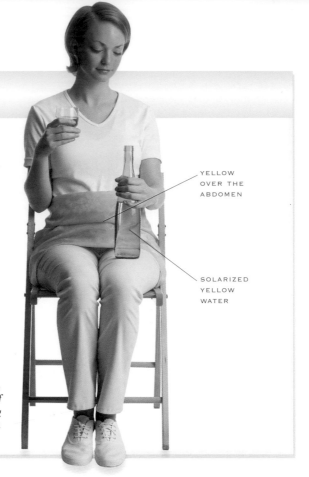

YELLOW OVER THE ABDOMEN

SOLARIZED YELLOW WATER

RIGHT *Yellow energy has strong, cleansing qualities. Combine a scarf around the abdomen with a stimulating drink of yellow solarized water.*

FOR STRESS AND HIGH BLOOD PRESSURE

Place a green scarf over your chest area while lying down. You could also lie on a green towel, sheet, or large scarf.

❧ You can also use turquoise, which is a mixture of blue and green. This refreshing colour is relaxing to the mind while acting as a mild tonic, leaving you feeling alert and renewed.

FOR NECK AND SHOULDER TENSION

Place a green scarf over the back of a chair or pillow. Lie against the chair or pillow with your eyes closed and visualize the colour green.

BELOW *Green will soothe away stress, while the after-effects of turquoise are rejuvenating.*

FOR HEADACHES AND TIRED EYES (INCLUDING FEVERS AND SUNSTROKE)

Place a dark blue scarf over your eyes while lying or sitting down comfortably. You can put the scarf over the head if you wish, especially if you are mentally tired. Rest your eyes by closing them for a minute and then open them for a minute or two, so that you absorb the blue light. Repeat this a few times until you feel rested.

☞ *If you have swollen and puffy eyes, you can use a blue scarf treatment or dip two pads of absorbent cotton into blue solarized water (see p 208), placing them on each eye. This will cool and soothe your eyes and help to take down the swelling.*

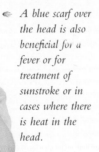

☞ *A blue scarf over the head is also beneficial for a fever or for treatment of sunstroke or in cases where there is heat in the head.*

LEFT ***Blue solarized water helps reduce redness and swelling.***

FOR HEALING PAIN (BURNS, STINGS, AND BITES)

If you have a wound, make up a blue bandage or sling and place it over the affected area. Deep blue is an excellent pain healer. It has antiseptic and cooling properties. Colour visualization and colour breathing (see p 226) will help reinforce the action of the blue bandaging.

☞ *Bites and stings can be quickly relieved by placing a drop of neat lavender oil on the wound and then covering it with a small square of blue fabric or blue bandage.*

ABSENT HEALING USING SILK

By directing colour energy to others we can give immediate comfort and relief to people anywhere in the world. Since colour healing works through sympathetic resonance, the more sensitive the person is to this type of vibrational healing, the more immediate and better the results will be.

Send colour for absent healing in these ways:

☞ The first is by mentally sending waves of colour to a person by visualizing the person being filled and then surrounded by the colour.

☞ The second is to obtain a photograph or something belonging to the person to be healed. A sample of handwriting, an object belonging to him or her, or a lock of hair would be suitable. Cover the photo or object with a colour filter or coloured silk square and leave in the natural light. I keep photographs of friends and family by a window and regularly cover different photos with coloured filters if I feel the person needs a particular colour energy.

☞ If you wish physically to send someone colour energy, dab a small piece of silk of the appropriate colour with an essential oil that relates to the colour frequency. Place the piece of silk on your left palm and hold your right palm over it. Energize the silk by mentally directing healing energy into it, and, asking that the energy be absorbed by him or her (say the name). Place the silk in a folded piece of paper and send it to the person who needs healing.

BELOW ***Draping a coloured silk cloth over the picture of someone who is absent will send them healing energy of that colour.***

COLOUR BATHS

We can give ourselves a colour energy bath by soaking in warm water to which specific colouring has been added. The colours will not stain the skin and you will find the colour energy revitalizes your whole being.

There are now a few commercially available bath salts and essences that colour the bath water. Turquoise is one colour I particularly love to use as a colour bath. Soaking in an orange bath (coloured with a few drops of food colouring) is extremely relaxing if you are feeling emotionally drained. In fact, you can soak in a bath coloured in many different colours to either soothe, heal, or invigorate. It is still difficult to find commercially made pure dyes for the bath, although you can make several yourself using natural dyes and nonstaining colourings used in cooking.

It is a good idea to combine colour with fragrance for your bath, so use a few drops of essential oil too. Do not have the water too hot because this puts pressure on your heart, conflicts with the colour energy, and evaporates the oil. It would be ideal if the water were barely above body temperature so that you can feel comfortable and relaxed without being cold.

Cooler water aids soothing colours such as blue, green, and violet; while more stimulating yellow, orange, and red can be used in water of a slightly higher temperature.

COLOUR AROMA HERBAL BATHING

If the idea of bathing in coloured water does not appeal to you, you can use flowers, herbs, or essential oils that correspond to that colour frequency instead. Combining colour baths with essential oils is an excellent treatment for tension and other forms of stress as well as exhaustion. After a colour bath your skin will also feel more supple and the aroma will be longer lasting.

The water temperature can be quite hot, but let the water run in first before adding the oils, so they don't evaporate before you get in. If you have dry skin, rub a scented oil on your body after bathing.

BELOW *Highly restorative, a turquoise bath will cleanse and revive the aura and rid it of harmful negative vibrations.*

MAKE SURE WATER IS NOT TOO HOT, BECAUSE THIS WILL DISTORT THE COLOUR ENERGY

BATHING AT NIGHT IS BETTER THAN BATHING IN THE MORNING BECAUSE IT GIVES THE DEPLETED AURA TIME TO REFORM

ADD A FEW DROPS OF YOUR FAVORITE ESSENTIAL OIL TO YOUR BATH FOR MAXIMUM BENEFIT

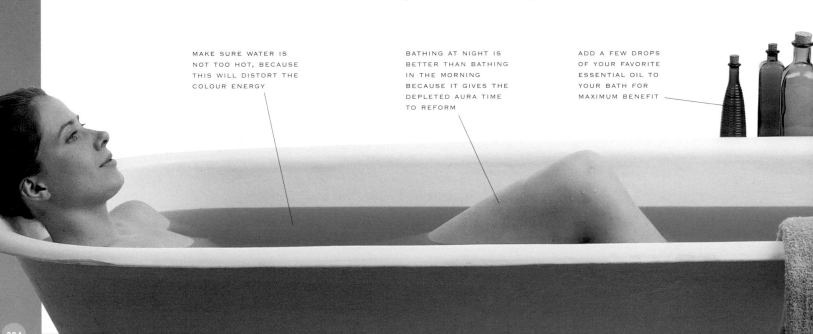

THERAPEUTIC QUALITIES OF COLOUR BATHS

RED

vitality, strength, power, and courage; helps you meet a demanding day, giving an extra reserve of energy

PINK

love, kindness, consideration, unselfishness; a pink bath will rid you of irritation and aggression – its sympathetic and supporting energy will surround you with love and protection

ORANGE

happiness, independence, resourcefulness; helps find practical solutions, uplifts and brings out laughter and joy

YELLOW

optimism, clarity of thought and knowledge; life-giving, reminding you that you must first love yourself before you can love others

GREEN

balance, harmony, nature, self-control, and generosity; relaxes your thoughts, nerves, and muscles, and gives a feeling of peace and harmony

TURQUOISE

communication, confidence, and the power of speech; helps you strengthen your concentration and control your speech; aids communication and symbolizes truth

BLUE

cooling and cleansing, peace, tranquillity, and wisdom; spaciousness like the ocean and sky; blue embodies the spirit of healing

INDIGO

understanding, intuition, meditation, and mysticism; you are not alone, but part of the universe; let your intuition and wisdom guide you

VIOLET

inspiration, beauty, art, and the spirit; purifies your thoughts, and inspires; this is an artist's colour vibration; violet will surround you with beauty and high ideals

---

The essential oils used are basically either stimulating or relaxing. The stimulating ones correspond to the energizing rays of red/orange and yellow, and the relaxing ones correspond to the blues and greens of the soothing end of the colour spectrum.

Every floral essence is a mixture of Yin and Yang (*see* p 76), and while it may be predominantly Yin or Yang it is never wholly one or the other. The plant world is predominantly green, and the animal world red. Our own physiological spectrum normally runs from red to yellow. Red gives us a feeling of excitement, restriction, warmth and movement, so we call it Yang. Violet on the other hand gives us the feeling of space, rest, and the female and we call it Yin.

By using essential oils we are also treating ourselves with the properties of coloured rays.

YIN AND YANG IN THE COLOUR SPECTRUM

YANG   YIN

RED   VIOLET

ABOVE *The spectrum runs from the invigorating oranges and reds to the cooling blues and greens.*

Here are some bath oil recipes that you can try yourself at home, and a guide to help you make up your own recipes.

PINK ROSE PETAL BATH

Pink is the colour of love, and since ancient times roses have been renowned for the loving and healing vibrations they emit.

- Pick two handfuls of rose petals – you can use white, pink, or red. Run a warm bath, not too hot, and add a few drops of rosewater or essential oil of rose. Throw on the petals.

- Enjoy the wonderful perfume, and feel the warm, loving, feeling that your bath will give you.

LEFT *Try to use freshly picked rose petals that are still plump and waxy. If they are not fresh they will lose their potency.*

LEFT *Run a warm bath before adding a few drops of rose essential oil. Add the oil once the bath is ready to prevent the oil from evaporating.*

LEFT *Add two handfuls of rose petals to the bath before getting in. Soak for around 20 minutes to gain the full benefit.*

WINTER BATH (RED-ORANGE)

This bath will help ward off colds, stimulate circulation, and energize your mind and body. It uses the warming energy of the red ray.

- Add 1 drop of black pepper, 2 drops of juniper, and 3 drops of lavender oil to the bath water.

APHRODISIAC BATH (RED-ORANGE)

This uses the stimulation of the red ray, and orange and brown, energizing the base and sacral chakras allowing you to feel connected to your physical energy.

- Blend 1 drop of ylang-ylang, 4 drops of sandalwood, and 1 drop of jasmine oil, and add to a warm bath.

WARMING YELLOW MUSTARD FOOTBATH

Yellow is a stimulating and warming colour, and while improving circulation does not raise the heartbeat.

- Put 2tbsp/30ml of mustard powder into a bowl of hot water.

- Steep your feet for 10 minutes to get your circulation going and your legs feeling warm.

MORNING BATH (GOLDEN YELLOW)

The morning bath is tonic, invigorating, and antidepressant, using the warmth and stimulation of the orange and yellow ray.

- Blend 2 drops of sandalwood, 3 drops of rosemary, and 2 drops of juniper oil, and add to a warm, not hot, bath.

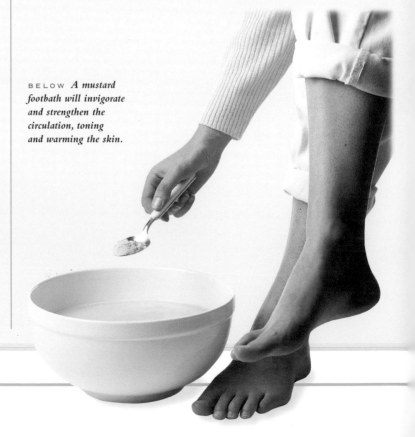

BELOW *A mustard footbath will invigorate and strengthen the circulation, toning and warming the skin.*

LEMON BATH (YELLOW)

A lemon bath is refreshing, relaxing, and cleansing. It uses the acidic quality of the yellow-green ray.

❧ *Add the juice of half a lemon, 4 drops of lemon oil, and 1 drop of geranium oil to a cool bath.*

SUMMER BATH (GREEN–YELLOW)

Cooling, refreshing, and invigorating, this bath helps with water retention and stimulates the lymphatics for good circulation and clear skin. The colours green, blue, turquoise, and lavender are all in the summer bath.

❧ *Add 2 drops of neroli, 2 drops of fennel, 3 drops of grapefruit, and 1 drop of peppermint to the bath.*

❧ *Make sure the water is very slightly warmer than body temperature.*

EVENING BATH (GREEN–BLUE–VIOLET)

Sedative and relaxing, the evening bath is for those who have difficulty sleeping. Lavender and violet rays are represented in this bath.

❧ *Place two handfuls of fresh herbs in a circular piece of cheesecloth and tie it up to form a pouch. Hang under the running faucet while your bath fills.*

❧ *Add 3 drops of marjoram (for aching muscles), 1 drop of camomile (sedative), and 4 drops of lavender (mentally relaxing). Add to a warm bath.*

1. *For a relaxing evening bath, you can use sprigs of fresh herbs in a warm bath instead of oils if you prefer.*

2. *Once you have selected your herbs, place them in a circular piece of cheesecloth and secure with thread.*

1. *Tie your bag of herbs securely on to your mixer faucet or hot faucet so that it is hanging directly beneath the flow of water.*

2. *When you run your bath, ensure the water is flowing through the bag, transferring the herb essences to the water.*

BATH TO CLEANSE THE AURA (TURQUOISE)

We can cleanse ourselves from the bad vibrations collected from other people and places in our aura (see p 212). Take a 20-minute bath in a warm tub of water containing 1 cup/250ml of sea salt and 1 cup/250ml of baking soda; this bath harmonizes with the turquoise ray. This may leave you very weak because it draws large quantities of energy out of the body, so make sure you rest afterward to replenish yourself.

LEFT *Turquoise is a deeply cleansing colour. A turquoise bath will help to revive a congested aura.*

COLOUR-ENERGIZED WATER TREATMENTS

Making and taking colour-energized water or milk is totally safe, and you can make home remedies for many ailments extremely quickly and inexpensively this way.

ABOVE *Solarization is an age-old practice. The contents of these Ancient Egyptian glass storage vessels would have been solarized.*

The Ancient Egyptians used their understanding of the effect of coloured rays to create exquisite bowls with encrusted jewels, and bottles, jars, and plates of coloured glass in which they placed food, drink, and healing potions. These were placed in the sunlight so that the colour of the glass or the gemstones filtering the sunlight would energize the contents with a particular colour energy. In India, colour-solarized milk forms part of Ayurvedic medicine.

Some of these ancient methods are again becoming common practice. For instance, some manufacturers of water filters are colouring them – blue, turquoise, and green glass or plastic. The water from these always tastes much fresher and cooler than water that is poured from clear glass.

Brightly coloured glass bottles and storage jars are appearing in a variety of different stores, and can be filled with oils, herbal vinegar, bottled fruit and many other foods. Try decanting a cough mixture or herbal remedy into an appropriately coloured bottle to enhance its effects.

Drinking water that has been energized or "solarized" with the red or orange ray has been found to have a tonic action, while yellow-solarized water has a cleansing and purgative effect, similar to lemon or grapefruit juice. Blue slows water putrefaction. The magnetic colours red, orange, yellow, and magenta have a stimulating action so are better taken in the morning. They can be drunk a tumbler at a time. The electrical colours of green, blue, indigo, and violet should only be sipped – not more than a half a wine glass at a time. They have a sedating action, so are best taken during the latter part of the day.

RIGHT *When left in the light, the colour of the glass or plastic container will have a very different effect on the water it holds.*

BLUE HAS A SEDATIVE EFFECT

ORANGE WILL HAVE A TONIC ACTION

GREEN, LIKE BLUE, IS CALMING

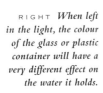

MAKING SOLARIZED WATER

Y ou can treat yourself to a glass of colour-charged water every day. Solar-energized water can be made by covering the glass container with a coloured filter. Commercially produced colour photographic filters are made of translucent plastic material and have the same effect on water as coloured glass. They have a precise and specific colouring that allows only the vibration of that particular colour to pass through. Coloured filters can also be bought from colour therapy suppliers.

The best water to energize is rain water, pure filtered water, or spring water. Fill a glass with the water and wrap the filter around it, securing it with a piece of tape. Put the glass in the sunlight for 30 minutes. (It does not have to be a sunny day for the light rays to penetrate.) You can also use a bottle made from coloured glass.

1. Use the purest water you can find – rain water, filtered water or spring water are best. Pour the water into a glass.

2. Cover the glass with the filter and secure with a piece of tape. Leave the glass in the light for 30 minutes.

CONDITIONS THAT CAN BE TREATED USING ENERGIZED WATER

RED

Use for sciatica and to activate the nerves and blood. Use if lethargic, if unduly tired, or if hands and feet are cold. One glassful between meals is helpful for anemia. It will raise the blood pressure. Do not use on those who have tempers, anger, are violent, have heart trouble, varicose veins, or skin rashes.

ORANGE

Used to drain blocked lymphatics and to free phlegm. Good for cramps and spasms, as well as for asthma, wet coughs, fever, digestive problems, difficult menstruation, kidney problems, and colitis. Draws boils and abscesses.

YELLOW

Cleans sluggish conditions and constipation. Activates the motor nerves and creates energy in the muscles. Increases the vital flow of fluids in the body. Stimulates the spleen, liver, pancreas, and kidneys. Sip a small amount before meals.

GREEN

A nerve sedative and tonic. Relieves head colds, hay fever, neuralgia, and sunburn or skin irritations. Use for shock or in first aid.

BLUE

Combats an overactive thyroid. Use also for kidney problems and diarrhea. It has antiseptic effect on minor cuts and bruises. Gargle with it for a sore throat or mouth ulcers. Sip before a meal. For colitis and biliousness, sip half a wine glass daily. To help "hot flashes" take three times a day before meals.

INDIGO

For migraine and headaches. For heat rash or sunburn, drink to cool the system. Use as a gargle for a sore throat. Bathe sore, tired, or inflamed eyes.

VIOLET

For those suffering from asthma, nervous tension, and mental disturbances. Also use for purification and regeneration of infected cells.

MAGENTA

Good for improving circulation and the skin and when you lack energy.

ABOVE *Water energized with the blue ray has an antiseptic, cooling effect, taking the heat out of any symptoms. It should be sipped slowly.*

BACH FLOWER REMEDIES AND FLOWER ESSENCES

*Flowers contain solar energy, because they absorb and store sunlight.
The colour, scent, and shape of a flower all combine to send out a powerful
magnetic frequency. This healing vibration can be captured in water since it
is an excellent conductor of electromagnetic currents and retains their
imprint. The resulting flower essence retains the flower's healing frequency.*

BACH FLOWER REMEDIES

The healing power of flowers became widely recognized at the end of the 19th century, mainly because of the discoveries of Dr. Edward Bach, a London physician, bacteriologist, and then homeopath, who believed that disease is simply a manifestation of negative thoughts such as fear, anxiety, grief, and despair. The way to heal people, he believed, was to heal the negativity of thought that can cause physical disease.

Bach classified all emotional problems into seven major groups: fear, uncertainty and indecision, insufficient interest in present circumstances, loneliness, oversensitivity, despon-

RIGHT *Flower remedies are excellent for treating the emotional problems that can lead to physical illness.*

dency or despair, and overcare for the welfare of others. Thirty-eight remedies were developed, diluted homeopathically so that none of their original material remained, to heal every negative aspect of the seven types of emotional illnesses. A few drops of the remedy are taken diluted in fresh spring or rain water.

Colour therapy is similar to homeopathy in that it is the frequency of the healing vibration and not the quantity that is important. Flower essences contain light vibrations, the strength of which depends on the colour of the flower. The essences also reflect the different colour frequencies that relate to the state of mind being treated.

COLOURS AND BACH FLOWER ESSENCES

COLOUR	MIND STATE	ESSENCES
red/green	uncertainty	Cerato, Scleranthus, Gentian, Gorse, Hornbeam, Wild Oat
pink/green	loneliness	Water, Violet, Impatiens, Heather
orange/blue	oversensitivity to influence of others and ideas; despondency and despair	Agrimony, Centaury, Walnut, Holly, Larch, Pine, Elm, Sweet Chestnut, Star of Bethlehem, Willow, Oak, Crab Apple
golden-yellow turquoise	lack of interest in present circumstances	Clematis, Honeysuckle, Wild Rose, Olive, White Chestnut, Mustard, Chestnut Bud
yellow/violet	fear	Rock Rose, Mimulus, Cherry Plum, Aspen, Red Chestnut
magenta/green	overcare for others	Chicory, Vervain, Vine, Beech, Rock water

MAKING YOUR OWN FLOWER ESSENCES

Ingrid von Rohr, naturopath and colour therapist, suggests the following method for preparing your own essences.

SOLAR METHOD

- ✑ Take a thin glass bowl and fill it with the purest water available.
- ✑ Scatter the flowers over the surface of the water so it is covered.
- ✑ Let the bowl stand for 3 or 4 hours in sunlight, then remove the flowers carefully and pour the water into clean bottles until they are half full.
- ✑ Top up with approximately the same volume of brandy or cognac.
- ✑ From these stock bottles, make up a dosage solution by adding a few drops to a bottle containing 1–1½ fl oz/20–30ml spring water.

1 *Fill a thin glass bowl with purified water and scatter the flowers over the surface.*

2 *Let the bowl stand for 3 or 4 hours in the sunlight.*

3 *Pour the water into a clean bottle until half full and then add the same volume of brandy or cognac.*

An alternative to the solar method is the "boiling method."

THE BOILING METHOD

- ✑ Boil the flowers in pure water for about half an hour.
- ✑ Sieve through cheesecloth and half fill your bottle with the essence, then top up with brandy.

COLOUR ENERGIZING

- ✑ *Place a colour filter around the glass containing your diluted flower essence and place it in sunlight for several minutes.*

- ✑ *If you wish to use two complementary colours, alternate the colours with each successive treatment. Make sure you have an even number of doses of each colour.*

- ✑ *You can use a crystal quartz pendulum to test when a flower essence is fully energized.*

Flowers and leaves from healing plants can also be wrapped directly around flower essences or aromatherapy carrier oils. Wrap golden-yellow marigolds or green comfrey leaves around skin creams and lotions. Rose petals imbue emotional healing to a bath essence, while violet flowers promote healing and help regeneration of tissue.

COLOUR ENERGIZING FLOWER ESSENCES

Flowers work to heal on many levels, and their colours are an important part of their unique healing properties. Flower essences can be imbued with the related colour energy for a more synergistic effect.

Another method that I like to use for colour energizing flower essences is to place the dosage bottle under a coloured glass pyramid with the same proportions as the Great Pyramid of Giza. These do not need to be very large; a base 3 in/9cm square is sufficient.

HEALING
THROUGH THE AURA

*To understand colour therapy properly, we need to understand
the concept of the aura. According to this concept, we have not only a
physical body but also several more subtle bodies, which link to the
emotional, mental, and spiritual levels of our selves.*

ABOVE *Clairvoyants
have been aware of
the existence of auras
for centuries.*

RIGHT *The vibration
of energy in the aura
radiating out from the
body has been caught
on camera.*

These vibrate at such a fast rate that they are invisible to the human eye, and radiate colour vibrations, which spread out around us in bands of light forming an "*aura*." The aura is made up of three distinct layers or subtle bodies radiating outward from the physical body. The physical body is the most dense and is the one we can see, while the subtle bodies are invisible to everyone except those with "psychic" vision. Although the orthodox medical profession in the West consistently denies the existence of the aura and subtle bodies, knowledge of them has been claimed by healers and people with clairvoyant vision for thousands of years.

BANDS OF THE AURA

- *The first band of vibrations in the aura is a thin band of energy known as the etheric body, which is an exact duplicate of the physical body, but because it vibrates at a higher rate it is invisible to the naked eye. The etheric body acts as a type of vibrational sieve, allowing vibrations from the other subtle bodies to flow into the physical body and vibrations from the physical body to flow outward.*

- *The second band of energy in the aura is the astral or emotional body. This extends around us for up to about a yard (a little under a meter) and is made up of a changing array of colours that reflect our moods and emotions.*

- *Extending outward from the astral body is the mental body, and this band of colour energy is filled with energy from our thought waves. This mental energy interacts with the astral and etheric bodies, so it influences the type of energy balance in these areas. So if you are thinking negative thoughts these will have permeated through your other subtle bodies and will be having a direct influence on your emotional and physical well-being.*

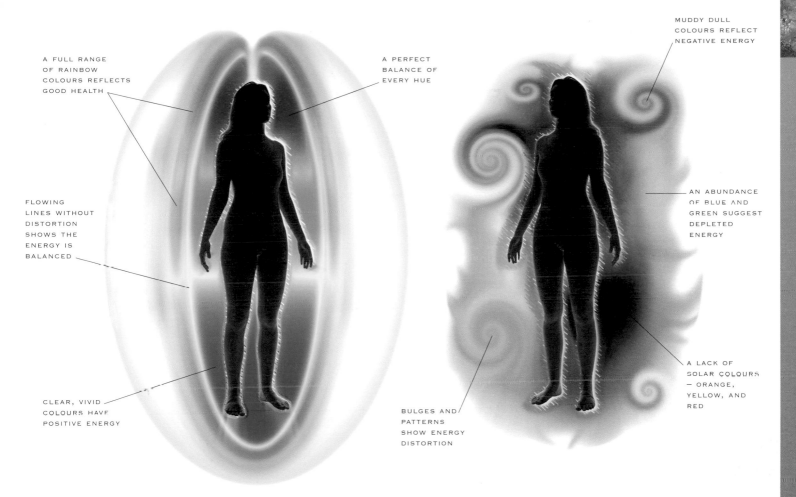

A FULL RANGE
OF RAINBOW
COLOURS REFLECTS
GOOD HEALTH

A PERFECT
BALANCE OF
EVERY HUE

MUDDY DULL
COLOURS REFLECT
NEGATIVE ENERGY

FLOWING
LINES WITHOUT
DISTORTION
SHOWS THE
ENERGY IS
BALANCED

AN ABUNDANCE
OF BLUE AND
GREEN SUGGEST
DEPLETED
ENERGY

CLEAR, VIVID
COLOURS HAVE
POSITIVE ENERGY

BULGES AND
PATTERNS
SHOW ENERGY
DISTORTION

A LACK OF
SOLAR COLOURS
— ORANGE,
YELLOW, AND
RED

Our aura is made up of many beautiful colour vibrations forming an egg shape around the physical body. The colours of the aura reflect our physical, emotional, mental, and spiritual states.

The vital energy from light rays, with its seven component colours, provides us with the nourishment we need to keep us in perfect health. However, if the vital life-giving force embodied in the seven healing rays becomes blocked then imbalances of energy occur. When this happens certain colour energies build up in some energy centers of the body (called chakras, *see* p 214), while others become depleted of energy. Problems in any of these areas show up as bulges or patterns in the shapes of the aura, and energy distortions show up there, too. Eventually our physical body interprets these energy imbalances as physical illness and manifests a whole array of different symptoms.

Our physical form cannot exist in isolation from our mental, emotional, and spiritual bodies. These aspects of our psyche are constantly interacting with one another. Many of our physical feelings are altered by our thoughts and expectations. Building our mental strength and tuning into our intuition influences the colours in our auras, changing negative expectations to positive ones.

THE COLOUR OF AURAS

When we are completely balanced and in perfect health, our aura will be a beautiful rainbow, for each cosmic ray will be able to flow through us without obstruction. As well as giving off our own colour vibrations, we also absorb light energy through our aura. Light energy is drawn into the auric egg, which acts like a prism, breaking down the light into its component colour elements.

ABOVE LEFT *When we are at ease with ourselves and the world, light is able to pass through our system, creating an aura of all the rainbow colours.*

ABOVE RIGHT *If one of our energy centers becomes blocked, our aura will appear distorted with an imbalance of colours.*

THE CHAKRAS

Each colour vibration is absorbed into the body through a system of seven body energy centers located at different points along the spine, known as chakras, which are directly linked to nerve centers.

ABOVE *Each of the seven chakras relates to a different colour vibration. When one of the chakras is out of balance, others are affected.*

Each chakra absorbs a certain vibration of light in the form of one of the major coloured rays, and then distributes it through the body. If the energy force is blocked at any particular level, there will be a buildup of energy at that level, causing a distortion that will then start affecting other areas of our being. The particular colour vibration to which a chakra is sensitive can be used to energize and balance the center and its related body systems, organs, and glands.

The centers that attract each of the rays are as follows.

- **red:** lowest center located at the base of the spine
- **orange:** splenic center in the small of the back
- **yellow:** middle of the back, the solar plexus
- **green:** heart center between the shoulder blades
- **blue:** throat or thyroid at the base of the skull
- **indigo:** third eye, the pineal gland
- **violet:** crown of the head, the pituitary gland

Each colour also affects the energy center above and below it, and certain energy centers have balancing effects with each other. For example, although yellow links to the digestive system, green and orange will also affect digestion.

There are three main ways we can attract and direct colour harmony into the etheric body.

- The first is by opening our chakras so that colour energy can flow freely through us. We can then direct this energy either with our mind or through our hands. In this way we can perform self-healing or heal other people.

- The second way is by making use of light instruments to expose the whole aura to colour energy. This is known as colour irradiation.

- The third way is known as chromatherapy and involves directing light toward a chakra or part of the body in order to heal that particular area. If we concentrate the colour energy into a narrow beam of light, it acts as a laser, the vibrations of which can be used to stimulate an acupressure point or foot reflex. You can also use fingers to apply pressure on the meridian points on the body, face, hands and feet, sending colour energy mentally along these channels.

The chart opposite illustrates the colour frequencies sympathetic to specific organs, glands, body systems, and chakras.

ENERGY CHANNELED THROUGH THE FINGERS CAN HELP MOVE ENERGY ALONG THE BODY

LEFT *Concentrate on sending a particular colour energy through your body, directing it to the chakra or part of the body that needs healing.*

BODY POWER CENTERS AND COLOURS

COLOUR	ENERGY CENTER	GLANDS	ORGANS	BODY SYSTEMS
red	base	adrenals	kidneys	muscular, system, arterial blood
orange	sacral (hara, dantian)	reproductive organs	ovaries, testes, stomach, colon	reproductive system
yellow	solar plexus	pancreas	liver, gall bladder, spleen	digestive system, nervous systems
green	heart	thymus	heart, lower lung	circulatory system, parasympathetic nervous system
blue	throat	thyroid, parathyroids	throat, upper lung	respiratory system
indigo	third eye	pituitary	eyes, nose, ears	skeletal system, venous blood
violet	crown	pineal	brain	central nervous system
magenta	etheric/spirit	glands related to meridians	acupuncture points, foot reflexes	meridian system

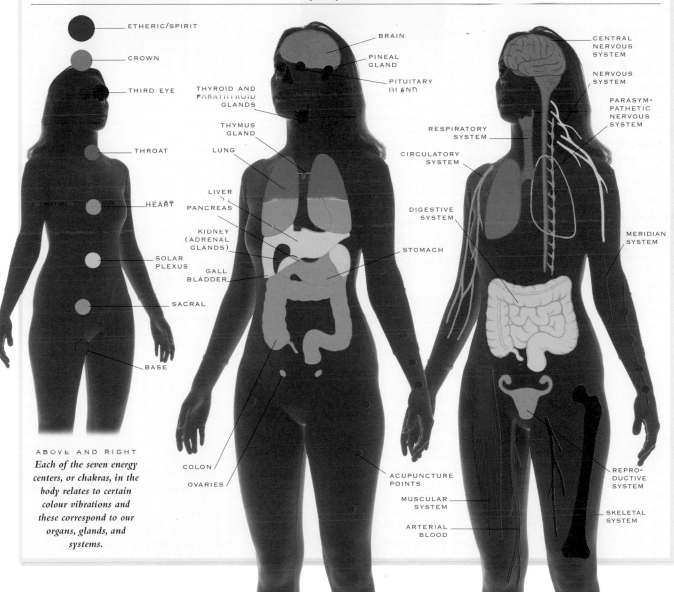

ETHERIC/SPIRIT

CROWN

THIRD EYE

THROAT

HEART

SOLAR PLEXUS

SACRAL

BASE

THYROID AND PARATHYROID GLANDS

THYMUS GLAND

LUNG

LIVER

PANCREAS

KIDNEY (ADRENAL GLANDS)

GALL BLADDER

COLON

OVARIES

BRAIN

PINEAL GLAND

PITUITARY GLAND

STOMACH

ACUPUNCTURE POINTS

MUSCULAR SYSTEM

ARTERIAL BLOOD

CENTRAL NERVOUS SYSTEM

NERVOUS SYSTEM

PARASYMPATHETIC NERVOUS SYSTEM

RESPIRATORY SYSTEM

CIRCULATORY SYSTEM

DIGESTIVE SYSTEM

MERIDIAN SYSTEM

REPRODUCTIVE SYSTEM

SKELETAL SYSTEM

ABOVE AND RIGHT
Each of the seven energy centers, or chakras, in the body relates to certain colour vibrations and these correspond to our organs, glands, and systems.

DAILY EXERCISES TO OPEN UP THE CHAKRAS

Hatha yoga, the yoga of physical movement, massages and energizes our internal systems. The following basic exercises will also open the chakras. Try to visualize the corresponding colours for each chakra when you are performing these exercises. You can also use the massage technique when giving a massage, aromatherapy, or colour treatment to somebody else.

EXERCISE TIPS

- *Wear loose-fitting, comfortable clothes.*
- *Try to wear cotton or another natural fiber, which lets the skin breathe naturally. Choose quiet or neutral colours.*
- *Remove all jewelry and watches.*
- *Do not eat for at least 2 hours before you exercise.*

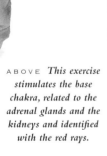

Red chakra – base of the spine

- Stand with your feet wide apart and your feet and knees outward at a comfortable angle, so that you can bend your knees as deeply as you are able without it hurting or straining.
- Move up and down several times, and now try to swing your pelvis as far forward and as far backward as you can.
- Rock backward and forward a few times in this way as you move down. Keeping your knees bent rock your pelvis back and forth in this position. Then slowly return to the starting position.
- Repeat three times.

MASSAGE

With your open palm, gently tap the base of your spine until you feel heat in this area and energy rising.

ABOVE *This exercise stimulates the base chakra, related to the adrenal glands and the kidneys and identified with the red rays.*

Orange chakra – reproductive organs

- Stand with your feet apart and knees slightly bent. Rock your pelvis back and forth as in the previous exercise.
- Now imagine you are in a cylinder and with your pelvis make a rotating, circular movement. Do this several times in both directions.

MASSAGE

With your open palm, rub your lower back and front pelvic region making figures of eight with your hands. This is gently warming and soothing.

Yellow chakra – solar plexus (stomach)

- Jumping – this requires a partner; one holds the other's hands firmly while the latter jumps up and down. If you aim to do this regularly it is well worth investing in a small trampoline.
- The jumping motion encourages lymphatic drainage, as well as releasing tension in the solar plexus. The jumping movement makes breathing deeper and more steady.

MASSAGE

With your palm open, massage your stomach in a circular movement. This action is very soothing.

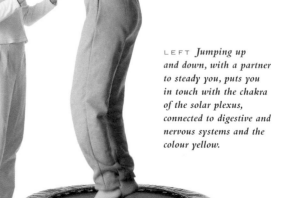

LEFT *Jumping up and down, with a partner to steady you, puts you in touch with the chakra of the solar plexus, connected to digestive and nervous systems and the colour yellow.*

Green chakra – heart

✍ Stretch out your arms above your head, breathe in and out deeply and slowly. Now stretch out your arms to the sides and relax in this position. You should feel your chest expanding and stretching out.

✍ To open the front of the heart chakra, find a fat cushion or bolster and lie on your back with the cushion under your shoulder blades.

✍ For the back of the heart chakra, kneel down and stretch your arms out in front of you on the floor. Now slide back so your bottom rests on your toes. Stretch out for a few minutes, then slide your arms away in front of you until your bottom is now over your knees. Repeat four times.

✍ Now relax with your arms down by your sides and rest your shoulders on the floor with your chest on your knees.

MASSAGE

With your left hand loosely making a fist, tap your thymus gland just over the heart seven times. This exercise is best done in the morning. You can also gently massage the chest. Place your left forefinger on the thymus gland and form figures of eight with your right hand around the body, passing through the thymus gland each time. Repeat five times.

Blue chakra – thyroid

✍ Move your head forward and backward, then from side to side, repeating the motion several times. Now roll your head slowly around in both directions several times.

✍ Move your shoulders up and down, then roll them forward and then backward to loosen them. The throat chakra also responds very well to sound, so hum or sing.

MASSAGE

Gently tap each side of the neck and each shoulder. You can work your way down the arms and up again.

Violet chakra – third eye

✍ Move your (open) eyes up and then down, then left, then right. Now roll them around to every corner of your vision in both directions.

✍ Look up and left and then down and right, then swap over the directions, looking first up and right, followed by down and left.

✍ Now rub your palms quickly together until they are hot. Cup your open palms over your eyes, and the warmth from your palms will soothe and relax them.

MASSAGE

Using your second and third finger together, gently press the third eye area between your eyebrows. You can anoint the third eye with a drop of lavender oil.

White chakra – crown

✍ Rub the crown of your head in a clockwise direction with your right hand.

✍ You can also give yourself a head massage, much the same as you would do when washing your hair. Feel how it relieves headaches and clears the head. A head massage is wonderful for people who are losing their hair, or are angry or generally heated because the head is where energy blockage is often held.

MASSAGE

Make small circles just above the crown of your head with your hand.

ABOVE *Rubbing the top of your head in a clockwise motion stimulates the crown chakra that affects your brain and central nervous system.*

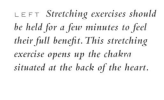

LEFT *Stretching exercises should be held for a few minutes to feel their full benefit. This stretching exercise opens up the chakra situated at the back of the heart.*

DIRECTING COLOUR
ENERGY IN THE BODY

Colour is just another form of wavelength, a vibration. Since thought is a vibration too, we can think strong positive thoughts and they will travel through us and influence our physical being.

DIRECTING COLOUR ENERGY WITH THE MIND

We can add colour to our thought waves for added success. Focusing on a colour can help our concentration and make our thought waves stronger, like holding a magnifying glass through which light rays are concentrated. We cannot see the focusing of these light rays through the magnifying glass, yet the evidence of the burning paper proves its power to us.

Visualization techniques (*see* p 226) are widely used to aid relaxation and sleep, and in the treatment of cancer and other diseases where available treatments are insufficient. Cancer patients are taught to focus mentally on the cells in the infected area and visualize them as complete, disease free, and completely healthy. The colour violet is used to cleanse cells in the disturbed area. The dense vibration of purple/violet also has a marked influence on all types of pain. Many people have dumbfounded doctors by their powers of recovery and have fought off serious illness by using these methods.

Visualization works because the mind can affect the body. Our etheric body is an exact duplicate of the physical body, but vibrates at a much higher, lighter rate than the heavier, denser physical body. This is why it is not visible to the naked eye. Some researchers, for instance using high-energy photography, have discovered that diseases may often appear in the etheric body long before they manifest in the physical body.

POSITIVE VISUALIZATION

By using strong concentrated thoughts, which are only vibrations in themselves, we can influence the physical body through the etheric body. If we can change the vibration patterns in the etheric, the physical body will also take on the new pattern. Visualization gets our desired blueprint across to the etheric body, so we must visualize what we want, and not what we don't want – in other words, visualize positively, not negatively. We must visualize the perfect state or perfect health, or concentrate on the perfect functioning of our bodies.

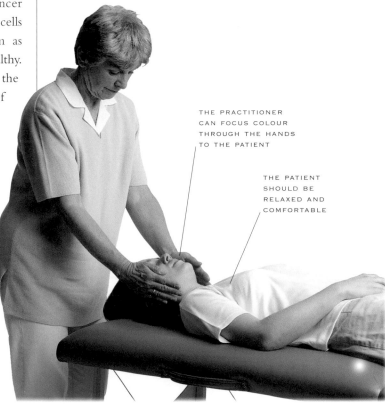

THE PRACTITIONER CAN FOCUS COLOUR THROUGH THE HANDS TO THE PATIENT

THE PATIENT SHOULD BE RELAXED AND COMFORTABLE

RIGHT *Patients can be helped by a practitioner to focus healing colour to diminish an area of pain or disease.*

218

ACHIEVE A
CALM AND
BALANCED
STATE

ADOPT A
RELAXED
POSITION

LEFT *Before channeling colour vibrations, prepare yourself for 5 minutes so that you feel calm and in touch with your higher self.*

of mind. The methods that are given in this section can help balance your body system prior to giving healing treatment.

Colour healing needs to take place in an airy and quiet environment where you won't be disturbed. Ideally you should have bathed before the treatment and should be wearing clean, neutral-coloured clothes (a protective dark blue is good when giving chromatherapy treatments), because both skin and clothing can pick up and hold negative energy. The quality and lightness of the food that you eat beforehand will also influence your energetic system.

AURA POLLUTION

Alcohol, drugs and smoking all create pollution in our aura, so you should refrain from these if you wish to perform colour healing.

CHANNELING COLOUR ENERGY THROUGH THE HANDS

Channeling colour through the hands can be used to direct colour energy either to our own or someone else's body. If we wish to perform colour healing on another person we first have to ensure we are in a balanced state ourselves. Any imbalances in our system will distort the colour vibrations, so we will pass on contaminated energy. To avoid this, it is important that we begin by cleansing our system as much as possible and practice colour healing only when we are healthy and in a peaceful state

Before you can channel colour energy, you will need to still your mind and connect with your intuition and spiritual forces. You can do this by sitting quietly for 5 minutes, practicing cleansing breathing (*see* p 228) using white light and mentally opening each chakra as you draw your attention up to your third eye or brow center. If you are giving healing to another person visualize yourself circled in a protective white or golden light.

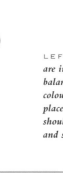

NEUTRAL-
COLOURED
CLOTHING

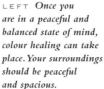

LEFT *Once you are in a peaceful and balanced state of mind, colour healing can take place. Your surroundings should be peaceful and spacious.*

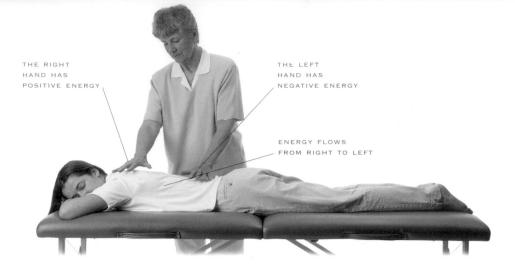

THE RIGHT
HAND HAS
POSITIVE ENERGY

THE LEFT
HAND HAS
NEGATIVE ENERGY

ENERGY FLOWS
FROM RIGHT TO LEFT

POLARIZING HEALING TREATMENTS

This method moves blocked energy within the chakras, restoring a natural flow of energy through the system. Like all living things the human body contains electrical energy, with positive and negative polarities. These polarities affect our electrical circuits and can create confusion in the mind and body. Each hand possesses a different dominant polarity – the left hand corresponds to the north pole and is negative, while the right hand corresponds to the south pole and is positive.

In colour healing, the healer's left hand is the receiver or contains negative polarity while the right hand is the transmitter or positive force. Placing your left hand on the solar plexus, move your right hand to appropriate chakras or meridian points to complete the circuit. Remove your hands when you feel the flow of energy passing through your body and between your hands in a circular motion from right to left.

TONIC HEALING TREATMENT

This is a good treatment to give in the morning because it raises energy levels and feeds the immune system. To do this you need to channel orange light to the base of the spine and sacral chakra, moving your hands around the pelvis area until the person you are treating feels a warm glow in the lower spine. You can also channel orange light through the feet, feeding the solar plexus, which will distribute the stimulating effects throughout the system. Heat will be produced in deep structures, thus diminishing congestion especially in the lymphatics. Blood vessels dilate, increasing the blood supply. If a stronger treatment is required when someone is extremely exhausted, cold, or anemic, channel magenta light to the base of the spine, kidney area, and soles of the feet.

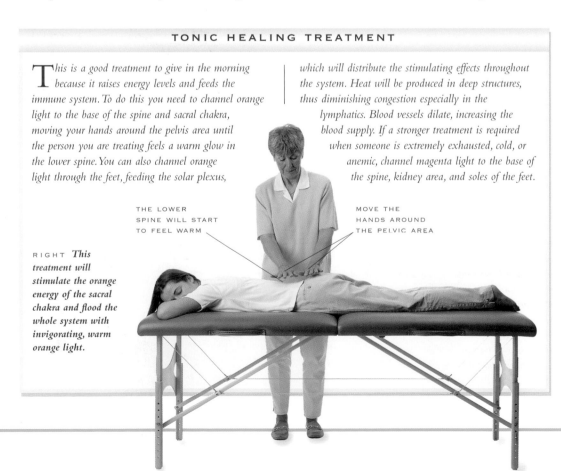

THE LOWER
SPINE WILL START
TO FEEL WARM

MOVE THE
HANDS AROUND
THE PELVIC AREA

RIGHT **This treatment will stimulate the orange energy of the sacral chakra and flood the whole system with invigorating, warm orange light.**

Pain relief

Pain, although unpleasant, is a necessary phenomenon for it is the only means of communication the body has to let us know that something is wrong and we must take immediate notice. Its discomfort forces us to make changes, especially at times when we have been ignoring telltale signs of imbalance for too long. It is essential to find out the cause of the pain and treat this problem at source. This may take some time and effort, but once harmony is restored the pain will disappear. So make sure you are treating the cause and not just the symptom. We should not concentrate on suppressing pain or healing pain itself, but rather should use colour healing for pain relief while the deeper causes are being treated.

EMOTIONAL AND MENTAL PAIN

ABOVE *When healing with green energy, visualizing bare feet on lush, summer grass will help.*

Many of us experience the feeling of heartache when suffering from the emotional pain of rejection or grief over the loss of a loved one. This type of pain often also affects us physically; it can take the form of a migraine headache, back and joint aches and generally manifests with many of the same symptoms as stress.

Green is the colour energy needed for this kind of pain, for green is nature's healer and teaches the lesson of nature's abundance, and that before we can go through a period of regeneration and growth the old needs to be broken down, followed by a period of change and rest.

Channel green through your hands by placing them over the heart. Breathe slowly and deeply until the tension held in the chest is released and a feeling of relaxation replaces it. An appropriate visualization to accompany this would be walking on soft green grass with bare feet and imagine the feeling of freedom that this brings.

PHYSICAL PAIN

Deep blue is an excellent pain healer. It also has antiseptic and cooling properties and aids the body's own healing process, accelerating the formation of new cell growth and scar tissue. You may wish to channel blue for pain healing, and in this case you need to visualize a ball of deep midnight blue light above your head. Absorb this blue and feel it traveling to your hands, and through them to the part of the body that needs healing. If healing someone else, place your hands over the painful area while you visualize the blue light entering the tissues and cells, cleansing and cooling as it progresses through the person's system. Tell him or her to try to go through the pain to a place where harmony and balance reign, and hold an image of a deep blue pool of light as the pain eases.

TRANSMIT THE BLUE VIBRATION FROM YOUR HANDS TO THE PAINFUL AREA

LEFT *The image of a deep blue ball of light above your head, from which you absorb healing energy, can help relieve pain.*

CHROMATHERAPY AND COLOUR ACUPUNCTURE

Many of our ailments can be treated directly with the use of coloured light. If you have some difficulty in attracting and directing colour energy using the hands and mind, an alternative is either to use certain light-emitting instruments over the whole body or to direct light to a certain part of the body.

RIGHT Colour therapists use directional light energy to treat a variety of ailments. Coloured rays are directed at different energy points on the body.

These have the added bonus of being visible to us or another person we are treating, and the colours themselves can be healing and comforting. Two techniques that use coloured light in this way are chromatherapy and colour acupuncture.

IRRADIATION AND CHROMATHERAPY

Light irradiation was first used by the Ancient Egyptians, who have left us evidence of their colour-healing treatments in their temples and writings. Small rooms were built around the courtyards in a temple complex. The rooms were floodlit with colour energy, which entered the room through stained-glass panels and gemstones set into the roof. Each room was designed to give a particular colour treatment.

In much more recent times this method has been used in certain psychiatric wards and hospitals, but the colour energy was reflected off the walls, which were painted a single colour and the light source in each room was also a specific colour. Many theaters to this day still have a "green room" where actors can relax before they go on stage.

There are various methods of treatment that are practiced by experienced colour therapists. Chromapaths give treatments by exposure of a body part to light filtered through coloured filters or a crystal. The light ray can also

RIGHT Colour therapy is thousands of years old. Evidence has been found in Ancient Egyptian writings of the practice and some of their temples were built with colour-treatment rooms.

be directed at different energy points on the body – a method known as colour acupuncture (*see* p 224) – or on the chakra centers.

CHROMATHERAPY AT HOME

Colour therapists sometimes use an artificial light source or light instruments to aid with colour healing and, although without training it is difficult to give ourselves complete chromatherapy treatments at home, we can use the same principles to give ourselves, family, and friends colour treatments using coloured lamps and filters, crystals, colour acupressure, and colour reflexology techniques.

COLOURED LIGHTS

There are several ways we can make use of light instruments as tools for assisting us with focusing colour energy.

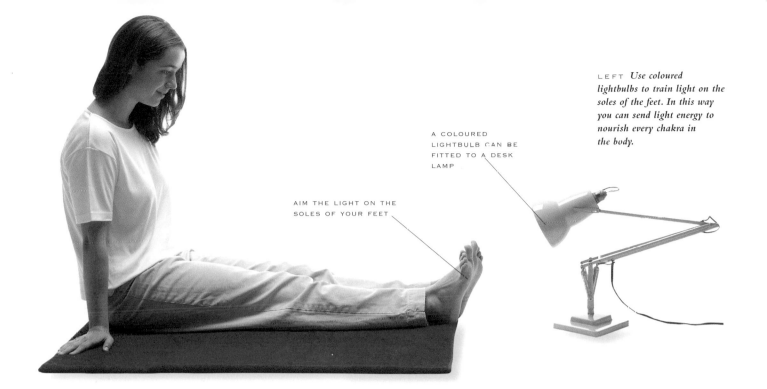

A COLOURED
LIGHTBULB CAN BE
FITTED TO A DESK
LAMP

AIM THE LIGHT ON THE
SOLES OF YOUR FEET

LEFT *Use coloured
lightbulbs to train light on the
soles of the feet. In this way
you can send light energy to
nourish every chakra in
the body.*

The first method is to use coloured light over the whole body. We can give ourselves an overall coloured light irradiation by fitting in a particular room or a table lamp lightbulbs of appropriate colours. (*See* p 137 for the effects of different-coloured lights.)

It is also possible to direct light irradiation on to our feet. The solar plexus reflex in the middle of the sole of the foot acts as a "junction box " through which we can send light energy to all the energy centers in the body. The warming, magnetic colours of red, magenta, orange, and yellow are particularly successful if directed through the feet because these colour energies are naturally drawn into the body through the feet. Do this by placing the light a little distance from the feet. Both feet need to be treated equally in order to keep the energy balanced.

FILTERS

An inexpensive way of giving a chromatherapy treatment without buying expensive specialized instruments is by using the same colour filters that we use to solarize water. By shining a light through them the colour vibration is directed to the affected part of the body or onto the relevant body energy center. Unless you have a specialized lamp that has a filter attachment, this method can be difficult to administer to oneself, so it is best to give this form of colour treatments to others when you feel confident to do so.

BELOW *Use a
coloured filter to direct
colour to an affected body
part or depleted chakra.
Cooling blue light is a
pain reliever.*

THE PRINCIPLES OF CHROMATHERAPY

The primary colours used in chromatherapy are red, green, and blue/violet; this is because chromatherapy is based on the theory of the physics of light and these are the primary colours of light – that is, they cannot be derived from the other colours, and when these three primary colours are projected as beams of light, mixing them results in white light. (*See* p 13 for more detail on this, and pp 83 and 215 for the effects of these three colours on the various glands and organs of the body, and on our systems overall.)

Colour vibrations work in pairs or with their complementary colour energy. Each colour naturally attracts its opposite and complementary energy just as magnets attract each other. This is why when we stare at a colour for a minute or so and then look away we see a temporary flash of the complementary colour.

Each complementary colour enhances the other – one energizing and the other calming. It is the rhythm created by alternating the colours that sets up a resonance that moves and balances energy in the tissues and cells. Consequently, in chromatherapy these colours are used in pairs – first the activating colour (the Yang colour – for an explanation of Yin and Yang *see* p 80), followed by the balancing or sedating colour (the Yin colour).

Chromatherapy treatments really need to be given regularly when treating illness, in groups of three treatments as often as necessary. Acute conditions may need a treatment every day for 3 days, while chronic conditions may require a treatment only once a week over a longer period of time. The healing properties of the colours are listed on pp 209 and 230; decide which ailments most need attention, and which mental or emotional symptoms you'd like to address. Apply treatment, using Yin and Yang colours, as follows.

TREATMENT SEQUENCE

TREATMENT	YIN COLOUR	YANG COLOUR	YIN COLOUR
1		7 minutes	2 minutes
2		5 minutes	4 minutes
3	3 minutes	3 minutes	3 minutes

COMPLEMENTARY COLOUR PAIRS IN CHROMATHERAPY

YANG (STIMULATING)	YIN (SEDATING)
red/pink	*green*
orange	*blue*
yellow	*violet*

COLOUR ACUPUNCTURE OR ACUPRESSURE

Colour therapy affects the electricity that keeps our bodies working. Electrical impulses carry the messages that travel through our nerves between the sensory parts of the body and the control centers in the brain and spinal cord, and each

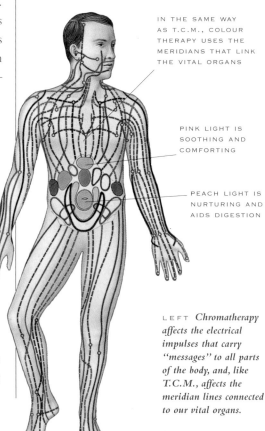

IN THE SAME WAY AS T.C.M., COLOUR THERAPY USES THE MERIDIANS THAT LINK THE VITAL ORGANS

PINK LIGHT IS SOOTHING AND COMFORTING

PEACH LIGHT IS NURTURING AND AIDS DIGESTION

LEFT *Chromatherapy affects the electrical impulses that carry "messages" to all parts of the body, and, like T.C.M., affects the meridian lines connected to our vital organs.*

muscle cell. In addition, according to Traditional Chinese Medicine, there are other electrical circuits known as meridians; most of these are associated with one of the body organs – the liver, kidney, small intestine, large intestine, stomach, spleen/pancreas, gall bladder, bladder, lung, heart, etc. – running between the head and the hands or feet. Certain points along these meridians where the resistance to the electrical current is lower (called acupuncture points or acupoints) are used to adjust and balance the energy in each organ system. These points can be influenced by inserting needles (acupuncture), pressure (acupressure), and also by coloured light, a technique known as colour acupuncture.

These practices need to be performed with caution, preferably by a qualified colour therapist, to avoid further imbalancing the meridians with the wrong colours. However, colour acupressure can be used safely; you can do this by pressing coloured marks or gems on the acupoints. Some colour healers also press the depression behind the ball of the feet with their middle fingers, this applies pressure to the first point on the kidney meridian, an important point used for calming and to increase the vital energy. It is quite comfortable to do this while resting your thumbs on the top of the foot.

LEFT *Use coloured gems or stones to apply healing colour pressure on certain acupoints.*

APPLYING PRESSURE ON THE BALL OF THE FOOT AFFECTS THE KIDNEY MERIDIAN

ABOVE *Colour acupressure can be performed safely in the comfort of your own home.*

COLOUR IRRADIATION/PRESSURE		
COLOUR	METHOD	USES
red	*foot pressure*	*exhaustion, coldness in lower limbs, anemia, chronic arthritis, lethargy, low blood pressure*
pink	*light irradiation or foot pressure*	*soothing, pacifying, emotionally supporting, promotes self-love, and helps loneliness and grief*
orange	*light irradiation or foot pressure*	*low libido, chronic asthma, SAD (seasonal affective disorder), phlegm in system, stiffness in joints, activates lymphatics*
peach	*light irradiation to whole body*	*warming and nurturing, aids digestion, good for children to help sleep and to provide comfort*
yellow	*foot pressure*	*nervousness, fear, skin cleanser, constipation, releases calcium deposits, helps obesity/diabetes by stimulating pancreas to make insulin, stimulating without raising the heartbeat*
green	*light irradiation on chakra, organ, or gland*	*shock, stress, normalizes circulation, hay fever, indigestion, emotional trauma, normalizes growth of cells*
blue	*light irradiation to whole body*	*acute pain relief, fevers, burns, sunstroke, depresses heartbeat, calming, acute bronchitis, acute asthma*
violet	*light irradiation to whole body*	*mental and nervous disorders, strengthens bladder and kidney, regulates potassium balance, controls hunger, cleans blood, varicose veins. Good for meditation because it raises consciousness and promotes alpha brain wave state*
magenta	*foot pressure*	*polarizes body's magnetic field, stimulating without raising heartbeat, warming but with a gentler action than red*

COLOUR-BREATHING VISUALIZATIONS

The power of positive thought is reinforced by creative visualization using colour, which can aid mental development, and peace of mind and spirit. Visualizations of this kind have been used over the centuries as an aid to meditation.

VISUALIZE A GOLDEN SUNSET TO HELP YOU UNWIND

ADOPT A RELAXING YOGA POSE

ABOVE *Colour visualizations used in combination with yoga are extremely therapeutic.*

RIGHT *Colour breathing involves envisaging beams of colour energy entering our etheric energy centers or chakras.*

Those who have practiced certain types of yoga, or spiritual healing techniques have used colour breathing with good results. In the West, medical science is now recognizing the healing power they contain. Visualizations are now used extensively to alleviate pain, in times of shock, for stress and distress, and in the treatment of serious illness.

Many methods of psychotherapy can help us identify and release deep-seated internal emotional blocks, which affect our health, but colour breathing and visualization help us unblock these channels psychically. Colour breathing makes use of the act of breathing together with the mental focus on colour. Using colour visualization is not merely a technique with instant visible results. A student does, however, need to understand the laws of colour and how to apply them through visualization. By learning how to colour breathe you can direct it, together with a source of life energy contained in the breath, to any part of your body – your glands, organs, even your face and eyes – or to protect inanimate objects such as your home and belongings. People who have been practicing colour breathing with care and understanding have reported dramatic changes in their

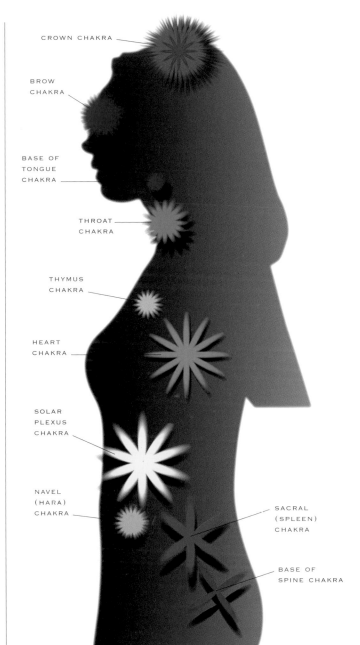

CROWN CHAKRA

BROW CHAKRA

BASE OF TONGUE CHAKRA

THROAT CHAKRA

THYMUS CHAKRA

HEART CHAKRA

SOLAR PLEXUS CHAKRA

NAVEL (HARA) CHAKRA

SACRAL (SPLEEN) CHAKRA

BASE OF SPINE CHAKRA

physical and mental health. The power of the positive mind coupled with the uplifting effects of the coloured rays are a winning combination.

The breath itself is coloured since the ethers are coloured and we continuously breathe into ourselves the colours of the people, places and objects around us. If someone is depressed, or has been smoking, they will breathe out gray or brown, and their dirt is superimposed on our energy centers when we inhale. Each of our centers or chakras also accumulates negativity by our thoughts and actions. We should aim to breathe in the life-giving colours we need and breathe out the dark, dirty colours that are polluting us internally.

We need therefore to focus our minds on a particular colour so that a positive blueprint will be picked up through the etheric body. If we consistently reprogram our blueprint on a daily basis, the message will get through to the conscious mind with very tangible results. Like learning to drive a car or ride a bicycle, we need to practice consistently before we internalize the process and do it automatically. It is also best to prepare ourselves before embarking on colour-breathing visualization by learning to breathe properly. Most of our breathing is so shallow we are depleted by it.

Linda Clark and Yvonne Martine, in their wonderful book *Health, Youth and Beauty through Colour Breathing*, tell us that if we want a happy life we must think happy thoughts. If we want a prosperous life we must think prosperous thoughts. If we want a loving life we must think loving thoughts. Whatever we send out mentally or verbally will come back to us in like form. You must, however, think these thoughts sincerely and not merely for your own gain, because you cannot deceive yourself, or that deceit will be mirrored back to you.

Self-discipline is needed for best effect. The following guidelines are essential for colour breathing to work well.

THINK OF A
HAPPY OCCASION

SIT IN A RELAXED AND
COMFORTABLE POSTURE

ABOVE
Imagining a happy occasion will promote positive thoughts.

❧ Visualize only what you wish to happen for your own highest good. Negative thoughts imprint themselves too. If you are constantly expecting the worst you are blocking out good vibrations from your system.

❧ Work out a colour-related affirmation and repeat it consistently. This is equivalent to mental "software," changing negative thought patterns into positive ones. So if you are prone to say things like, "It always happens to me," or "I am no good/ugly/stupid/unlucky," these thoughts will be constantly reinforced in your system.

❧ Concentrate and visualize strongly. Thought is a vibration and a stronger vibration will work better than a weak one. The mind needs to be focused in order to send out pure and resonant thought waves. These strong vibrations will override the mass of worried and confused thoughts swirling around the head.

❧ Add colour for extra vibrational effects to your visualizations and affirmations. This is the general overall plan for achieving youth, beauty, and health. Use colour affirmations to focus on the qualities you want to enhance.

ABOVE *Stretch upward from the waist, extending the upper body.*

CLEANSING BREATH TO OPEN CHANNELS FOR COLOUR VIBRATIONS

Colour visualization is much more effective if you first cleanse the body with slow, deep, cleansing breathing. You can do this standing or kneeling, or sitting cross-legged if you find this position comfortable. (Never undertake this exercise on a full stomach.)

🌿 Stretch out of the waist, pulling your upper body out of the stomach.

🌿 Visualize an imaginary thread attached to the top of your head, pulling you upward. This opens the chest and lungs. You can use a chair or wall to help you sit straight if you are not sure of your position.

🌿 Raise and lower both your shoulders a couple of times to relax them.

🌿 Now breathe slowly through the nostrils, filling first the lower part of the lungs and diaphragm. As the air descends into the lungs it will push forward the front walls of the abdomen, giving your internal organs a gentle squeeze.

🌿 Now fill the middle part of your lungs with air, extending the ribcage. Then top up the breath into your upper chest and throat. Hold it a second and then exhale slowly.

🌿 Breathe rhythmically and evenly.

RHYTHMIC COLOUR BREATHING – PRANAYAMA

Colour visualization can be especially effective if you combine it with yogic breathing. Pranayama is the Indian "science of the breath," which includes breathing in a rhythmic and balanced way. To perform pranayama find a comfortable sitting position where your back is straight and both feet are on the floor.

🌿 Gently close your right nostril with your thumb so that you cannot breathe through it and slowly exhale through your left nostril.

ABOVE *Relax, raise and lower shoulder, then breathe in.*

🌿 Inhale through your left nostril and then close it with your two middle fingers.

🌿 Exhale through your right nostril.

🌿 Keeping the left closed, inhale again through your right nostril, and so on.

🌿 Do not worry about taking deep breaths or holding your breath. Just relax and breathe comfortably and rhythmically.

🌿 Now combine the breathing with colour visualization. Our nostrils emit different colours; the right is positive and associated with the sun, the warming reds and oranges; and the left is negative and associated with the Moon, the blues and greens. Visualize these colours as you breathe.

CLOSE THE RIGHT NOSTRIL WITH YOUR THUMB AND EXHALE THROUGH THE LEFT NOSTRIL

ABOVE *We exhale different colours from each nostril; the right nostril is positive, the left is negative.*

EXHALE THROUGH RIGHT NOSTRIL

CLOSE LEFT NOSTRIL WITH TWO FINGERS

ABOVE *Colour visualization is enhanced when performed simultaneously with yogic breathing.*

COLOUR BREATHING AND MUSIC

Colour visualizations can be enhanced by listening to relaxing music while practicing them.

⟅ First lie comfortably on the floor, consciously relaxing each part of your body in turn.

⟅ Start with the toes and then feet, first tensing and relaxing each part, working up the body.

⟅ Roll your head gently from side to side, then open and shut your eyes, relax the ears and finally the whole head.

⟅ You can then breathe in and out slowly and deeply, surrounding yourself with the colour associated with the area needing treatment.

⟅ Hold this colour in your mind's eye for a few minutes. Alternatively surround your body with a rainbow, gold, or mother-of-pearl sheaf.

USING COLOUR BREATHING TO RELAX AND HEAL

The coloured cosmic rays have a powerful effect on our glandular system and its etheric counter-part, and the best way we can give ourselves a colour treatment is by getting into the daily habit of practicing colour visualizations. Paying atten-tion to the area of the body where the weakness first occurs will give us an insight into the area that needs to be healed and the correct colour to use. For instance, people who suffer from stomach ulcers have their tension lodged in their solar plexus, while those with shoulder problems carry their load literally on their shoulders. Each area, as we know, corresponds to one of the chakras, and we can start by practicing colour visualiza-tions to release tension in any of these areas.

We do not need to be restricted to the seven rainbow colours when using colour breathing. It also often happens when you are concentrating on colour breathing that you will experience changing harmonies of colour. Try to remember any colour that is particularly special because this colour may be meaningful to you at this time.

Colour breathing can be combined with colour affirmations (*see* p 236) to focus on the specific quality of the colour you are breathing. Close your eyes when saying and visualizing a colour affirmation. Breathe naturally, deeply and slowly, consciously taking the colour into you and letting it fill your whole being.

ABOVE *Imagine yourself surrounded by a rainbow. Also, listening to relaxing music can help to improve your colour visualizations.*

COLOURS TO USE FOR COLOUR-BREATHING VISUALIZATION

Red

The red cosmic ray is very powerful and should not be used by people with high blood pressure or circulatory troubles. The experienced colour healer and teacher Marie Louise Lacy suggests using rose pink, a softer version of red. Since red is a magnetic ray, imagine the rose pink rising through the soles of your feet.

PINK

Use for skin wrinkles, acne, sagging, puffiness and looseness and liver spots. Pink also gives support to feelings of loneliness, despondency, or despair. Use pink to heal if you are oversensitive to others' influences.

ROSE PINK

Use for creating loving rapport. It has also been used for organ regeneration. It is a sexual colour for a positive self-image as an attractive person.

SALMON PINK

This represents love for all humanity, and a self-sacrificing mother love.

Orange

Orange is the vitality ray, and like rose pink is drawn up through the soles of the feet.

Apricot/peach

This removes pain, but does not cure it. It is a powerful tonic, and flows through the glands, stimulating and vitalizing them. It is good for nervous exhaustion.

Yellow

Yellow is the colour of the sun. Use it when you are feeling depressed or lonely. Golden-yellow is a magnetic ray, drawn through the soles of the feet.

Gold

Gold is an overall healing colour to irradiate you from head to toe; it connects to the light of the higher spirit, restructuring the spiritual layers of the aura, protecting and charging the energy field with prana (life force). It is helpful for inner head problems, growths, and heart conditions. Use gold for fear, uncertainty, and when you show lack of interest in your present circumstances.

PALE GOLD

This is stimulating and illuminating to the mind and brain, spinal cord, and nervous system. It is excellent for depression.

Green

The green cosmic ray enters the body horizontally at the solar plexus; it is excellent for shock and nervous tension.

PALE GREEN

This can improve vision, eye injuries, or diseases not involved with circulation or nerves.

MEDIUM GREEN

This balances excesses and eliminates bad habits. Use it alongside a picture of what you wish to be. Green is the source of universal enrichment so use it to aid progress.

GRASS GREEN

Grass green restores rhythm and strength to the nerves. Use also for financial and material success. This must not be used for greed or for illegal gain, however, since it will always return to you somehow.

DARK GREEN

This shade purifies the blood and can be used for blood diseases and anemia. It is helpful for emotional uncertainty.

Blue

Sapphire blue is the first of the electrical rays, entering the body through the crown chakra. It has a calming, soothing and cooling effect, and is the colour of peace.

LIGHT BLUE

Light blue is electric, cooling and soothing, removing poisons from the tissues. If you suffer from insomnia use blue or lavender to induce sleep. It links us with our creativity.

SAPPHIRE

Sapphire is a general pain healer.

DARK BLUE

This shade enhances the powers of expression, gives psychological protection and authority.

TEAL BLUE

This shade helps heal bones and strengthen hair, nails, and teeth.

Turquoise

Turquoise transforms and can help you make a fresh start. It is good for lonely people, enhancing communication and creativity. It also removes excess fat when alternated with pink. It relieves respiratory ailments and arthritis. Use it to help people overconcerned for the welfare of others.

Indigo

This is the ray of knowledge and wisdom and is drawn into the body through the crown chakra. Indigo helps us get in touch with those things already inside us that we often cannot find.

Violet

Violet is the cosmic ray with the highest vibration and enters through the crown chakra. It works on the master glands and etheric center. It purifies, controls growth, and relieves pain. Use it for the treatment of shock or fear.

DEEP VIOLET

Can be used to cleanse cells in an infected area, and as a treatment for physical shock.

Purple

A cleansing breath for both physical and emotional disturbances. If you are in danger of any kind visualize the purple light beginning around your feet and working upward, enveloping your entire body, while asking for the disturbance to be removed. Immediately follow this with a cocoon of white light (see below).

White

White is an all-round colour of protection. Drawing a cocoon of white light around you from head to toe protects you from danger. Some people cleanse their entire house every morning by visualizing each room filled with white light. Use also to treat emotional shock and despair.

Silver

Silver gives a strong clearing of our energy field, balancing the feminine aspect.

COLOUR VISUALIZATIONS TO RELAX AND HEAL

The heart

Andrew Watson gives us several beautiful creative guided visualizations in his book *Healing Music*. Each exercise corresponds to a different chakra and you are asked to associate each area with a symbol, colour, and fragrance that you can recall with ease. I shall give you the visualization for the heart chakra; this controls the immune system, so is of vital importance to the healing process. The heart is "in healing terms, the transformer used to convert universal energy into the healing force or unconditional love."

✎ Sit or lie comfortably and relax your body and mind. Begin to imagine the closed bud of a flower you know will have 12 golden petals and a radiant blue center.

✎ As you visualize this, the sun rises over the horizon and shines down to warm and enliven this plant. The closed bud begins to open. Visualize the warming rays of the sun continuing to shine down as the golden petals gently draw back one by one, eventually revealing a glimpse of this beautifully radiant blue center.

✎ As the sun strikes the blue in the center of this opening bud, the center is energized and begins to spin on itself.

✎ As the 12 golden petals open fully outward the radiant

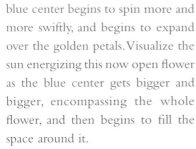

*RIGHT **Visualize the unfolding of a blue and yellow flower to heal the heart chakra.***

blue center begins to spin more and more swiftly, and begins to expand over the golden petals. Visualize the sun energizing this now open flower as the blue center gets bigger and bigger, encompassing the whole flower, and then begins to fill the space around it.

✎ Further and further the spinning radiant blue begins to fill the space around it.

✎ Further and further the spinning radiant blue center expands, gradually covering everything in its path until, like a large, whirling blue sun, it extends all the way to the horizon and beyond.

✎ As this radiant blue colour flows out over the Earth it encounters troubled spots around the world – for instance, places that are suffering from conflict, or disasters such as flooding, drought, or starvation.

✎ This radiant blue energy feels the pain and suffering of the various peoples, and feels too the pain of the ravaged Earth. As the sun continues to enliven the golden-petaled flower this radiant blue energy is able to flow around the whole planet bringing with it peace, harmony, and healing. As the world is healed, feel within yourself great joy in your heart.

✎ Gently become centered once again in yourself, and allow an image or symbol to form in your mind that would represent the quality of energy found within the heart.

BREATHING IN COLOUR

Standing with your hands outstretched, palms down, you breathe, in a colour. Breathe, in one colour at a time, starting with red and finishing with violet. First imagine red and then orange being drawn up through your feet, yellow entering your solar plexus then green through your chest, blue and violet through your crown.

EXHALING COLOUR

As you bend your knees push your arms down, bending the elbows and bringing them in to your body. At the same time breathe out the colour you have inhaled, through your mouth. Repeat until you have breathed in and out all the colours.

BELOW *To charge your aura with colour, practice visualization while doing these simple movements.*

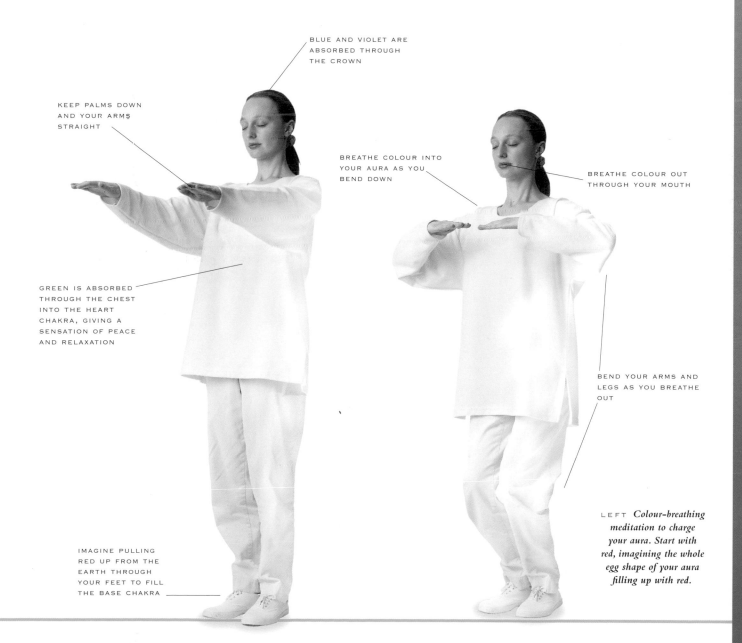

BLUE AND VIOLET ARE ABSORBED THROUGH THE CROWN

KEEP PALMS DOWN AND YOUR ARMS STRAIGHT

BREATHE COLOUR INTO YOUR AURA AS YOU BEND DOWN

BREATHE COLOUR OUT THROUGH YOUR MOUTH

GREEN IS ABSORBED THROUGH THE CHEST INTO THE HEART CHAKRA, GIVING A SENSATION OF PEACE AND RELAXATION

BEND YOUR ARMS AND LEGS AS YOU BREATHE OUT

IMAGINE PULLING RED UP FROM THE EARTH THROUGH YOUR FEET TO FILL THE BASE CHAKRA

LEFT *Colour-breathing meditation to charge your aura. Start with red, imagining the whole egg shape of your aura filling up with red.*

Visualization for general health

This is rejuvenating and invigorating.

Begin by visualizing yourself standing in a field of flowers. The flowers are of every beautiful colour and shade, and go on and on into the distance. Stand in the field and smell the sweet light scent of the flowers. Imagine the air you are breathing is filled with sparkling white light and feel this white light being drawn into your body.

As you breathe out see the cloudiness of the air as it meets the outside. With every breath feel the clean sparkling light reaching all parts of your body, and again see the grayish breath as you exhale. Continue breathing in this way, until your exhaled breath is clear, and you feel your lungs are filled with clean, fresh air.

Now see a large opalescent bubble forming around you. You are held in the center of the bubble and see how it shines when it catches the light. Your bubble starts to move, lifting you above the field of flowers. Feel how light and free you feel. You are carried higher and higher and at the same time feel your body revitalized and in perfect health.

Slowly let your bubble drift back to Earth. Feel that you are a new person transformed into a healthy, revitalized person. Let an image form in your mind that will represent how you are feeling. Open your eyes in your own time, and note down your symbol. Contemplate on this symbol in times when you need a pick-me-up.

You can also keep several crystals near you when you do this exercise. When you open your eyes you will find you are drawn to a stone. The stone will have absorbed the vibrations of health and energy and will give them out to you.

Visualization for nervousness and fear

Nervousness, which is the manifestation of fear, takes seat in the solar plexus just under your ribcage. When you are tense, your liver and pancreas create an excess of bile and you often feel sick.

Use this visualization when you are anxious, nervous, and feel knotted up under your ribcage. The only way of healing yourself is to dissolve your feelings of fear, which are merely projections of the mind.

RIGHT *Picture yourself in a field full of flowers of every colour to improve health and vitality.*

Imagine you are walking through a thick glade of trees, a gentle breeze is blowing and the sun is shining. You come to a stream, and you see how the banks are covered with deep, soft, dark green moss. Touch it, and feel how soft and cool it is. Look into the crystal-clear water, and watch it rippling over the smooth rounded stones. Look at the beautiful colours of the stones, the pale lilacs, the pale gray-greens, and the silvery whites.

Dip your hand into the water, and feel its freshness and cold-ness. Take a refreshing drink and imagine the cool pure water in your mouth, trav-eling down your throat into your stomach.

Now lie on your back on the green moss, and look at the pale blue sky. Listen to the gurgling stream and see the birds swirl high ahead. Feel relaxed and peaceful. Feel the warm sunshine on your skin. Exhale deeply and feel your chest open out.

Breathe in and out deeply again; experience the fresh cool air. All anxieties vanish, you can breathe deeply and peacefully, and you have nothing to worry about.

Everything will happen in its own time – there is no need to rush. The secrets of the universe will unfold when they are ready. Feel the warmth of the sun on your chest, and all around you. You are protected from all you fear by a sheath of golden light. Think of the colour yellow and a symbol to represent how you are feeling at this moment.

Open your eyes in your own time, and feel calm and protected, ready to face anything. Note down your symbol and use it to conjure up this feeling when needed.

LEFT *To heal feelings of fear, visualize yourself amid a lush green glade of trees suffused with soft, yellow sunlight.*

COLOUR AFFIRMATIONS

The coloured cosmic rays have a powerful effect on our glandular system and its etheric counterpart; one of the best ways we can give ourselves a colour treatment is by getting into the daily habit of using colour affirmations.

USE A RED PEN TO ENCOURAGE VITALITY

ABOVE
Affirmations written in colour can stimulate the feelings or attitudes to which you aspire.

An affirmation is a simple sentence that acts as a visual reminder to us of a positive attitude or emotion that we wish to encourage. I have used affirmations myself for many years to help me through times of crisis as well as to boost my creative energy. I find it best to write down my affirmation using felt pens of appropriate colours on a small piece of paper or card. A book of post-cards or sticky telephone message booklets is perfect for this purpose.

Stick or pin your affirmations around the house or place of work in positions you will pass several times a day. Good places include your dressing table, mirror, by the telephone, or in your purse or diary. Try to surprise yourself with these messages because every time you read them you will be reinforcing the positive thought.

THE QUALITIES OF COLOUR

The following are qualities with which the different colours are associated; each of them can be used in combination or alone.

RED

warm, strong, patient, alive, determined, friendly, courageous, vital, assertive

ORANGE

fun, enlivening, practical, humorous, creative, constructive, willing

YELLOW

logical, intelligent, clear-headed, orderly, happy, light, bright, articulate, forgiving

GREEN

balanced, efficient, sincere, harmonious, secure, free, contented, sharing

TURQUOISE

imaginative, youthful, sparkling, fresh, sensitive, elevating, clean, transformational

BLUE

peaceful, tranquil, calm, hopeful, faithful, trusting, flexible, reassuring, honest, united, accepting, healing

VIOLET

dignified, proud, intuitive, gracious, beautiful, modest, valuable, open

MAGENTA

mature, genuine, helpful, natural, yielding, compassionate, supporting, kind, considerate

COLOUR AFFIRMATIONS FOR WELL-BEING

RED

The rose pink cosmic ray is flowing through my veins giving me strength and courage and filling me with God's love.

The magnetic ruby rays are flowing up through my feet and legs, filling me with radiant energy and strength.

ORANGE

The orange cosmic ray is filling me with vitality and joy, recharging my etheric body and rejuvenating every cell in my body.

The orange ray of vitality flows up through my feet and legs, filling my whole body with strength and energy and releasing any energy blockages that prevent the golden life-force from filling every part of me.

YELLOW

The golden-yellow cosmic ray is permeating my body, mind and soul with divine love and wisdom.

The golden-yellow light is flowing into my body, permeating it and enlightening every part of it.

GREEN

The green cosmic ray is flowing through my heart and nervous system, bringing complete balance and harmony to all my being.

I am drinking in the emerald rays, knowing that I am full of balanced strength and am secure and free.

BLUE

The sapphire blue cosmic ray pours into my veins bringing healing into my mind, body, and etheric body.

I breathe in the electric, heavenly blue ray, which cools and calms me, making me feel relaxed and in a state of perfect peace.

INDIGO

The indigo cosmic ray helps me to receive the understanding and knowledge that would be helpful to me at this time.

The midnight blue light pours down into me, purifying my lungs and every cell in my body.

VIOLET

The violet cosmic ray flows into my glands and is healing every cell and part of my being.

I breathe in the purest amethyst violet ray, which is a healing tonic to every nerve in my body. It nourishes and uplifts me.

MAKING YOUR COLOUR AFFIRMATIONS

An alternative to the colour affirmations given above is to construct your own colour affirmation, basing it on words such as the following.

- *Every day, I (name) am made more (strong, friendly, etc.) and (relaxed, happy) by the colour (your colour).*

- *Through the colour (your colour) I (name) am becoming (calm, happy, well, etc.).*

For each colour I have given you two affirmations to promote either your physical health or your mental and spiritual well-being. Repeat the colour affirmation seven times for maximum effect. Colour affirmations can also be combined with colour-breathing visualizations (*see* pp 226–235) for added concentration on the colour being breathed in. It helps to close your eyes when visualizing and saying a colour affirmation.

LEFT *Affirmations placed around the house will serve as frequent reminders to encourage positive thoughts.*

PLACE A COLOURED AFFIRMATION BY THE TELEPHONE TO ENCOURAGE FEELINGS OF PEACEFULNESS

Through the colour blue I am becoming calm

CRYSTAL AND GEM HEALING

Crystals and gemstones are an inexhaustible source of energy that can be used to heal, balance, invigorate or tranquilize in a completely natural way.

We can wear gems set as jewelry, keep them close to us, or use them in our homes and surroundings to improve the quality of everyday life. Business executives can put a crystal in a pocket to enhance concentration and give confidence. There are also many benefits of drinking gem water, and interior decorators can place crystals in homes, hospitals, and offices to absorb the bad vibrations caused by smoke, pollution, V.D.U.s (visual display units) and other machinery. We can treat illness with various stones by laying them on or around the body. For example, a woman suffering from chronic bronchitis was able to treat her illness with an amethyst by laying it on her chest. Coloured gems and crystals can also be laid on the meridian points of the body to give colour acupuncture (*see* p 224).

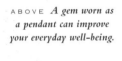

*ABOVE **A gem worn as a pendant can improve your everyday well-being.***

*ABOVE RIGHT **The gemstone has been employed for its spiritual powers since ancient times – turquoise was used by the Egyptians to ward off evil spirits.***

*RIGHT **The giving of rings is rooted in ancient tradition.***

GEMSTONES

Throughout history we have adorned our bodies with stones for decoration and for healing. The giving and receiving of engagement, wedding, and eternity rings is based on these ancient beliefs. Turquoise was used by the Egyptians, Tibetan Buddhists, Native Americans, and many Middle Eastern people for spiritual protection and healing. Both modern and traditional medicine and homeopathy use the healing powers of ground rocks and minerals.

In many cultures, including our own, some stones were believed to hold curses or bring illness. Many people still believe that wearing an opal or pearls will bring bad luck unless they are your birthstone. These customs originate from the knowledge that gemstones absorb and hold electromagnetic vibrations, which they can then release at another time with good or bad effects.

As white light passes through a gem, certain wavelengths may be filtered out; those that survive the passage give the stone its colour. The gem embodies the power of the coloured ray it reflects (*see* p 12–13). Sometimes the interaction of light with a gemstone produces not a single colour but several. Gems such as diamonds have the capacity to separate out the different wavelengths as light passes through them so that all the colours of the rainbow are produced. Other minerals also have this "fire quality" – for example, the fire opal. These stones should be worn alone, because they work on all the body energy centers.

SEMIPRECIOUS STONES

You do not need to use expensive precious gems to obtain the benefits they can bestow because semiprecious stones also embody the power and quality of the coloured cosmic ray required.

Each of us responds differently to different minerals and stones, and most of us have a very strong personal attraction to a particular gem or piece of jewelry. We will be drawn to stones we need, just as we are attracted to particular colours that we need, and it may indeed be the colour of the stone that attracts us.

The darker the colour, the denser and stronger the stone and the more "earthy" it is. A lighter colour will be operating on the same ray, but an octave (or more) higher. Its effects will be softer and more gentle. For example, the colour pink is a much softer spiritual form of love than the physical red of sexual love.

The density of the stone is also an indication of its qualities. The more opaque the stone, the nearer it is to earth and the greater its power. The more brilliant and sparkling the stone, the greater

its ability to stimulate and liberate the spirit and intellect. So if our nature is naturally physically strong and we are secure, stable, and methodical, we require the inspiration of the diamond, or sparkling clear light stones. If we have a tendency to live in a fantasy world we need the stabilizing effects of the physically grounding stones such as the agate.

Gems affect living things because they have similar internal structures to living organisms. All solid matter vibrates and each substance has its own frequency. Higher evolved precious gems reflect clearly their colour energy. They can be used to clear away negative vibrations by laying the stones on the appropriate area on or around the body. The stones themselves vibrate at the same rate as various colours that can clear blockages in us and then recharge our energies.

BELOW *A sparkling diamond will free the spirit of the naturally grounded person.*

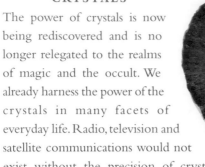

CRYSTALS

The power of crystals is now being rediscovered and is no longer relegated to the realms of magic and the occult. We already harness the power of the crystals in many facets of everyday life. Radio, television and satellite communications would not exist without the precision of crystals' vibrating energy fields. Computer technology and laser surgery both utilize the electromagnetic energy of crystals.

The power of a crystal can be experienced by everyone; simply hold one in the palm of your hand. Some types will radiate immense heat, while others will send tingling or shocklike feelings through your hands.

According to Theo Gimbel, "crystals are original sound forms," and "as sound is the powerful means by which form is created, the crystal captures the sound vibration of its creation." Marcel Vogel was a research scientist with IBM for 27 years, and was responsible for such developments as the magnetic coding for computer tapes and phosphors used in colour television images (phosphors are crystals that have impurities and emit light when excited by heat). He discovered that crystals capture powerful vibrations in their formation, and these remain locked in the gem and can be released, just as a videotape or CD plays back the vibrations locked into its memory. Crystals are also ultrasonic amplifiers, and this quality was used during World War I with crystal radio sets. In addition, crystals were placed at points where

communication cables were broken, to pick up the radio vibrations and amplify them.

Rock or mountain crystal is the best stone for healing, for it acts as a channel for the cosmic rays. This clear quartz is made up of silicon dioxide and emits an energy known as piezoelectricity, which means that when you stimulate one end of the crystal it sends an electrical charge to the other end. We can use this quality in healing

ABOVE *Rock crystal is a clear quartz that is made of silicon dioxide.*

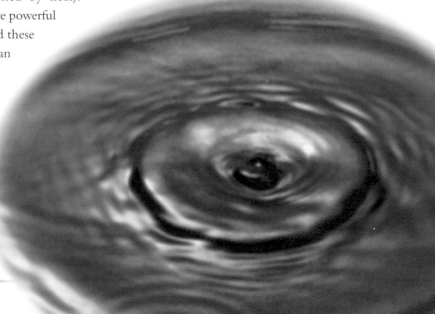

ABOVE *The healing properties of rose quartz are the result of its ability to conduct cosmic rays.*

RIGHT *Crystals can pick up thought vibrations, which move in a similar way to the circular patterns formed after a stone is thrown into water.*

by using the crystal to conduct energy. A crystal is both a receiver and ultrasonic transmitter of energy, and it is able to balance and harmonize the aura.

According to Vogel, crystals not only reflect sound and colour vibrations, but can also pick up our thoughts. He states that our patterns of thought vibration oscillate like a magnetic field. Thought is contained in geometric pattern forms in space, causing that space to oscillate. This movement in turn acts on matter, causing it to vibrate and to make a series of patterns that move outward into space around the body. These are similar to the circular patterns caused when throwing a stone into water.

Vogel discovered, while watching liquid crystals, that if he projected a thought into a crystal before it became solid it took the shape of his thought. If, for example, he thought of a flower, the crystal would take on the form of a flower. When we "think," we generate a pattern. This is "the energy that follows thought." Crystals are believed to respond to thoughts and emotions, and interact with the mind by interacting with these vibrating thought patterns in space.

A CRYSTAL PENDANT IS PROTECTIVE AND SUPPORTING, AND MAY DIAGNOSE CHAKRA IMBALANCE

LEFT *If you are a healer or work in a caring profession, wearing a crystal can enhance your energy field and protect your health.*

The ability of crystals to filter out or amplify certain vibrations can be used to protect or support us. If you are in any healing or counseling profession it is very useful to wear a crystal to protect your energy system and stay healthy. However, you should be sure that you wear the right one for your body. If the crystal is too strong it will increase your vibrations and eventually deplete your energy field. If, however, you choose a crystal that is slightly higher than your energy field, you will enhance your field. A clear quartz or amethyst crystal can be worn over the solar plexus to strengthen your field and make it less permeable. Rose quartz helps protect the heart when worn over the heart chakra.

We can also use crystals to diagnose distortions in the aura, and a crystal pendulum is very effective for diagnosing imbalances in the chakras. Finally, crystals can be programmed to perform a number of tasks - clearing and cleansing, balancing and harmonizing, protecting and healing.

The following list of colour frequencies outlines the characteristics of each of the colours of the spectrum and the areas of our character, mood, and physical being that they affect.

Often, one stone may be substituted for another of the same colour frequency; however, some stones have special effects.

Red-pink

RUBY, GARNET, AGATE, CARNELIAN, CORAL, ROSE QUARTZ

Red stimulates energy, heat, vitality, and regeneration of cells, blood, and tissue. Pink shades restore harmony where there is a conflict of emotion.

- Red stones (e.g. ruby) treat heart disease, circulatory problems, anemia, eye disease, and various mental troubles.

- Coral treats liver diseases, impure blood, high blood pressure, skin troubles, hemorrhoids, and sexual disease, and is good for meditation because it retains images and forms.

- Rose quartz treats mental disturbances and promotes friendship, self-love, forgiveness, and unconditional love.

ABOVE **The deep red of Carnelian is used to treat heart disorder.**

Orange

AMBER, TOPAZ

Orange balances the emotional body and digestive system, increases sexual potency, and boosts immunity. It also helps alcohol problems. It releases self-pity, lack of self-worth, and unwillingness to forgive.

ABOVE **Amber's subtle orange promotes emotional well-being.**

- Amber treats rheumatism, asthma, intestinal disorders, bone marrow, depression, and balances the endocrine and digestive systems. It lifts depression, absorbs negative energy, and promotes joy.

Yellow

ABOVE **Citrine rejuvenates the nervous system; it frees us to play and have fun.**

TOPAZ, CITRINE, YELLOW ZIRCON

Yellow charges the solar plexus area, strengthening nerves and promoting mental clarity.

- Topaz treats throat troubles, asthma, laryngitis, childhood infectious diseases, insomnia and shock, fever and burns, bites, itching, and infections, exhaustion and nervous trauma.

Green

EMERALD, JADE, TOURMALINE, MOSS AGATE

Green is for treating stress, balancing the emotions and general healing. Use it to combat jealousy and possessiveness.

- Emerald treats weak digestion, colic, cancer, skin problems, hypertension, heart troubles, and ulcers.

- Jade treats kidney and bladder problems, and eye trouble. It helps you detach yourself from your emotions and promotes clear thinking.

ABOVE **Moss agate's soothing green revitalizes and strengthens the mind.**

Blue

SAPPHIRE, AQUAMARINE, TURQUOISE, LAPIS LAZULI, BLUE LACE AGATE

Blue inspires mental control, clarity, creativity, and acceptance of responsibility for others. It inspires idealism and working for the good of others.

- Sapphire treats insomnia and nervousness. It gives a feeling of compassion.

- Aquamarine treats nerve pains, glandular troubles, and problems relating to the mouth, throat, and neck. Its balances our physical, mental, and spiritual bodies.

LEFT **Lapis lazuli is a stone of friendship and love.**

Indigo

SODALITE, AMETHYST

Indigo is a powerful colour associated with the right side of the brain, stimulating intuition and imagination. It also connects with and opens the third eye. It clears the head, is a strong sedative, and regenerates cells.

ABOVE **The intensity of sodalite's indigo triggers our powers of intuition.**

Violet/purple/lavender

AMETHYST, CLEAR CRYSTAL, SODALITE, SUGALITE

Violet is the colour of transformation. Purple connects to spirit and psychic protection, stimulating creativity and spiritual awareness; it also removes pain in deep tissue work. Lavender purges and cleans the energy field.

Amethyst treats emotional symptoms, insomnia and headaches, ailments from blood impurities, and alleviates hemorrhages. It is an energizing, transforming, and inspirational stone, helping break old patterns of thought and behavior. It has a marked effect on all pain – physical and emotional.

ABOVE **Amethyst helps to liberate us from entrenched behavioral patterns.**

Infrared

TIGER'S EYE

Infrared is very warming and energizing, with the ability to strengthen willpower and help us in times of stress where we need resistance and stamina. The orangey-brown colouring of tiger's eye gives it very grounding properties and its high iron content also resonates with the colour red. It treats skin diseases, headaches, and indigestion.

RIGHT **The warmth of tiger's eye enables us to put our feet back on the ground.**

Ultraviolet

ONYX

Ultraviolet's high vibrations aid concentration and help focus the mind.

Onyx provides us with structure in our life through grounding us with earth energies. It is used over the whole body following bacterial or viral infection.

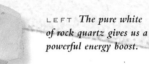

LEFT **The pure white of rock quartz gives us a powerful energy boost.**

White

DIAMOND, PEARL, ROCK CRYSTAL

White is used for charging our energy field, removing pain, and moving stagnant energy. It gives courage and confidence.

Diamond has the highest vibration and is the hardest of all gems. It removes negativity, and gives courage and confidence. It treats eye problems, paralysis, enlarged spleen, and epilepsy.

Pearl treats diabetes, asthma, digestive problems, gall stones, diarrhea, and menopausal difficulties. It gives the message of transmutation and struggle for inner growth. Never mix pearls with other stones because the conflict of energies will be mirrored back to the wearer. In fact, pearls absorb energy and mirror them back, which is why they are thought to be unlucky. Pearls help self-confrontation when you really need to be truthful to yourself.

Black

SMOKY QUARTZ, JET, OBSIDIAN

Black brings about a state of grace, silence, and peace with God and the infinite. Use it for protection against negative forces.

Smoky quartz creates a shield of protection when we are feeling under attack from other people or forces.

RIGHT **The black obsidian stone can protect us from harm.**

TREATMENT WITH CRYSTALS AND GEMSTONES

LEFT *Gems can be stored in soft cloth when not in use, but remember that they derive their energy from sunlight.*

Choosing crystals and gemstones

Choosing the crystals and stones you want to use will be a very intuitive decision. In general, the lighter the colour of the stone, the higher is the vibration. Clear luminous stones relate to the elements of Air and the Ether, which will draw up energy and connect it to the higher forces. Darker stones will contain more of the earth element and should be used on those who need to be "brought down to earth."

ABOVE *Blue lace agate has a high vibration because of its lightness.*

ABOVE *Aquamarine's luminosity gives it an ethereal quality.*

ABOVE *Carnelian's dark red has a grounding effect.*

Preparation

Stones should be carefully cleaned and programmed for the work they have to do. You need to remember they can pick up and store negative energy as well as good, and transfer this energy from one person to another. Cleaning is therefore essential to wash out or deprogram all the bad vibrations the stone has collected. You can do this by placing it in a bowl of salt water. Leave it there until you feel it is clean; the length of time to clean it varies so this is best done intuitively. You can also put the stone under running water.

Once the stone is clear, you are ready to program it. Place the gem in your right hand with the point facing away from your body. You need to be centered in your being to program it, and not in an emotional state. Quieten your mind

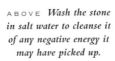

ABOVE *Wash the stone in salt water to cleanse it of any negative energy it may have picked up.*

and ask for help to program the stone for the "highest good." Program the stone with words like – "to balance and harmonize," "to bring peace and love," and "to heal and balance."

You are now ready to wear the stone or to place it where it will be of most benefit. If you are not using a gem immediately, wrap it carefully in soft material and

ABOVE *Ask the stone to perform your chosen task.*

put it away. Do not leave your stones in the dark too long though because, like us, gems get their energy and power from sunlight.

Treatment

Before beginning a colour treatment using gemstones it is best that the person to be treated has bathed to eradicate any negative vibrations picked up from other people or in their environment. A garment of white is the best type to work on, because there is no interference with the vibrations from the stones. A nightdress or loose shirt would be ideal. Some relaxation techniques and creative visualization before the treatment will promote an atmosphere of calm and relaxation (*see* p 232).

You may want to start by using a quartz pendulum over each chakra to identify specific blocks (see p 197). This method is a good visual guide, and one the patient may wish to see. The pendulum should rotate clockwise or anticlockwise alternatively as you move it over each chakra. (Its direction will depend on whether you are treating a man or a woman, for example, over

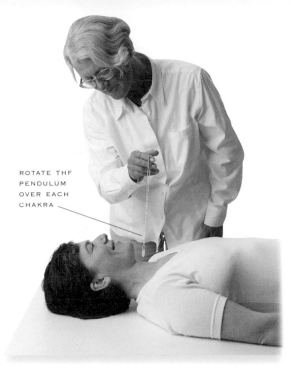

ROTATE THE PENDULUM OVER EACH CHAKRA

Now lay the point of the crown chakra crystal upward and the base stone downward. Point the crystals toward the spot to which you want the energy channeled.

With a sweeping movement starting from the crown chakra, stroke the aura down one side of the body and up the other, ending at the crown chakra once more.

You can place stones corresponding to the colours of the chakra centers: red on the base chakra, orange on the splenic center, and so on. You can place the stones on either the front or back of the body.

The stones will cleanse the aura, and balance and recharge any of the depleted energy centers. They work at a very deep level and often the person being treated falls asleep. If a gem falls off the patient during a treatment, do not replace it for it has done its job and the person no longer needs its energy.

LEFT A quartz pendulum is a useful diagnostic tool.

the crown chakra of a man it will register clockwise, while for a woman it will swing anticlockwise.) The wider the swing, the more open is the chakra; irregular movements indicate areas that are closed.

You may decide to treat certain areas, or you might want to give a good general balancing treatment. Follow this procedure.

You will first need to cleanse the aura by using clear quartz crystals laid at the crown chakra and between the legs.

BELOW A person's energy system is balanced and rejuvenated by healing treatment with stones.

RE-ENERGIZING

When laid on the body, crystal quartz possesses the power to decrystalize the knots that block the flow of energy.

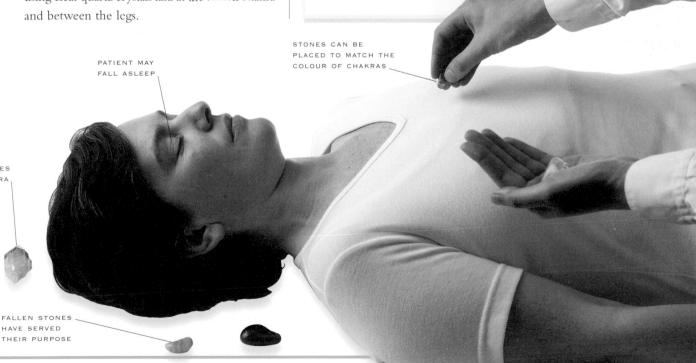

PATIENT MAY FALL ASLEEP

STONES CAN BE PLACED TO MATCH THE COLOUR OF CHAKRAS

CLEAR QUARTZ CLEANSES THE AURA

FALLEN STONES HAVE SERVED THEIR PURPOSE

ENDWORD

Fashion trends have a great influence on our choice of colours and style of furnishings. We are all part of a larger community and are constantly under pressure to emulate ideas seen in the media and stores. If we are not highly selective about the colours we use, we may be surrounding ourselves with harmful colours.

As individuals we should take only those elements from current trends and use only those colours best suited to our emotional and mental health. Each of us can contribute and change the taste and aspirations of the community in which we live. These changes can be positive and benefit the larger group if the individuals making up the group are well balanced, secure, and open-minded.

ABOVE *The colours with which we furnish our houses often reflect our social environment.*

COLOURS FOR THE FUTURE

If we look at the trends in colour preferences it will give us an insight into many aspects of the society in which we live. If we look back in time, we can see that as political and social tension builds, red becomes exceedingly popular. It has been adopted as the symbol of war and revolution throughout history. If war ensues we revert suddenly to dark muddy colours, in uniforms and camouflage suits. Colour becomes a luxury we have to do without. As war progresses and takes its toll and morale is low, strong idealist colours then come to the fore. The flamboyant hues of royal purple, bright fuchsias, and rich magenta serve to lift the spirit and give hope, and are often incorporated into the designs on banners and flags. This same colour pattern emerges during years of great economic depression.

After any time of conflict comes a period of soothing typified by lovely pastels; we need the healing properties of colours mixed with white. We turn then to beautiful misty blues and greens, the colours that belong to healing, higher aspiration, and ideals. Light blue promotes and releases creative energy, and soft greens allow us empathy with others and our environment.

The colour white has played a prominent part in our buildings in the last two decades. This preference for white walls, tiles, and furniture was partly a reaction to the dark, heavy interiors of the war years, and white has become a symbol of the modern home. It reflects light and makes a room bright, airy, and unobstructive, but it also can be sterile and draining. If you need a light, bright environment, choose an off-white, ivory, mushroom, or cream paint.

NATURAL COLOURS AND THE ENVIRONMENT

With our added awareness of the major environmental problems facing our world, the trend in the 1990s has been toward more natural colours. Our adoption of natural tones and pigments shows that we are opening up our awareness and love for our earth. Terra-cotta, turquoise, green, ocher, and old gold have become increasingly popular; these mimic the natural colours in our environment and make us feel more in touch with nature. Even the light tints we are using are soft – ivory, cream, peach and blue-gray, are much more like organic pastels found in the colours of flowers and rocks.

As we go forward in time we see our world in turmoil and crisis. Old orders and ideals are being broken down – and this is a painful and frightening ordeal for us all. We need to lift our vibrations and those surrounding us with lovely natural pastels, silver, pearl, and gold to heal our spirit and to lift us up into the new millennium.

BELOW *Suzy Chiazzari*

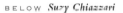

Once your heart as well as your eyes have been opened to colour, its special power will transform your life. When you work sympathetically with colour you will be touched with a divine spark bringing joy and peace to all those whom you meet. In this way we can spread the light, which will help create a better world.

GLOSSARY

A

ABSENT HEALING
Directing colour mentally or through the heart chakra to others who are not present.

ADDITIVE MIXING
Projection of colours of light together to form a new colour.

AFFIRMATIONS
Short sentences repeated many times for their positive effect on the mind.

ASTRAL BODY
One of the subtle bodies, which are invisible to ocular sight; it is filled with vibrations emitted by our emotions.

AURA
Electromagnetic protective envelope of colours and sounds, which surrounds every living thing.

B

BACH FLOWER REMEDY
Flower essence containing light vibrations depending on the colour of the flower.

BETACAROTENE
The orange-yellow pigment in plants (e.g. carrots and squashes).

BICOMPLEMENTARY COLOURS
The colours on either side of a complementary colour.

BIORHYTHMS
The natural body clock, which regulates our sleep patterns and energy levels.

C

CHAKRAS
Centers of energy located within our subtle etheric body, and connected along the spine, acting as a channel through which light flows. Colours from each chakra extend into the aura.

CHANNELING
Opening the chakras to create a channel through which light energy can flow. This energy can be channeled out through the hands for healing.

CHOLERIC
Body type in which the element of Fire is dominant, with a tendency toward overactivity, bad temper, and nervousness.

CHROMATHERAPY
System of directing artificial light on or around the body for healing.

COLOUR ACUPUNCTURE
Directing a light ray to different energy points (acupoints) on the body, to adjust and balance the energy in each organ system.

COLOUR AROMA HERBAL BATHING
Use of flowers, herbs, or essential oils that correspond to a colour frequency in a bath.

COLOUR BATHING
Soaking in a bath in which a specific colourant is added to the water.

COLOUR BREATHING
Technique making use of breathing together with mental focus on colour.

COLOUR-ENERGIZED WATER
Containers of water placed in the sunlight so that the colour of the glass or a gemstone filters the light, energizing the contents with a particular colour energy.

COLOUR THERAPIST
Therapist who uses colour to diagnose the deep causes of physical and mental problems and then introduces different colours into the energetic system to restore harmony.

COLOUR VIBRATIONS
Vibrations that exist in their own right and have a powerful effect on all parts of our being. Each colour

has a particular wavelength, frequency, and effect upon us.

COLOUR WHEEL
A wheel formed by placing the primary and secondary (and possibly further) colours in order around a circle.

COMPLEMENTARY COLOURS
Colours that when mixed together create white light. Each colour has an opposite but complementary partner, which it attracts.

CONES
Colour-sensitive cells in the retina.

CRYSTALS
Substances found naturally in the earth that have powerful electrical and magnetic qualities and can absorb and amplify light waves.

D

DOWSING
Using the hands or a pendulum to find energy changes (e.g. in the human body).

E

ELECTRICAL COLOURS
The colours blue, indigo, and violet, which have a sedating, cooling, and calming action and are drawn into the body through the head.

ELEMENTS
The elemental forces in the Universe; according to Traditional Chinese Medicine there are five – Earth, Wood, Fire, Metal, and Water – and according to Greek tradition there are four – Earth, Air, Fire, and Water.

ESSENTIAL OILS
Oils made from distilling certain parts of plants, reproducing the very essence of the plant and vibratory pattern of sunlight.

ETHERIC BODY
The first band of the aura, which is an exact duplication of the

physical body but vibrating at a higher rate and invisible to the eye.

F

FLUORESCENCE
The emission of electromagnetic radiation, especially light, resulting from bombardment of a substance with other forms of electromagnetic radiation.

FOOD IRRADIATION
The bombardment of food with ultraviolet light.

H

HOLISTIC MEDICINE
System of medicine that treats the whole person rather than the symptoms of the disease alone.

HUE
The quality of the colour itself; it usually refers to the colours on a colour wheel or mixtures of primary colours.

L

LIGHTNESS (LUMINOSITY)
How close a colour is to white or black.

LYCOPENE
A red pigment in plants (e.g. tomatoes).

M

MAGNETIC COLOURS
The colours red, orange, yellow and magenta, which have a warming, stimulating action and are drawn into the body through the feet.

MELANCHOLIC
Body type in which the element of Earth is dominant, and prone to depression and lethargy.

MENTAL BODY
Subtle body extending outward from the astral body, filled with energy from thought waves.

P

PASTEL
A soft delicate hue; a light tint.

PHLEGMATIC
Body type in which the element of Water is dominant, with a tendency to moodiness and emotionality.

PINEAL GLAND
A gland inside the brain that is sensitive to light, and controls seasonal rhythms.

PRIMARY COLOUR
A colour that cannot be made from other colours, or a basic colour that generates the other colours.

R

RETINA
A layer of light-sensitive cells at the back of the eye.

RODS
Light-sensitive cells in the retina that allow us to see in dim light, but do not record colour, only shades of gray.

S

SAD (SEASONAL AFFECTIVE DISORDER)
A group of health problems (e.g. sleep and emotional problems) caused by lack of light or incorrect light wavelengths.

SANGUINE
Body type in which the element of Air is dominant, generally ruddy in appearance.

SATURATION
The intensity of a colour from pale to dark.

SECONDARY COLOUR
A colour formed by mixing two primary colours in approximately equal proportions.

SHADE
A darker version of a colour created by mixing it with black.

SOLAR-ENERGIZED WATER
Water energized by covering a glass container of it with a coloured filter.

SOLAR RAY THERAPY
Bathing in a tub of water covered with a sheet of coloured glass, silk, or cotton, which acts as a filter.

SOUL COLOURS
The colours to which we are attracted over a long period of time, even our entire life, reflecting our personality traits and potential.

SUBTRACTIVE MIXING
Mixing of pigment colours to form a new colour.

T

TINT
A pale version of a hue created by mixing it with white.

V

VIBRATIONAL MEDICINE
Medicine utilizing the powerful vibrations of the electromagnetic spectrum.

VISUALIZATION
Harnessing the mind through the imagination so that thought vibrations can be used to help the healing process.

Y

YIN-YANG
In Chinese philosophy, the two primary forces of energy in the Universe. Yin is feminine and represents darkness, while Yang is masculine and represents light.

YOGA
Holistic therapy developed from an ancient form of movement and meditation that balances the body and mind.

FURTHER READING

Andrews, Ted, **SACRED SOUNDS,** LLEWELLYN PUBLICATIONS, 1995

Birren, Faber, **COLOUR PSYCHOLOGY AND COLOUR THERAPY,** CITADEL PRESS, 1950

Brennan, Barbara Ann, **HANDS OF LIGHT,** BANTAM BOOKS, NEW YORK

Brennan, Barbara Ann, **LIGHT EMERGING,** BANTAM BOOKS, NEW YORK, 1996

Chancellor, Philip, **HANDBOOK OF THE BACH FLOWER REMEDIES,** KEATS PUBLISHING, NEW CANAAN CT, 1971; C.W. DANIEL, SAFFRON WALDEN, UK, 1985

Clark, Linda and Martine, Yvonne, **HEALTH, YOUTH AND BEAUTY THROUGH COLOUR BREATHING,** CELESTIAL ARTS, MILLBRAE CA, 1976

Chiazzari, Suzy, **THE HEALING HOME,** EBURY PRESS, UK, 1998

Cousins, David, **A HANDBOOK FOR LIGHT WORKERS,** BARTON HOUSE PUBLISHING, UK, 1993

David, W., **THE HARMONICS OF SOUND, COLOUR AND VIBRATION,** DEVORS PUBLICATIONS, MARINA DEL RAY CA, 1980

Downer, John, **SUPERSENSE,** BBC BOOKS, LONDON, 1988

Garland, Sarah, **THE HERB GARDEN,** FRANCES LINCOLN, UK, 1984

Gimbel, D.C.E. Theo, **HEALING THROUGH COLOUR,** C.W. DANIEL, SAFFRON WALDEN, UK, 1980

Grieve, Mrs. A., **MODERN HERBAL (2 VOLS),** DOVER PUBLICATIONS, NEW YORK, 1931; HAFNER PRESS, NEW YORK, 1974

Hay, Louise L., **YOU CAN HEAL YOUR LIFE,** COLEMAN PUBLISHING, FARMINGDALE NY, 1984; HAY HOUSE, 1987

Itten, Johannes, **THE ART OF COLOR,** VAN NOSTRAND REINHOLD, NEW YORK, 1969

Jackson, Carole, **COLOR ME BEAUTIFUL,** BALLANTINE BOOKS, NEW YORK, 1981

Jekyll, Gertrude, **COLOUR SCHEMES FOR THE FLOWER GARDEN,** (1ST EDN 1896) ANTIQUE COLLECTORS CLUB UK, 1982

Jekyll, Gertrude, **ON GARDENING,** STUDIO VISTA, LONDON, 1966

Lacy, Marie Louise, **KNOW YOURSELF THROUGH COLOUR,** AQUARIAN PRESS, WELLINGBOROUGH, UK, 1989

Lacy, Marie Louise, **THE POWER OF COLOUR TO HEAL THE ENVIRONMENT,** RAINBOW BRIDGE PUBLICATIONS, 1996

Lansdowne, Zachary F., **RAY METHODS OF HEALING,** SAMUEL WEISER, NEW YORK, 1993

Luscher, Dr. Max (trans. Ian Scott), **THE LUSCHER COLOR TEST,** WASHINGTON SQUARE PRESS, 1969

Mella, Dorothee, **SELF-IMAGE COLOUR ANALYSIS,** MICHAEL JOSEPH, UK, 1990

Pearson, David, **THE NATURAL HOUSE BOOK,** CONRAN OCTOPUS, LONDON, 1989

Sellar, Wanda, **DIRECTORY OF ESSENTIAL OILS,** C.W. DANIEL, SAFFRON WALDEN UK, 1992

Steiner, Rudolph, **COLOR,** RUDOLPH STEINER PRESS, BLAUVELT NY, 1992

Wills, Pauline, **COLOUR THERAPY,** ELEMENT BOOKS, SHAFTESBURY, UK, 1993

Wills, Pauline, **THE REFLEXOLOGY OF COLOUR THERAPY WORKBOOK,** ELEMENT BOOKS, SHAFTESBURY, UK, 1992

Wilson, Annie and Bek, Lilla, **WHAT COLOUR ARE YOU?,** AQUARIAN PRESS, WELLINGBOROUGH, UK, 1987

THE COMPLETE BOOK OF COLOUR

USEFUL ADDRESSES

Affiliation of Crystal Healing Organizations (A.C.H.O.)
46 Lower Green Road
Esher
Surrey KT10 8HD
England

American Alliance of Aromatherapy
PO Box 750428
Petaluma
California
94975-0428 U.S.A.

American Aromatherapy Association
PO Box 3679
South Pasadena
California
U.S.A. 91031

American Crystallographic Association
PO Box 96
Ellicott Station
Buffalo
NY 14205-00963
U.S.A.

American Holistic Medical Association
Suite 201
4101 Lake Boone Trail
Raleigh
NC 27607
U.S.A.

Dr. Edward Bach Centre
Mount Vernon
Sotwell
Wallingford
Oxon OX10 0PZ
England

Nelson Bach U.S.A. Ltd
Wilmington Technology Park
100 Research Drive
Wilmington, Massachusetts
01887-4406 U.S.A.

British Register of Complementary Practitioners
PO Box 194
London SE16 1QZ
England
(send large S.S.A.E.)

Colour and Reflexology
9 Wyndale Avenue
Kingsbury
London NW9 9PT
England
tel: 0181-294 7672

Colour Therapy Association
P O Box 16756
London
SW20 8ZW
England

The Essential Oil Company Ltd
100 Enterprise Place
Dover
DE 19901
U.S.A.

Flower and Gem Remedy Association
Suite 1
Castle Farm
Clifton Road
Deddington
Oxon OX16 0TP
England

FSL Limited
Unit 1
Riverside Business Centre
Victoria Street
High Wycombe
Bucks HP11 2LT
England
(for light therapy)

Hygeia College of Colour Therapy
Brook House
Minchinhampton Hill
Avening
Near Tetbury
Glos GL8 8NS
England
tel: (01453) 832150

The International Association for Colour Therapy (I.A.C.T.)
PO Box 3
Potters Bar
Herts EN6 3ET
England

International Society of Professional Aromatherapists
Hinckley and District Hospital
and Health Centre
The Annexe
Mount Road
Hinckley
Leicestershire LE10 1AG
England

Iris International School of Colour Therapy
Farfields House
Jubilee Road
Totnes
Devon TQ9 5BP
England
tel: (01803) 868037

Natural Food Associates
PO Box 210
Atlanta
TX 75551
U.S.A.

School of Electro-crystal Therapy
117 Long Drive
South Ruislip
Middlesex HA4 0HL
England

INDEX